YAOI

Stories

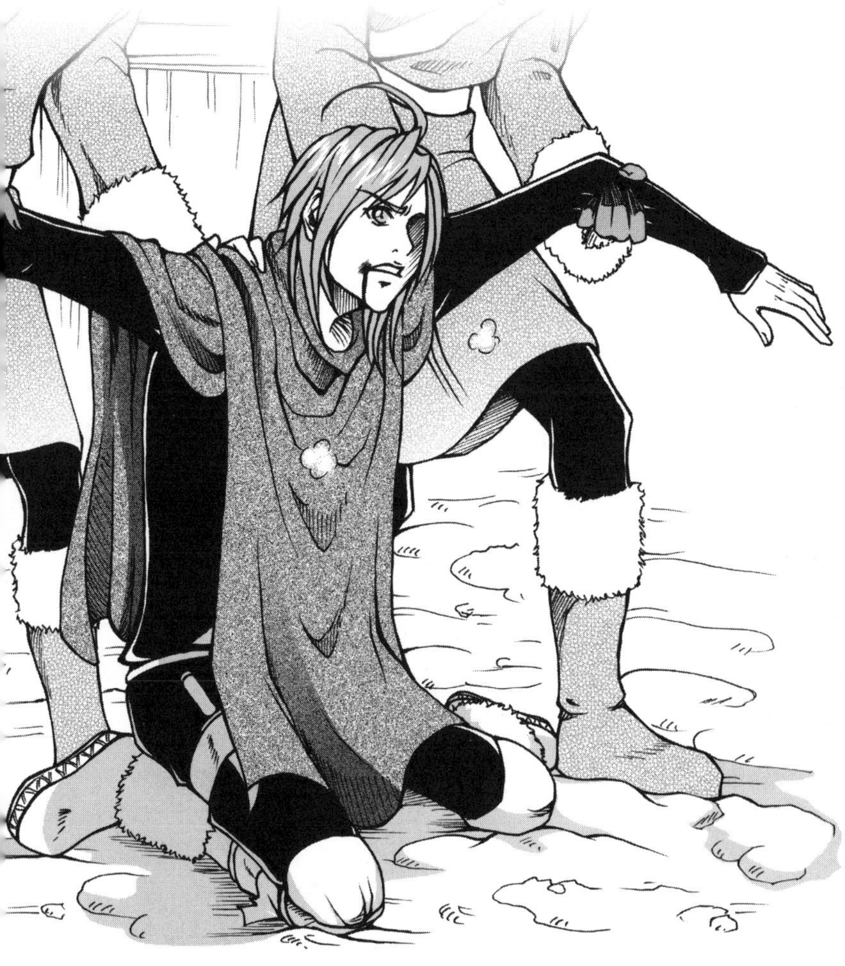

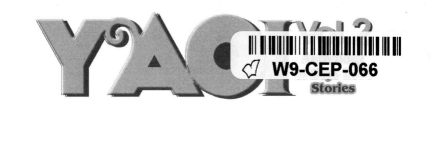

Yaoi: An Anthology of Boys Love Volume 2

Cover color by Lancer Mona, Cover linework by Studio Xian Nu

Divided
Story and Letters by Christine Schilling, Art by Studio Xian Nu

Servant
Story by Yamila Abraham, Art by Jablay Studios,
Letters by April FitzGerald

Edited by Kellie Lynch

Printed in the United States of America

ISBN: 978-1-933664-27-9

Published by Yaoi Press LLC. First printing February 2008.

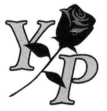

www.yaoipress.com
www.everythingyaoi.com
www.yaoijamboree.com
www.y-curious.com

10 9 8 7 6 5 4 3 2 1

SUNN

The young Sunn is on his way to become second in command of his tribe. He'll be under his older brother Raffe, who he idolizes.

RAFFE

The tribe of the Eurydis has known prosperity under the leadership of Raffe, even if some of his methods are questionable.

CICLO

Ciclo is a member of a tribe of 'barbarians.' He becomes the prisoner of Raffe and Sunn.

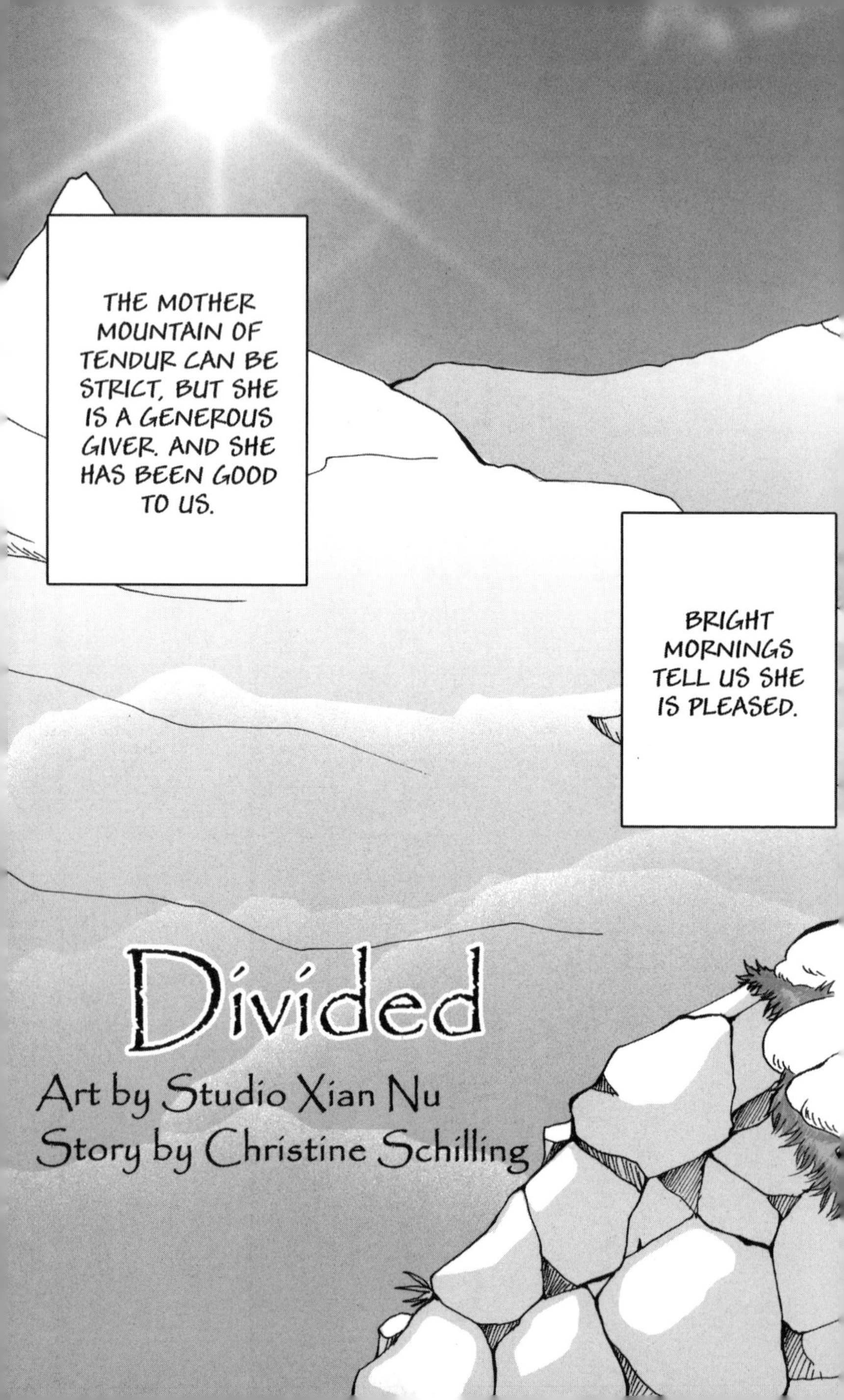
THE MOTHER MOUNTAIN OF TENDUR CAN BE STRICT, BUT SHE IS A GENEROUS GIVER. AND SHE HAS BEEN GOOD TO US.
BRIGHT MORNINGS TELL US SHE IS PLEASED.
Divided
Art by Studio Xian Nu
Story by Christine Schilling

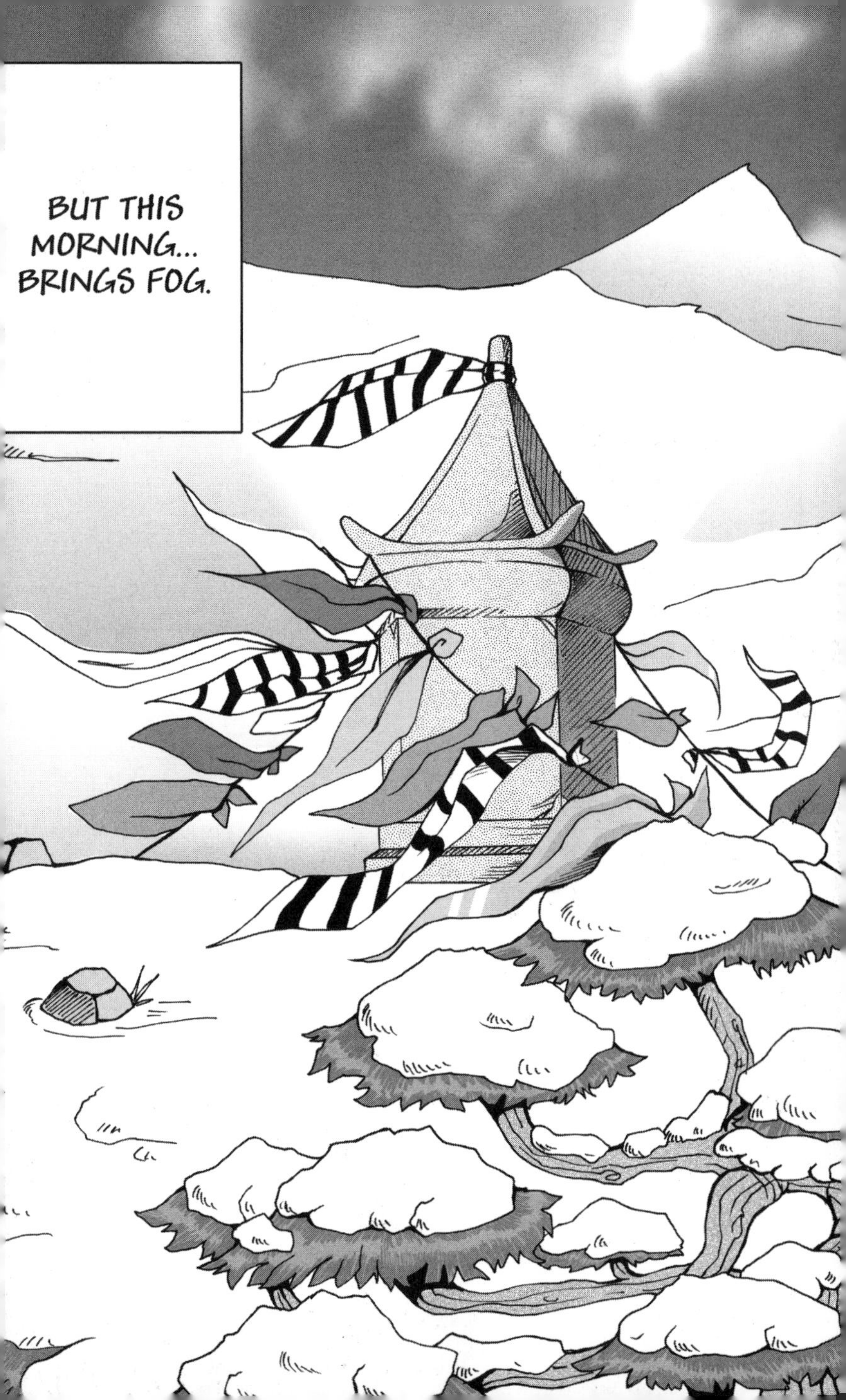
BUT THIS MORNING... BRINGS FOG.

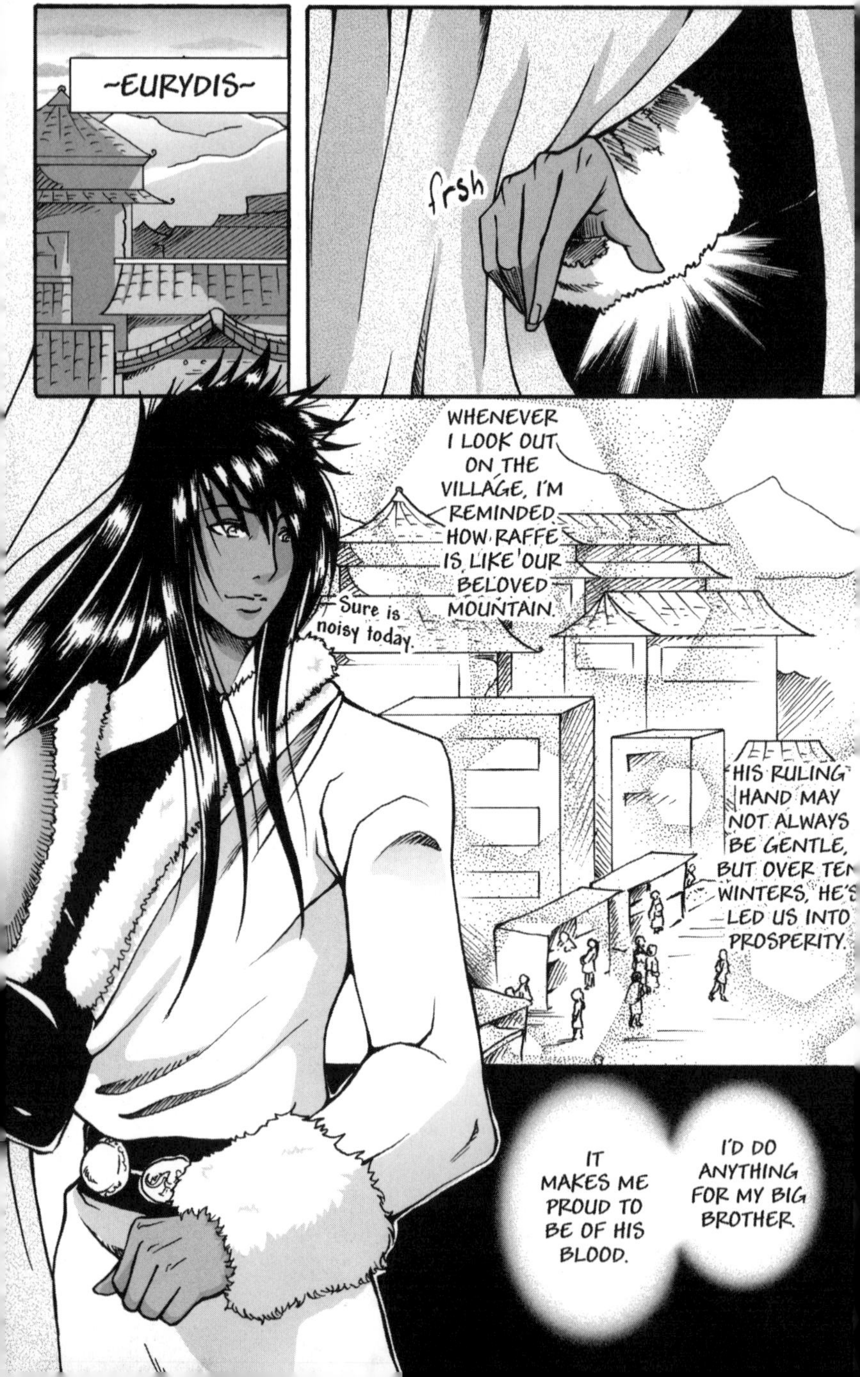

~EURYDIS~
frsh
WHENEVER I LOOK OUT ON THE VILLAGE, I'M REMINDED HOW RAFFE IS LIKE OUR BELOVED MOUNTAIN.
Sure is noisy today.
HIS RULING HAND MAY NOT ALWAYS BE GENTLE, BUT OVER TEN WINTERS, HE'S LED US INTO PROSPERITY.
IT MAKES ME PROUD TO BE OF HIS BLOOD.
I'D DO ANYTHING FOR MY BIG BROTHER.

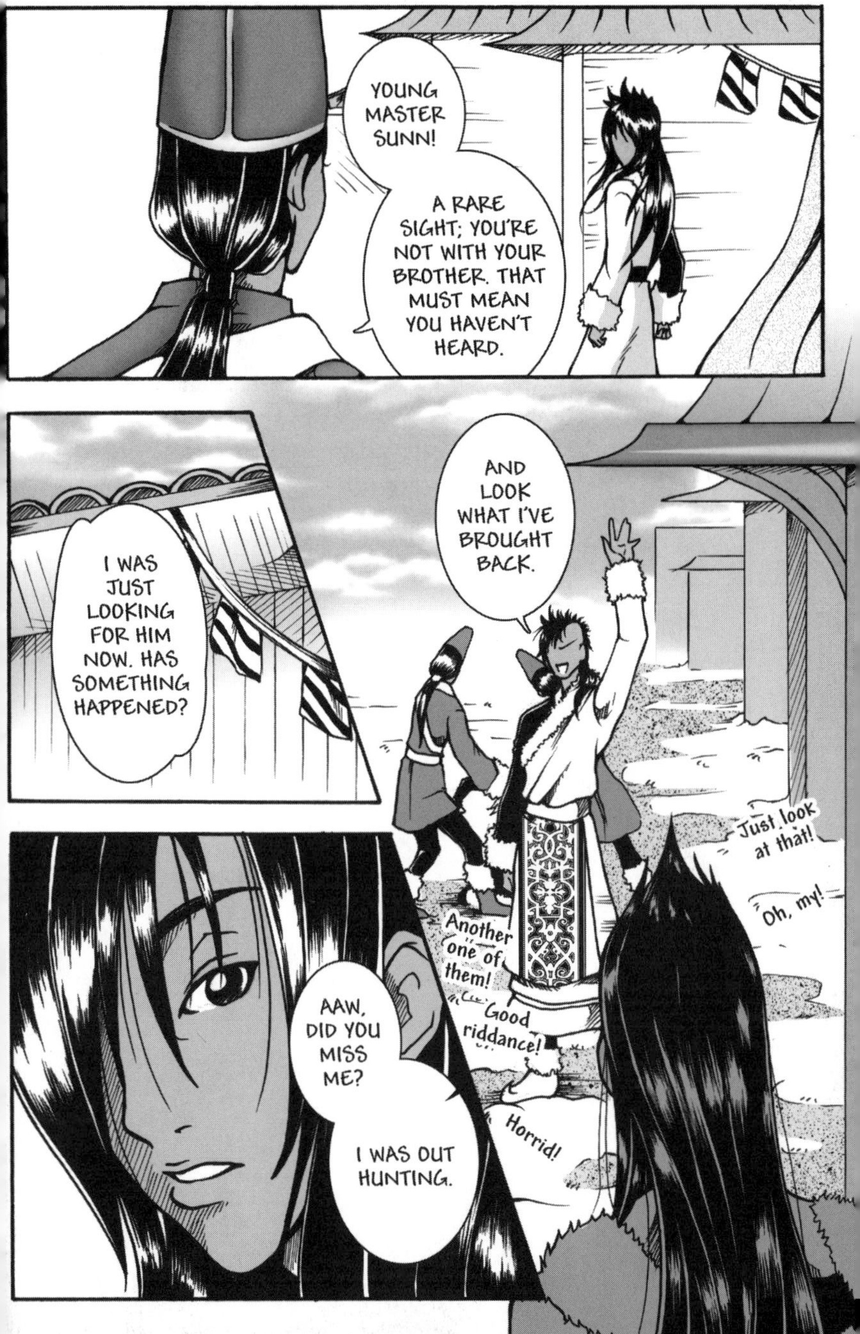
YOUNG MASTER SUNN!
A RARE SIGHT; YOU'RE NOT WITH YOUR BROTHER. THAT MUST MEAN YOU HAVEN'T HEARD.
I WAS JUST LOOKING FOR HIM NOW. HAS SOMETHING HAPPENED?
AND LOOK WHAT I'VE BROUGHT BACK.
Just look at that!
Oh, my!
Another one of them!
Good riddance!
Horrid!
AAW, DID YOU MISS ME?
I WAS OUT HUNTING.

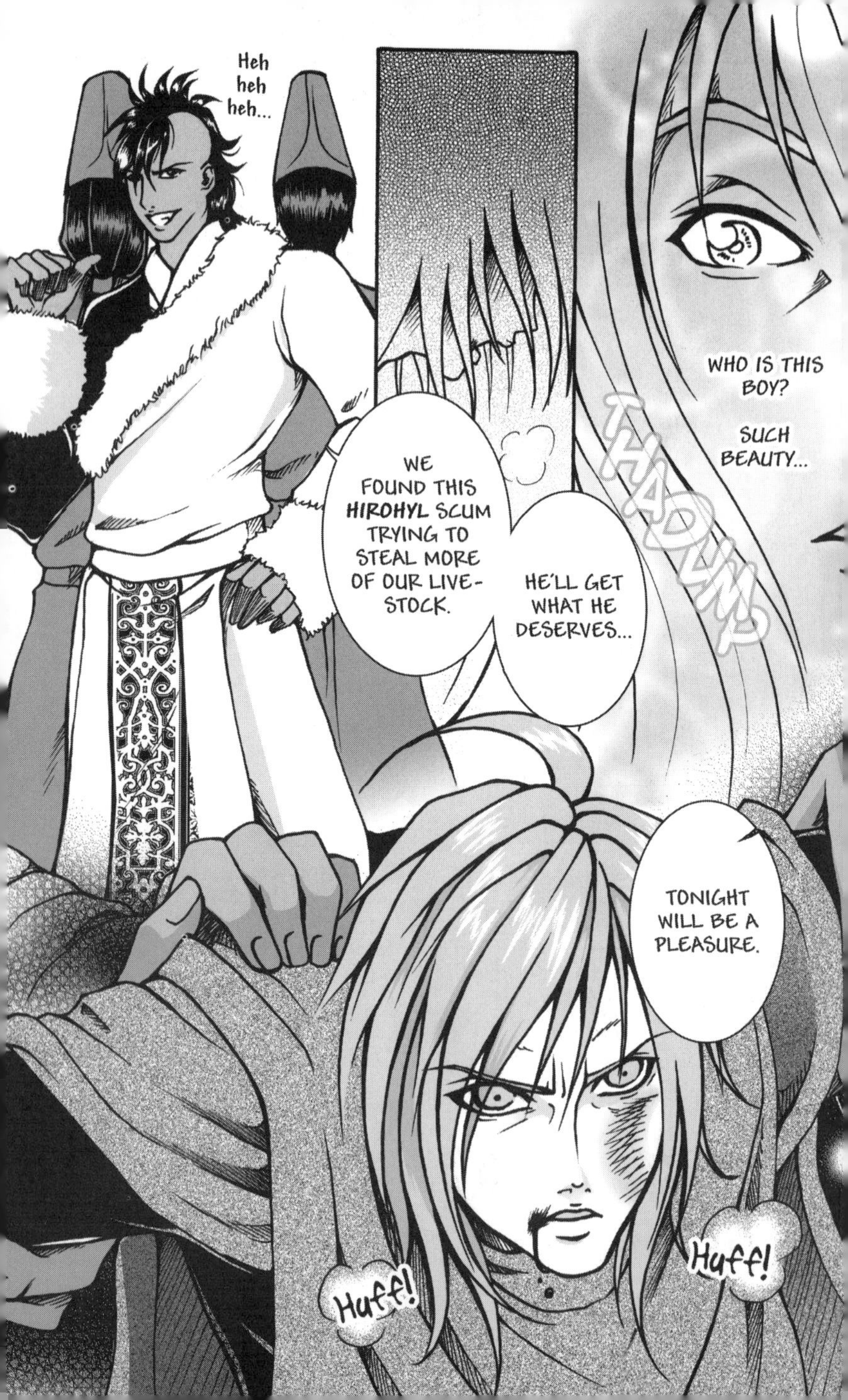

Heh heh heh...
WE FOUND THIS HIROHYL SCUM TRYING TO STEAL MORE OF OUR LIVE-STOCK.
HE'LL GET WHAT HE DESERVES...
WHO IS THIS BOY?
SUCH BEAUTY...
THADUMP
TONIGHT WILL BE A PLEASURE.
Huff!
Huff!

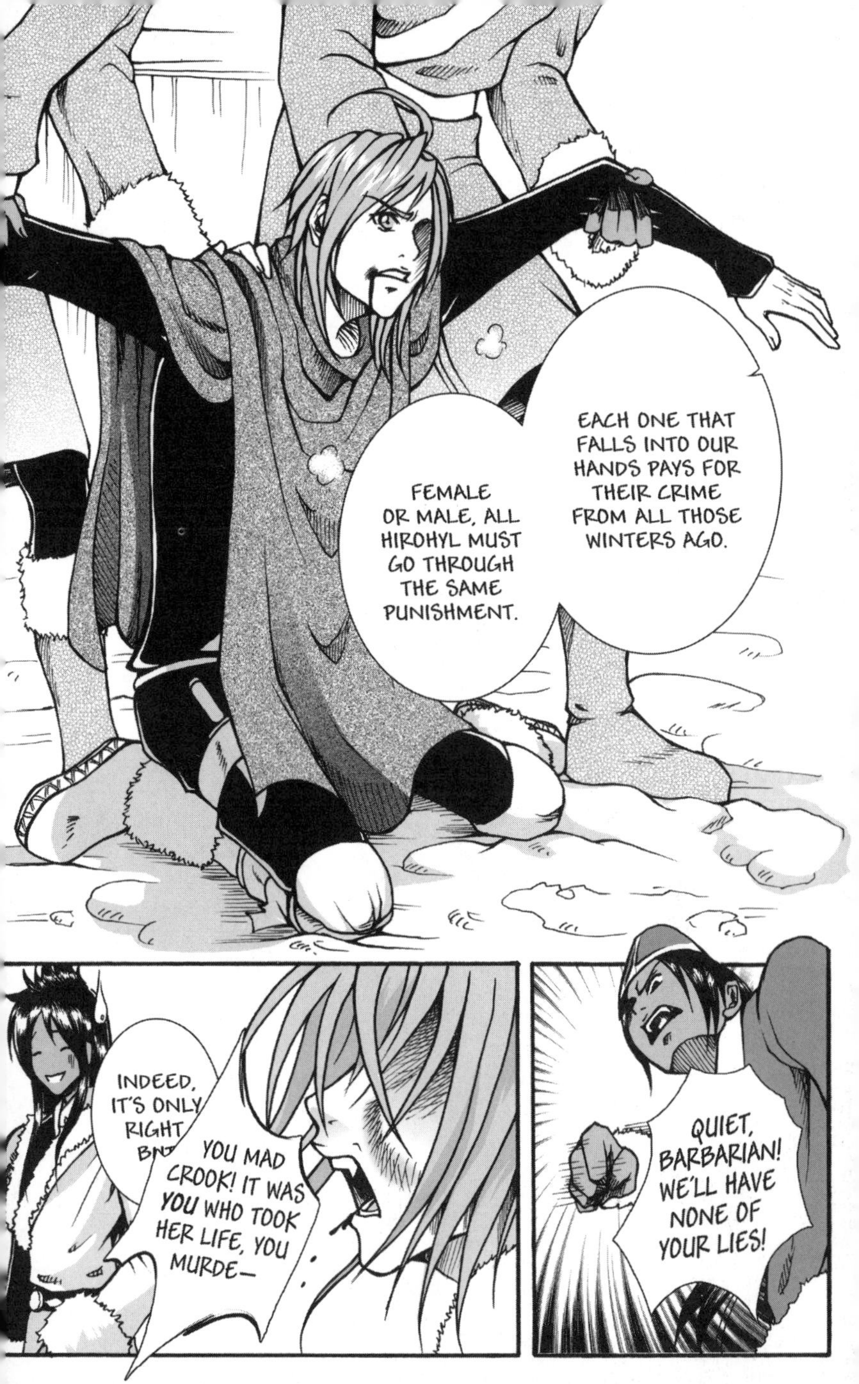
FEMALE OR MALE, ALL HIROHYL MUST GO THROUGH THE SAME PUNISHMENT.
EACH ONE THAT FALLS INTO OUR HANDS PAYS FOR THEIR CRIME FROM ALL THOSE WINTERS AGO.
INDEED, IT'S ONLY RIGHT
YOU MAD CROOK! IT WAS YOU WHO TOOK HER LIFE, YOU MURDE—
QUIET, BARBARIAN! WE'LL HAVE NONE OF YOUR LIES!

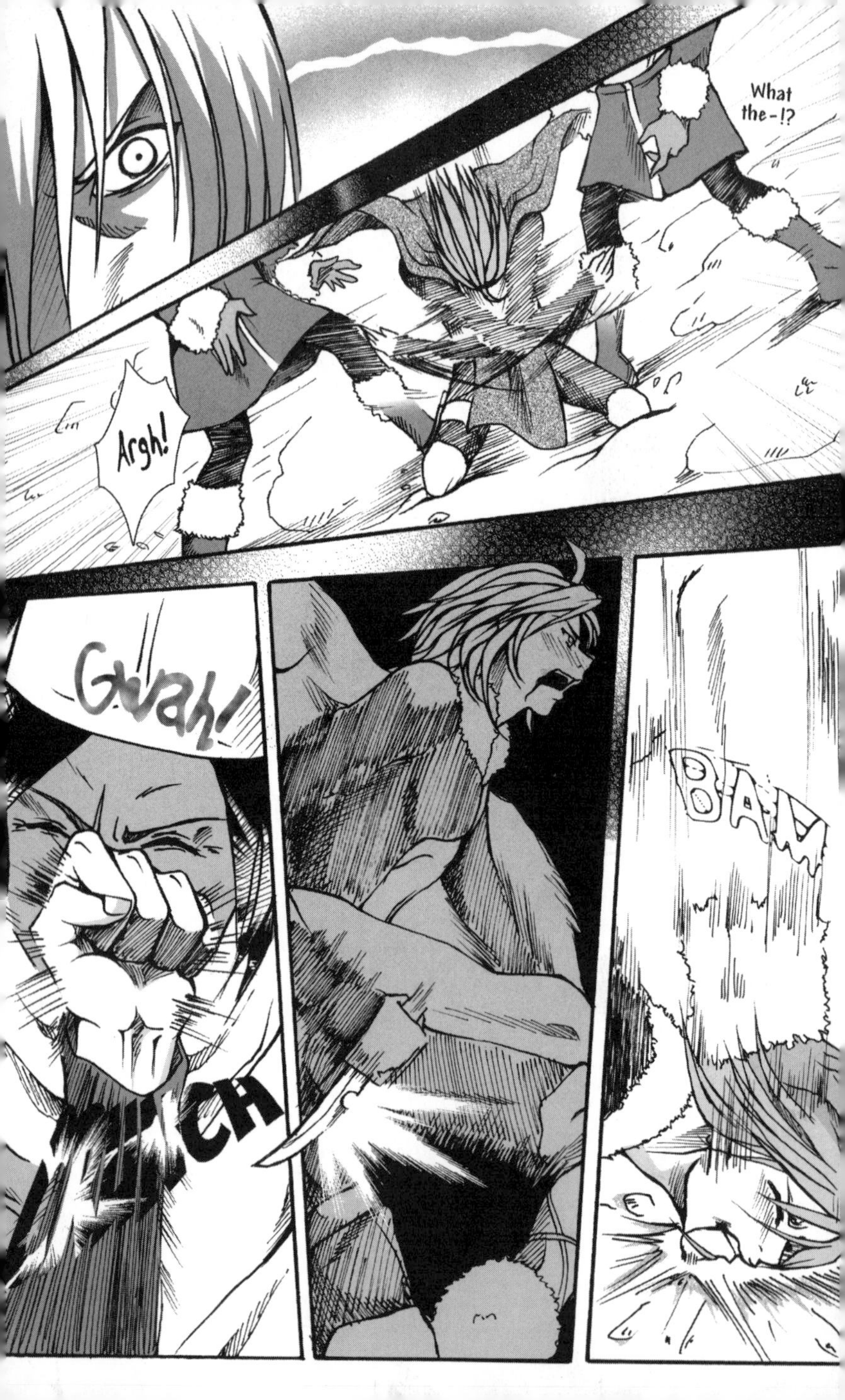
What the-!?
Argh!
BAM
Gwah!

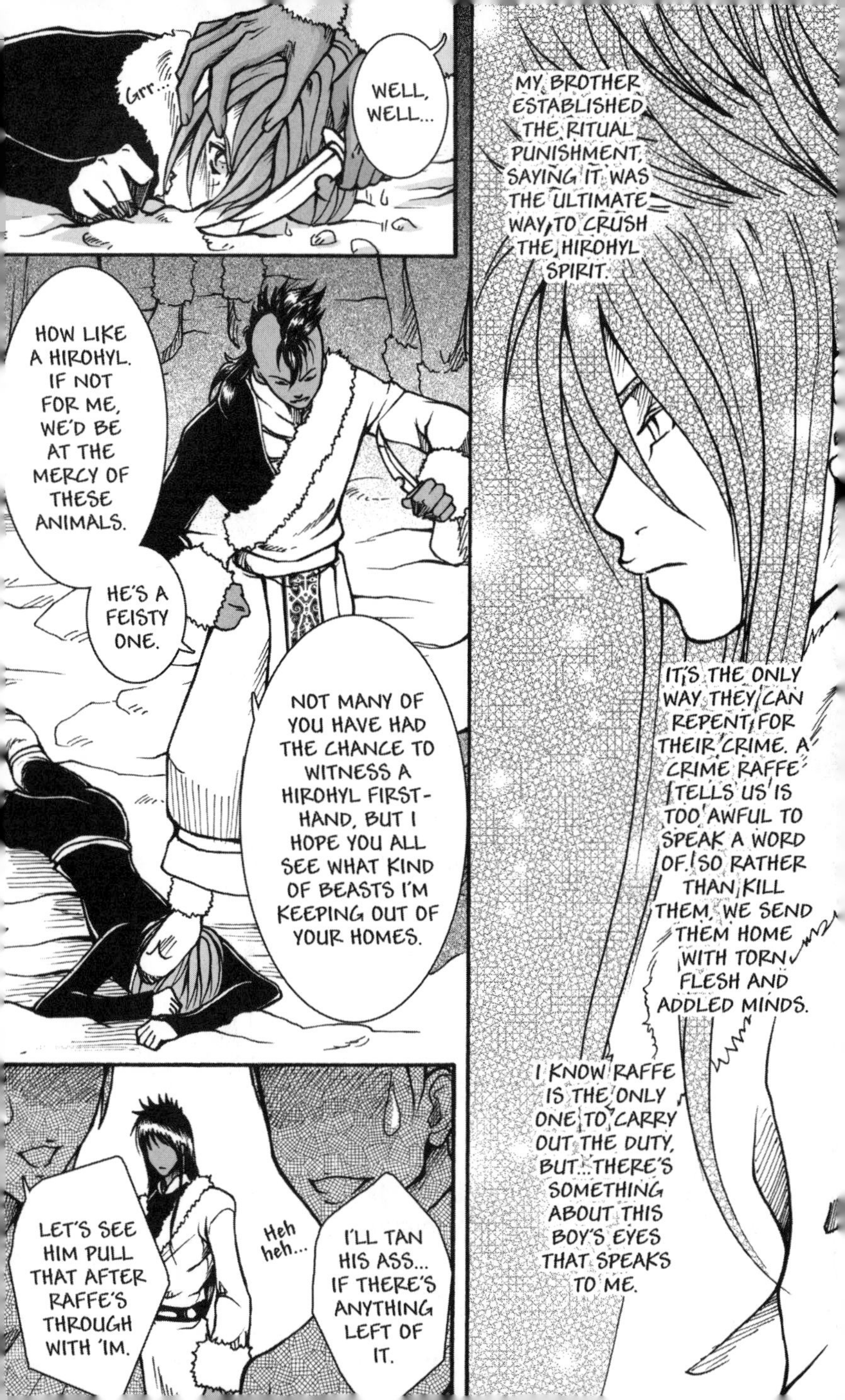
Grr...
WELL, WELL...
HOW LIKE A HIROHYL. IF NOT FOR ME, WE'D BE AT THE MERCY OF THESE ANIMALS.
HE'S A FEISTY ONE.
NOT MANY OF YOU HAVE HAD THE CHANCE TO WITNESS A HIROHYL FIRST-HAND, BUT I HOPE YOU ALL SEE WHAT KIND OF BEASTS I'M KEEPING OUT OF YOUR HOMES.
LET'S SEE HIM PULL THAT AFTER RAFFE'S THROUGH WITH 'IM.
Heh heh...
I'LL TAN HIS ASS... IF THERE'S ANYTHING LEFT OF IT.
MY BROTHER ESTABLISHED THE RITUAL PUNISHMENT, SAYING IT WAS THE ULTIMATE WAY TO CRUSH THE HIROHYL SPIRIT.
IT'S THE ONLY WAY THEY CAN REPENT FOR THEIR CRIME. A CRIME RAFFE TELLS US IS TOO AWFUL TO SPEAK A WORD OF. SO RATHER THAN KILL THEM, WE SEND THEM HOME WITH TORN FLESH AND ADDLED MINDS.
I KNOW RAFFE IS THE ONLY ONE TO CARRY OUT THE DUTY, BUT...THERE'S SOMETHING ABOUT THIS BOY'S EYES THAT SPEAKS TO ME.

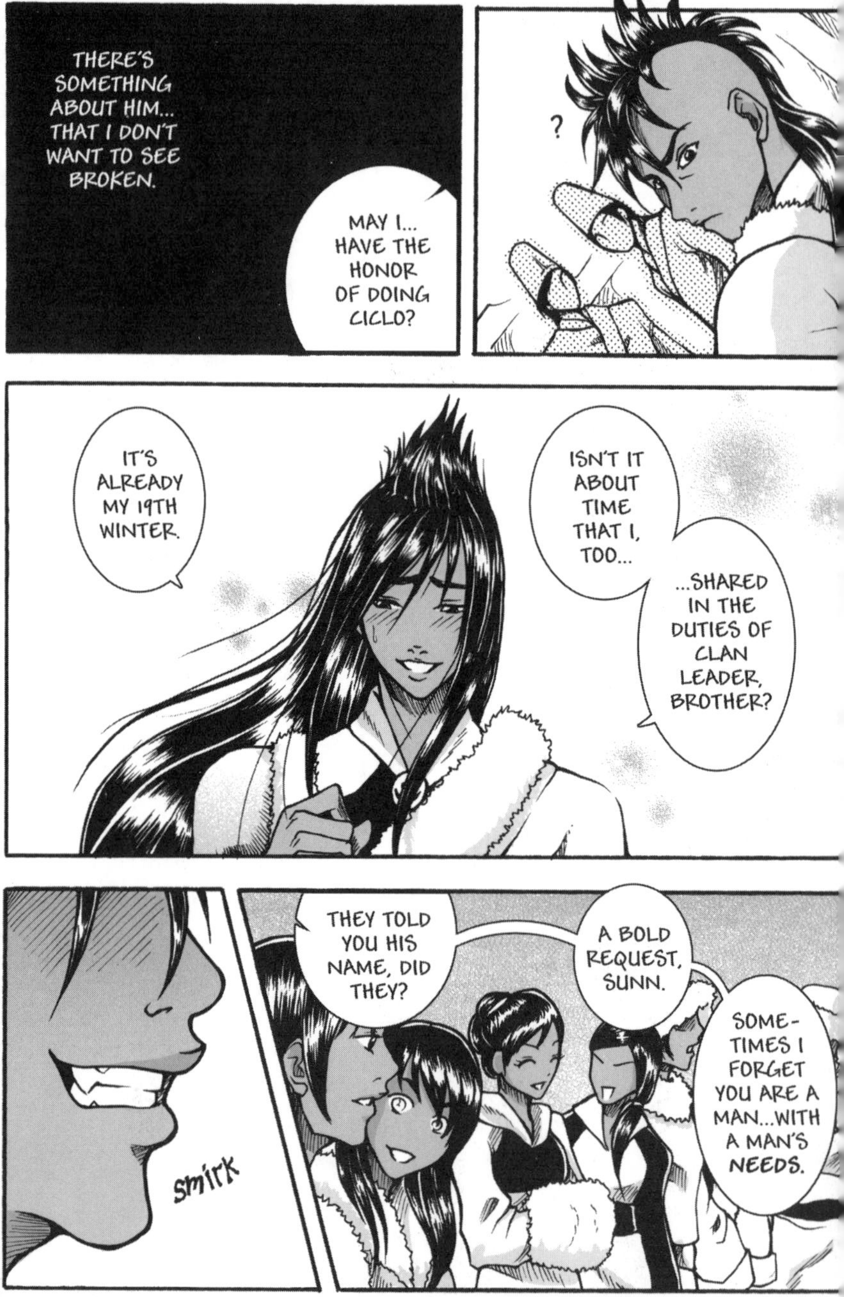
THERE'S SOMETHING ABOUT HIM... THAT I DON'T WANT TO SEE BROKEN.
MAY I... HAVE THE HONOR OF DOING CICLO?
?
IT'S ALREADY MY 19TH WINTER.
ISN'T IT ABOUT TIME THAT I, TOO...
...SHARED IN THE DUTIES OF CLAN LEADER, BROTHER?
smirk
THEY TOLD YOU HIS NAME, DID THEY?
A BOLD REQUEST, SUNN.
SOME-TIMES I FORGET YOU ARE A MAN...WITH A MAN'S NEEDS.

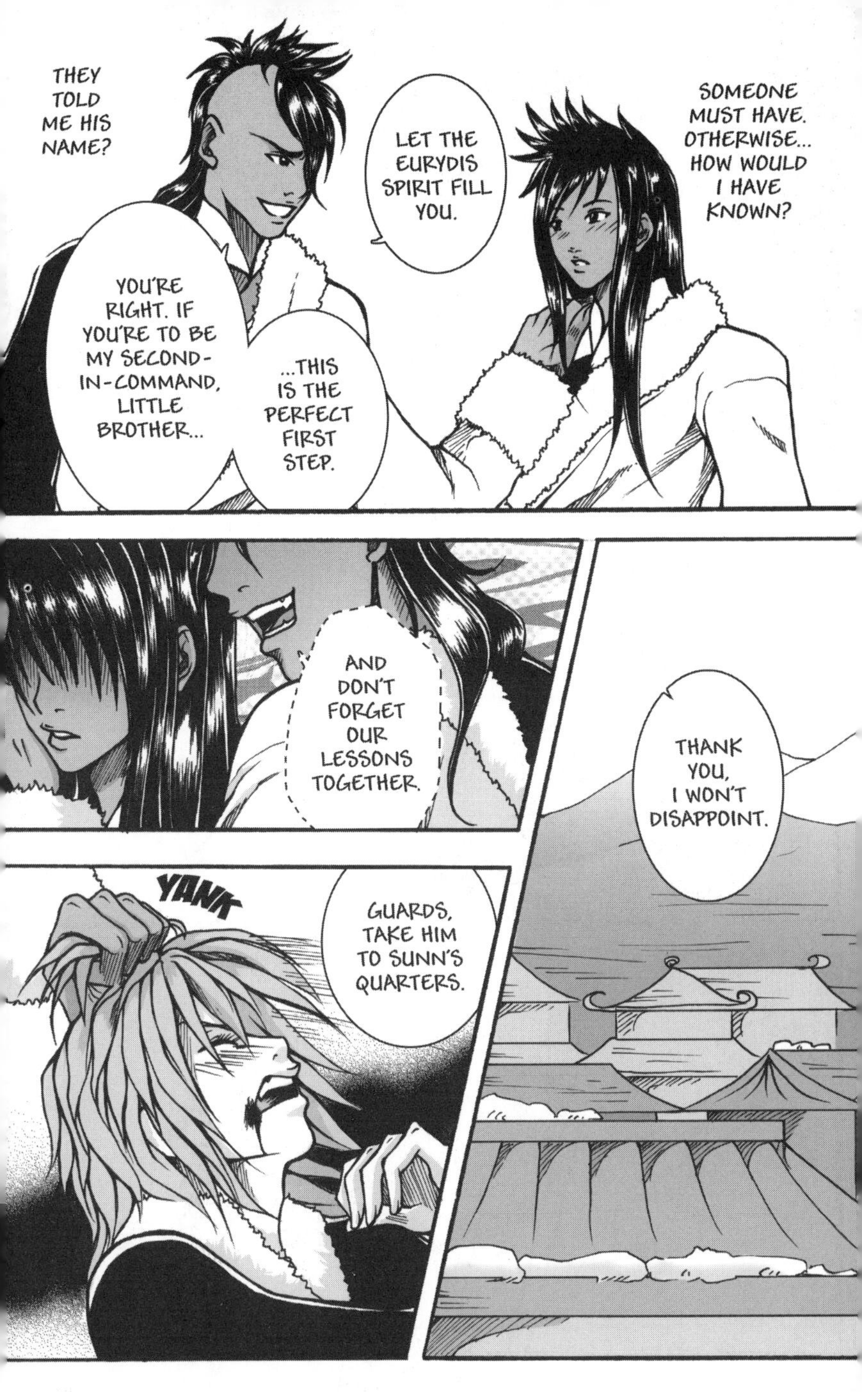
THEY TOLD ME HIS NAME?
SOMEONE MUST HAVE. OTHERWISE... HOW WOULD I HAVE KNOWN?
YOU'RE RIGHT. IF YOU'RE TO BE MY SECOND-IN-COMMAND, LITTLE BROTHER...
...THIS IS THE PERFECT FIRST STEP.
LET THE EURYDIS SPIRIT FILL YOU.
AND DON'T FORGET OUR LESSONS TOGETHER.
THANK YOU, I WON'T DISAPPOINT.
YANK
GUARDS, TAKE HIM TO SUNN'S QUARTERS.

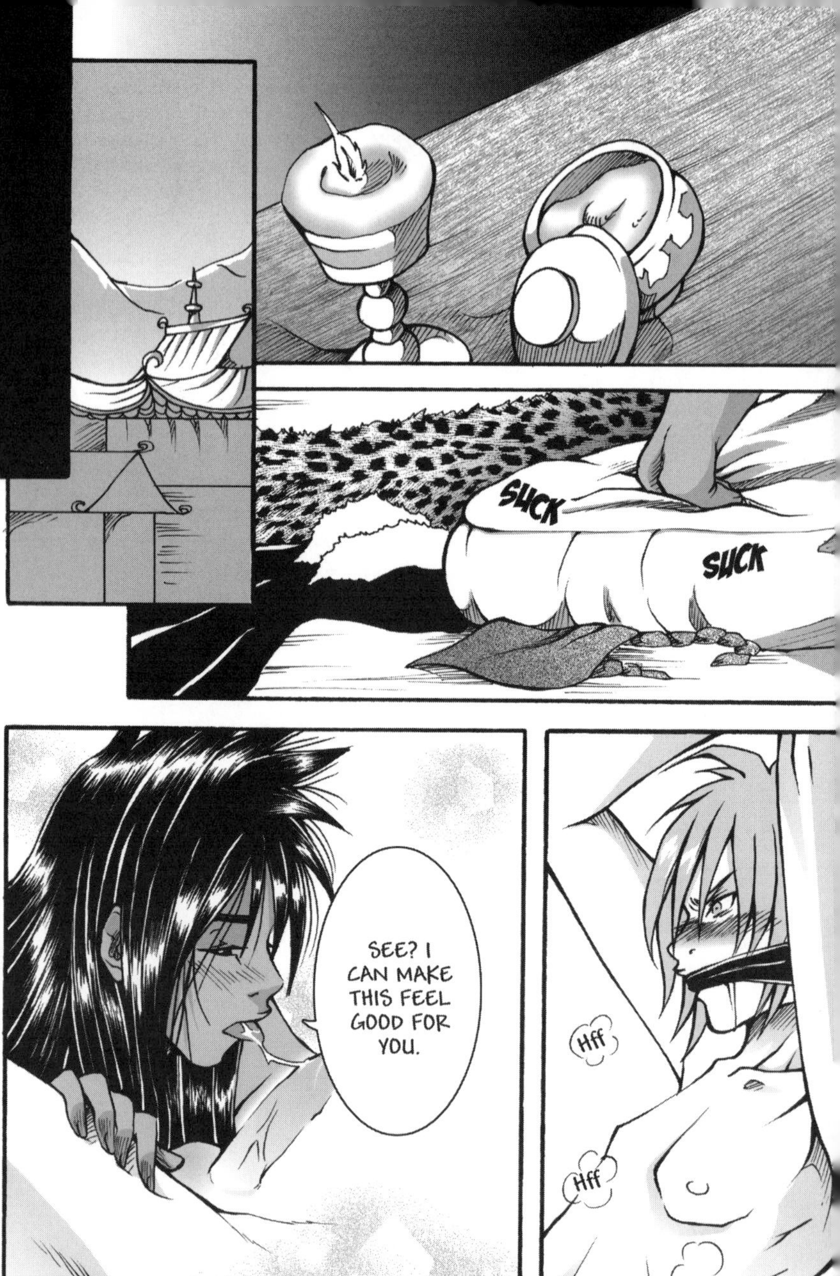
SUCK
SUCK
SEE? I CAN MAKE THIS FEEL GOOD FOR YOU.
Hff
Hff

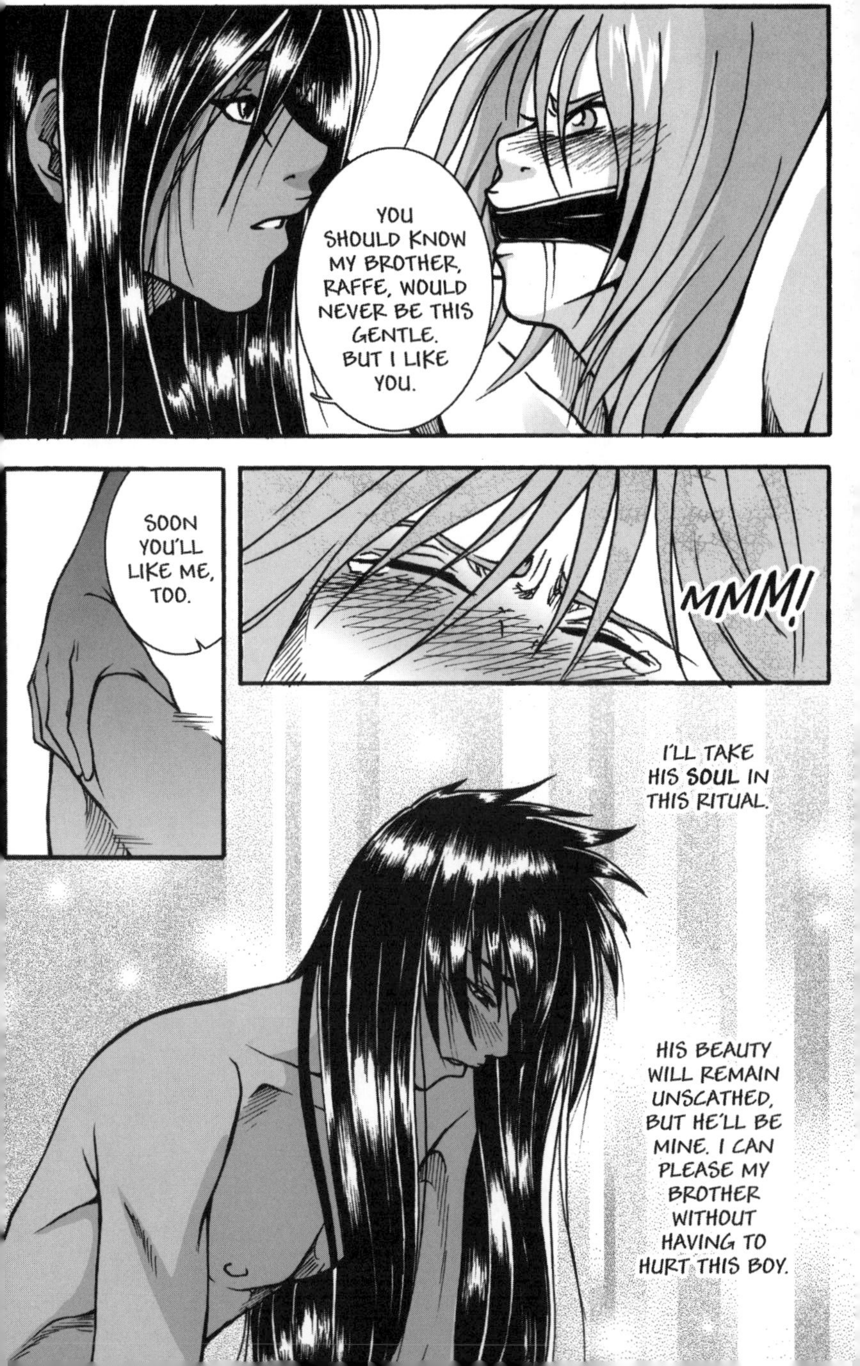
YOU SHOULD KNOW MY BROTHER, RAFFE, WOULD NEVER BE THIS GENTLE. BUT I LIKE YOU.
SOON YOU'LL LIKE ME, TOO.
MMM!
I'LL TAKE HIS SOUL IN THIS RITUAL.
HIS BEAUTY WILL REMAIN UNSCATHED, BUT HE'LL BE MINE. I CAN PLEASE MY BROTHER WITHOUT HAVING TO HURT THIS BOY.

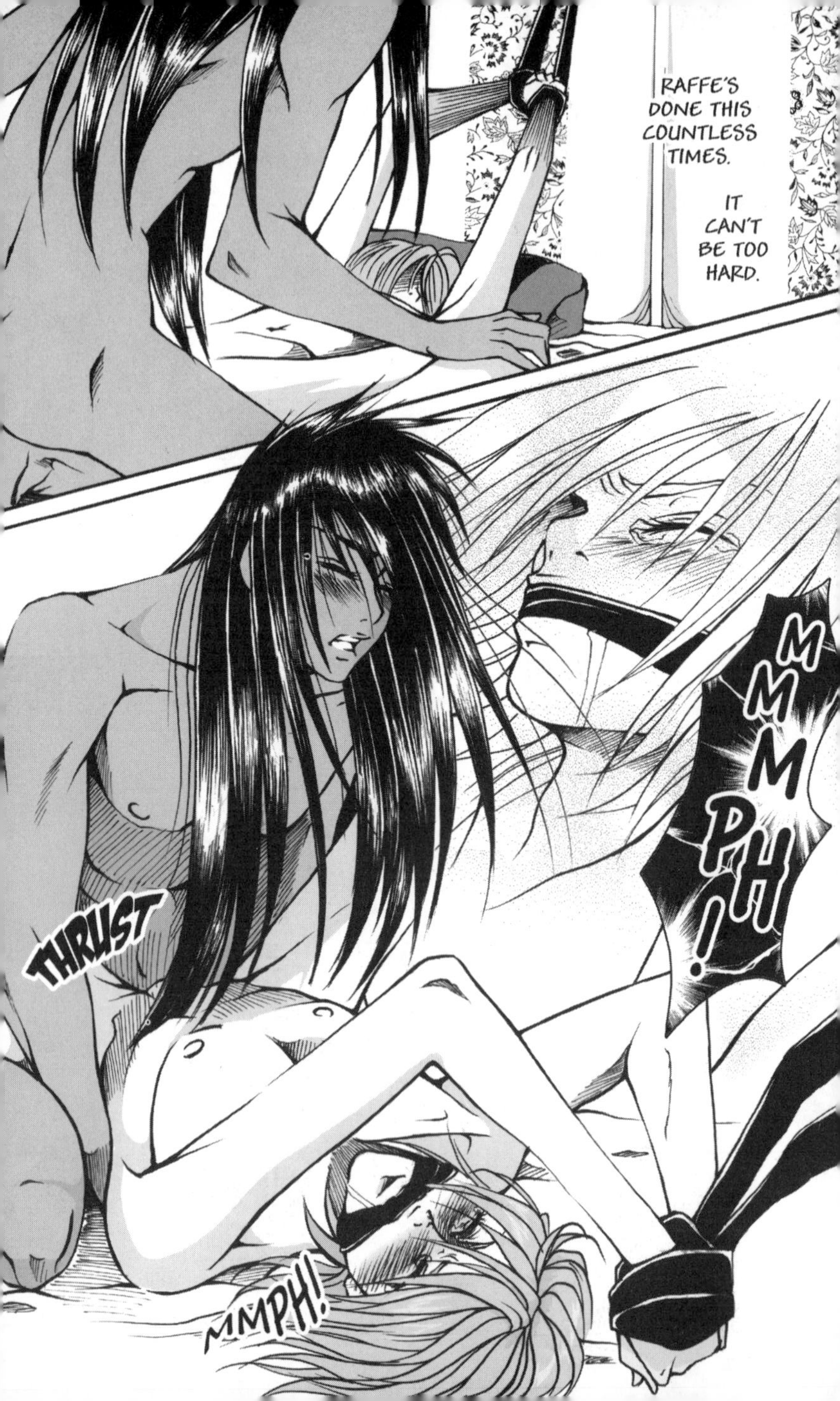
RAFFE'S DONE THIS COUNTLESS TIMES.
IT CAN'T BE TOO HARD.
MMMPH!
THRUST
MMPH!

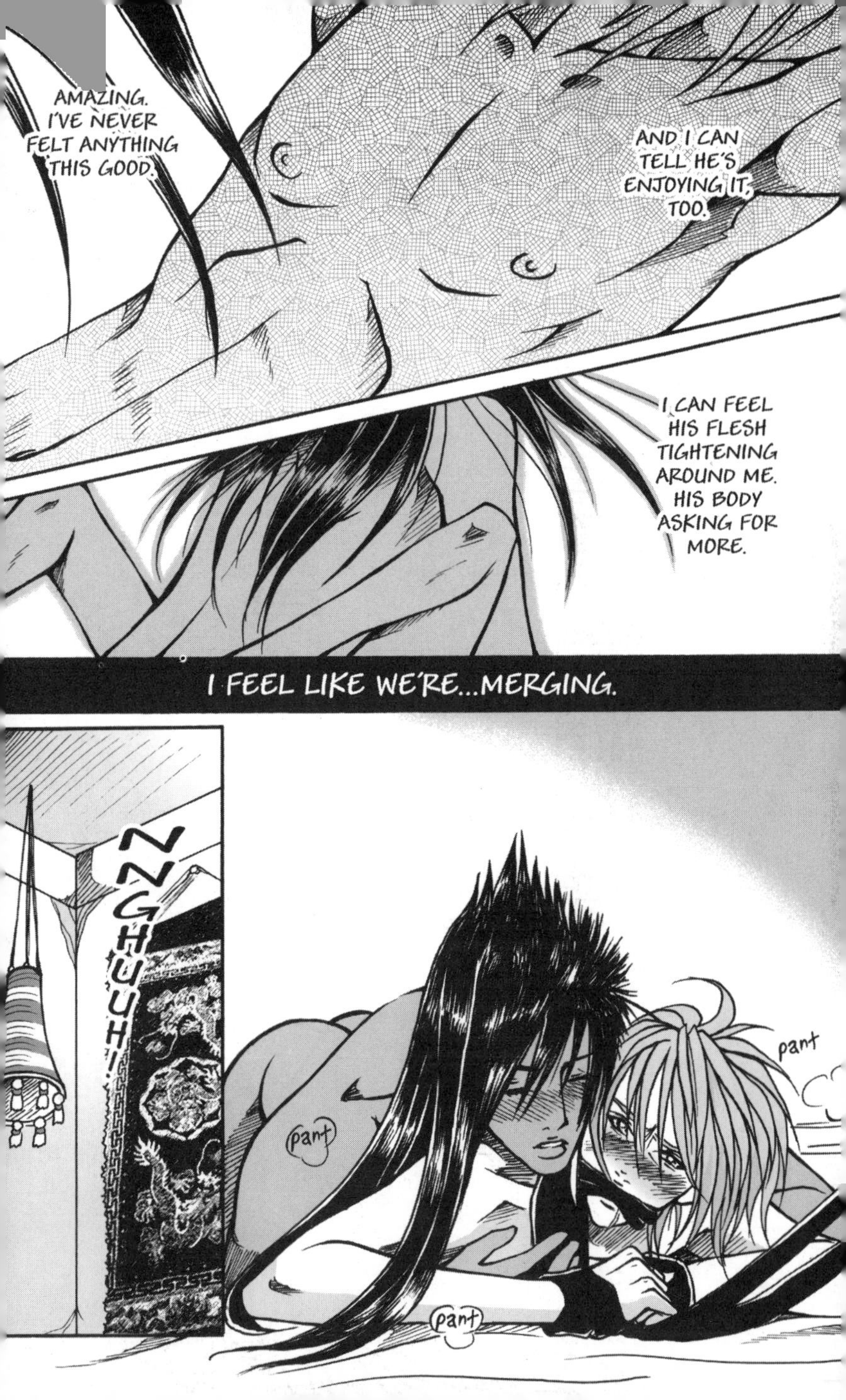
AMAZING. I'VE NEVER FELT ANYTHING THIS GOOD.
AND I CAN TELL HE'S ENJOYING IT, TOO.
I CAN FEEL HIS FLESH TIGHTENING AROUND ME. HIS BODY ASKING FOR MORE.
I FEEL LIKE WE'RE...MERGING.
NNGHUUUH!
pant
pant
pant

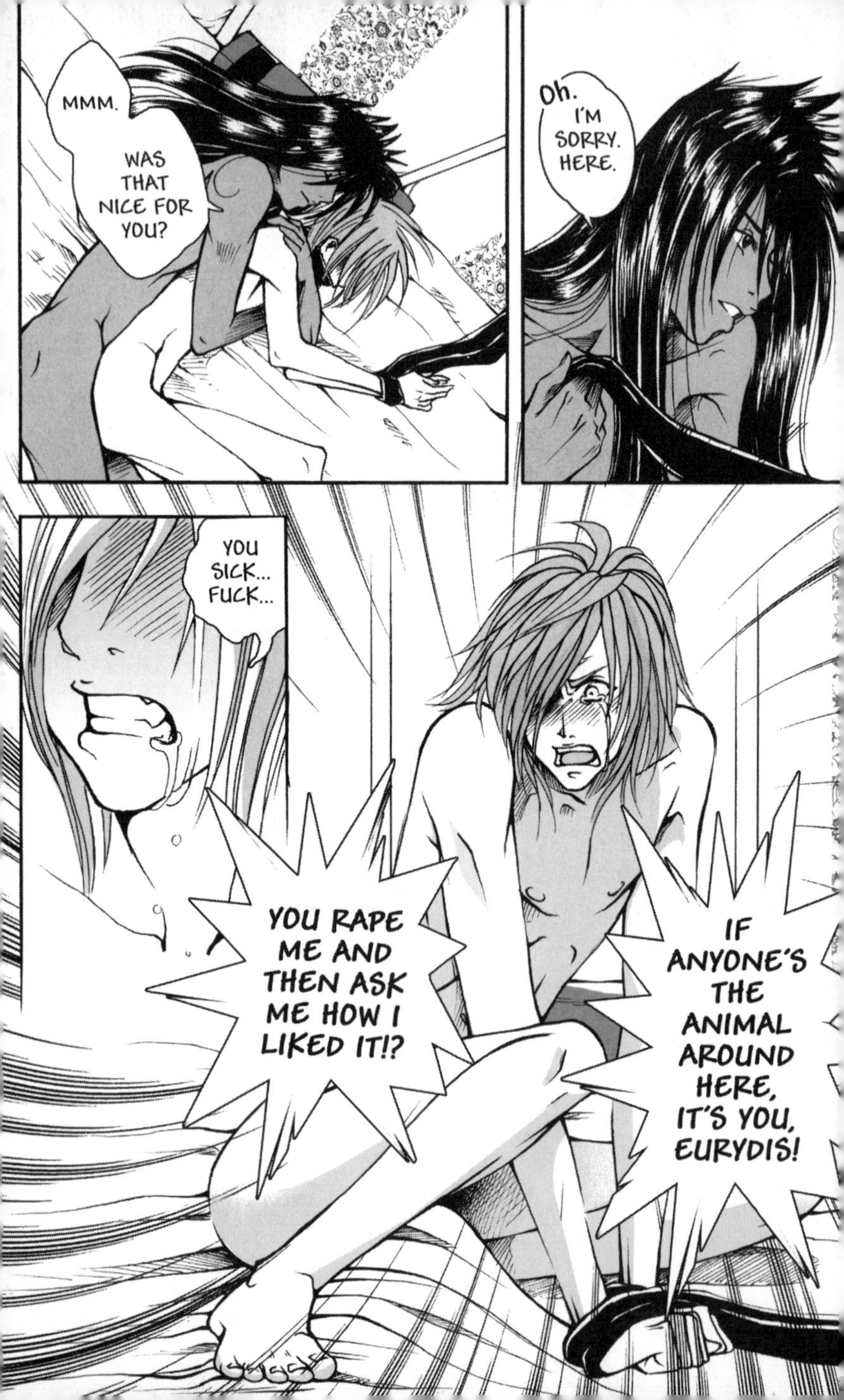
MMM.
WAS THAT NICE FOR YOU?
Oh. I'M SORRY. HERE.
YOU SICK... FUCK...
YOU RAPE ME AND THEN ASK ME HOW I LIKED IT!?
IF ANYONE'S THE ANIMAL AROUND HERE, IT'S YOU, EURYDIS!

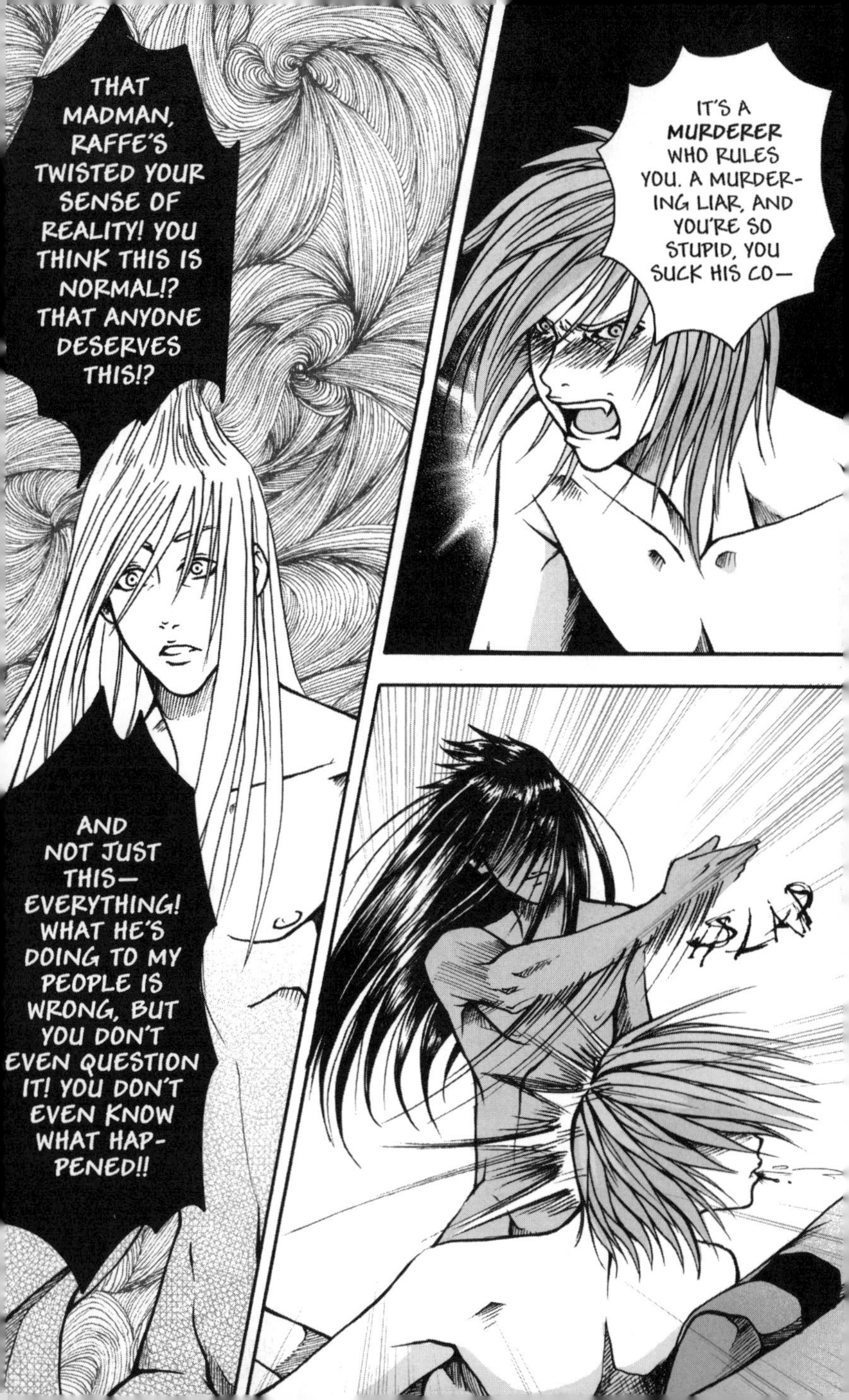
THAT MADMAN, RAFFE'S TWISTED YOUR SENSE OF REALITY! YOU THINK THIS IS NORMAL!? THAT ANYONE DESERVES THIS!?
AND NOT JUST THIS— EVERYTHING! WHAT HE'S DOING TO MY PEOPLE IS WRONG, BUT YOU DON'T EVEN QUESTION IT! YOU DON'T EVEN KNOW WHAT HAP-PENED!!
IT'S A MURDERER WHO RULES YOU. A MURDER-ING LIAR, AND YOU'RE SO STUPID, YOU SUCK HIS CO—
SLAP

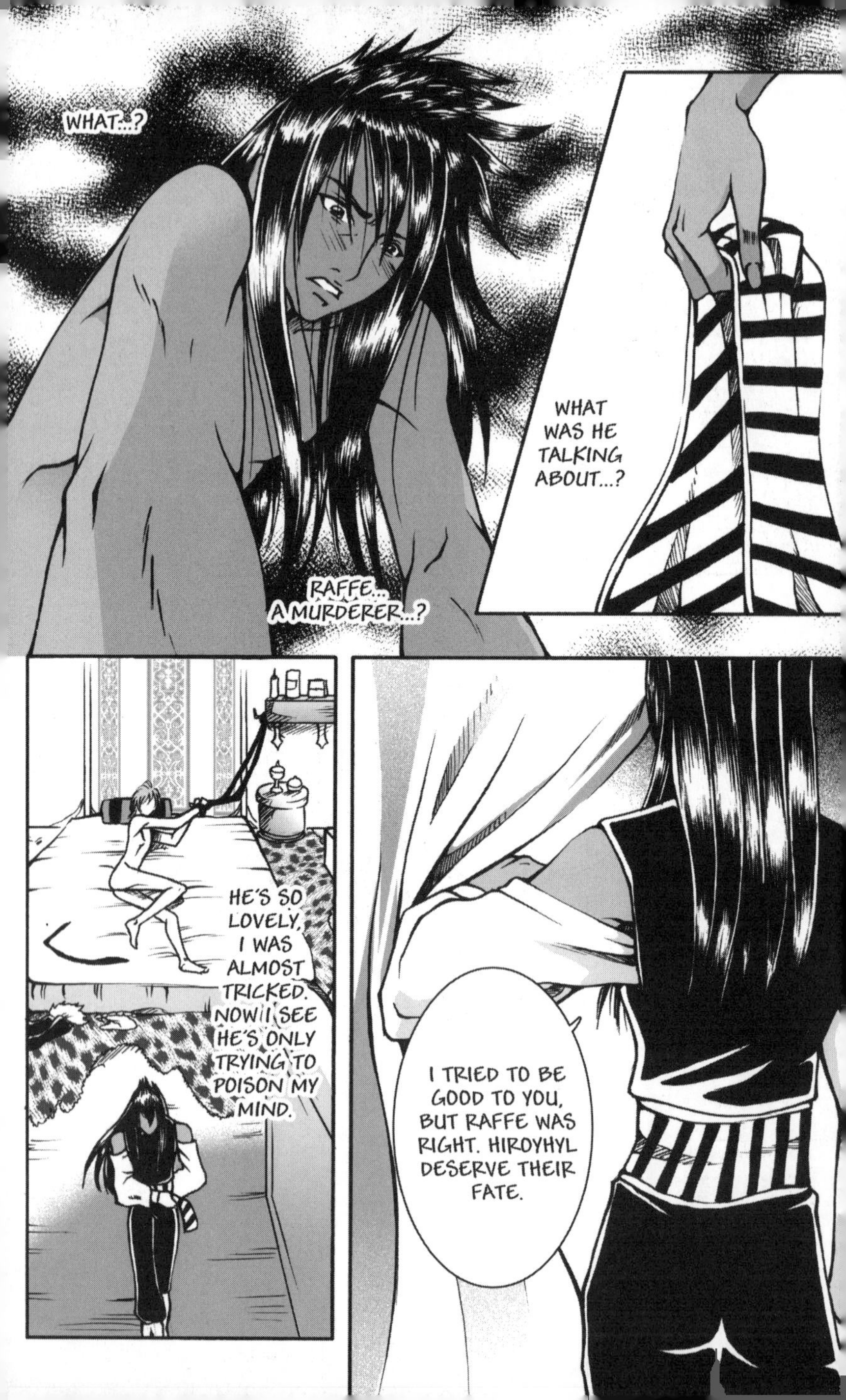
WHAT WAS HE TALKING ABOUT...?
WHAT...?
RAFFE... A MURDERER...?
I TRIED TO BE GOOD TO YOU, BUT RAFFE WAS RIGHT. HIROYHYL DESERVE THEIR FATE.
HE'S SO LOVELY, I WAS ALMOST TRICKED. NOW I SEE HE'S ONLY TRYING TO POISON MY MIND.

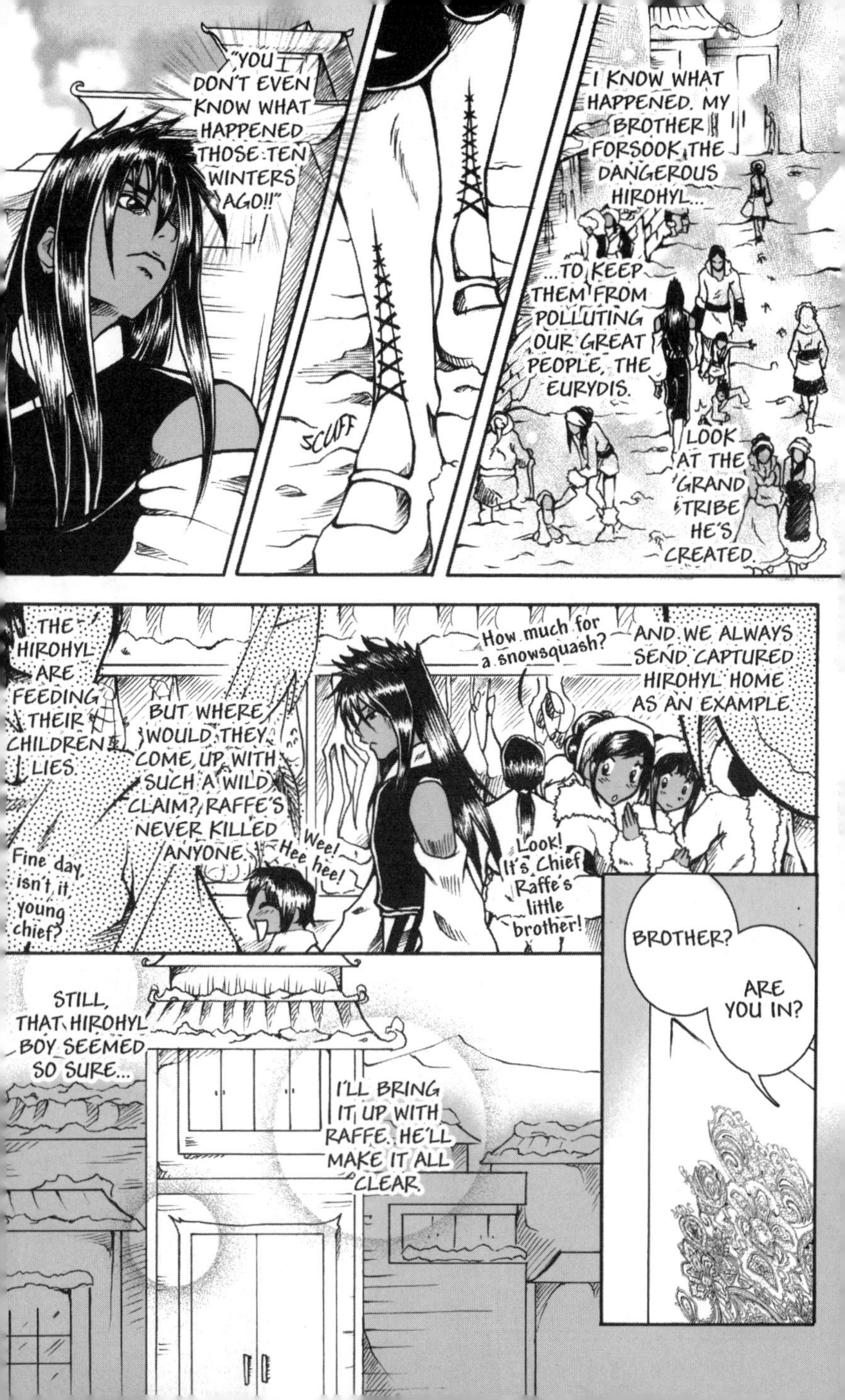
"YOU DON'T EVEN KNOW WHAT HAPPENED THOSE TEN WINTERS AGO!!"
SCUFF
I KNOW WHAT HAPPENED. MY BROTHER FORSOOK THE DANGEROUS HIROHYL...
...TO KEEP THEM FROM POLLUTING OUR GREAT PEOPLE, THE EURYDIS.
LOOK AT THE GRAND TRIBE HE'S CREATED.
THE HIROHYL ARE FEEDING THEIR CHILDREN LIES.
BUT WHERE WOULD THEY COME UP WITH SUCH A WILD CLAIM? RAFFE'S NEVER KILLED ANYONE.
How much for a snowsquash?
AND WE ALWAYS SEND CAPTURED HIROHYL HOME AS AN EXAMPLE.
Fine day, isn't it, young chief?
Wee! Hee hee!
Look! It's Chief Raffe's little brother!
STILL, THAT HIROHYL BOY SEEMED SO SURE...
I'LL BRING IT UP WITH RAFFE. HE'LL MAKE IT ALL CLEAR.
BROTHER?
ARE YOU IN?

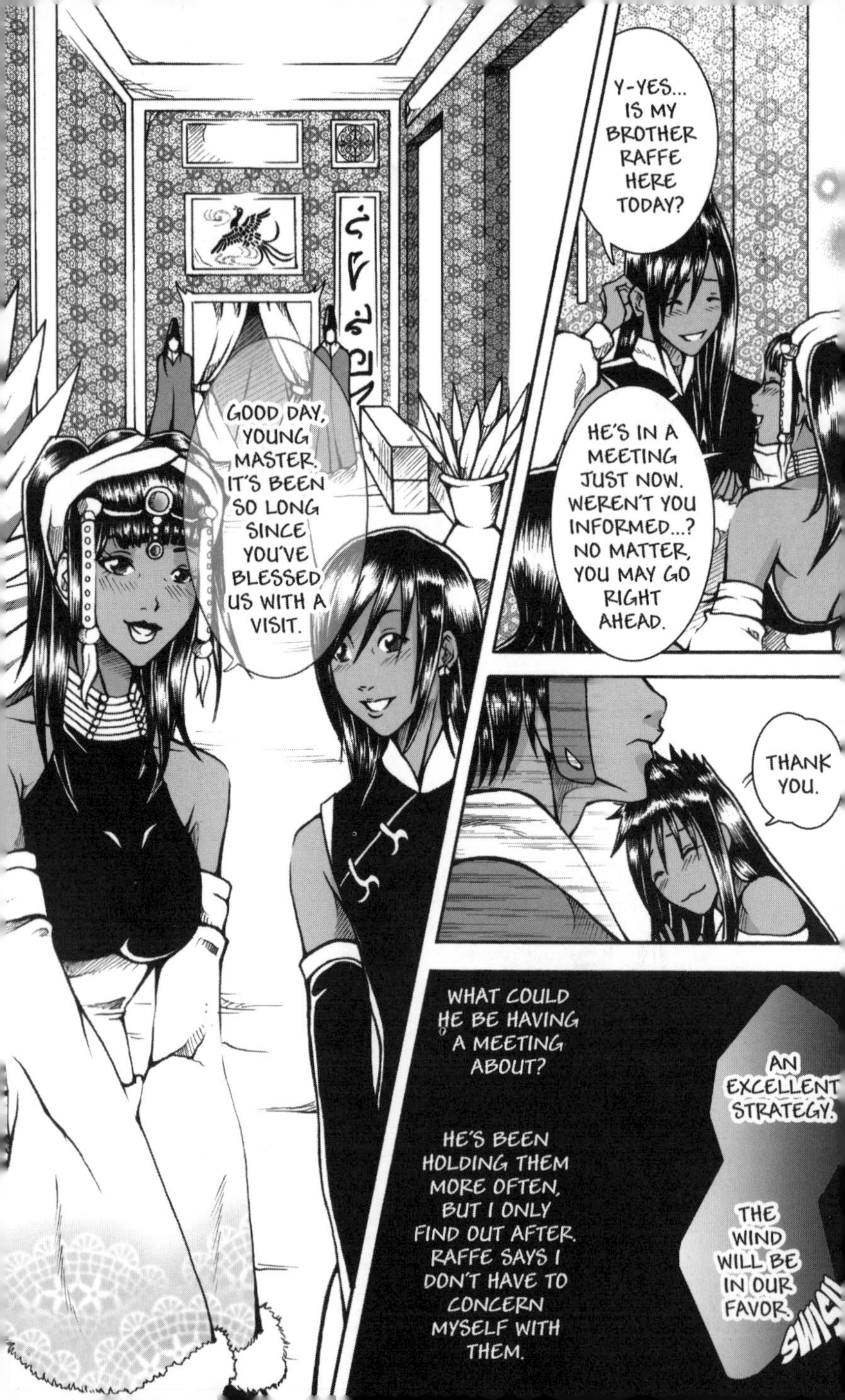
GOOD DAY, YOUNG MASTER. IT'S BEEN SO LONG SINCE YOU'VE BLESSED US WITH A VISIT.
Y-YES... IS MY BROTHER RAFFE HERE TODAY?
HE'S IN A MEETING JUST NOW. WEREN'T YOU INFORMED...? NO MATTER, YOU MAY GO RIGHT AHEAD.
THANK YOU.
WHAT COULD HE BE HAVING A MEETING ABOUT?
HE'S BEEN HOLDING THEM MORE OFTEN, BUT I ONLY FIND OUT AFTER. RAFFE SAYS I DON'T HAVE TO CONCERN MYSELF WITH THEM.
AN EXCELLENT STRATEGY.
THE WIND WILL BE IN OUR FAVOR.

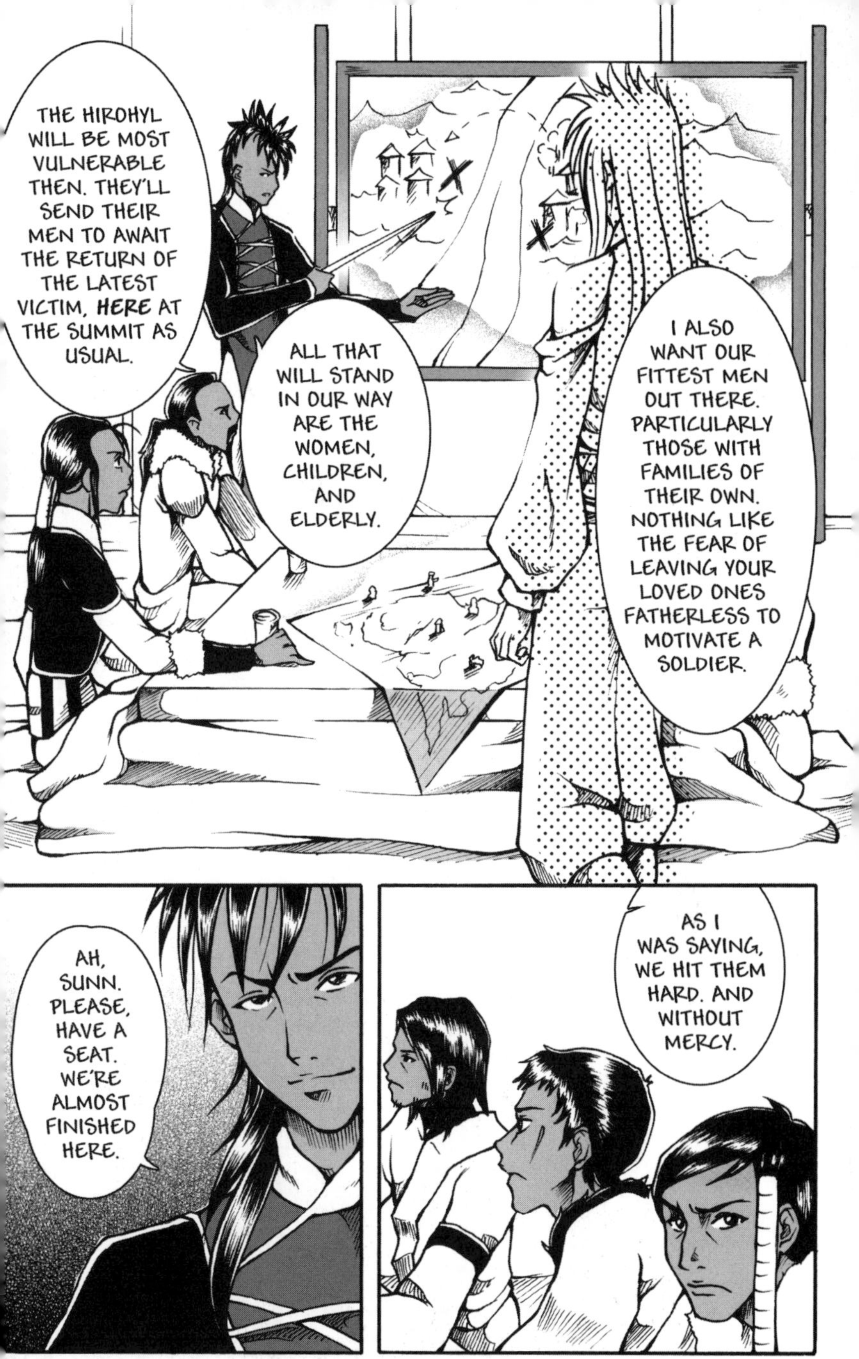
THE HIROHYL WILL BE MOST VULNERABLE THEN. THEY'LL SEND THEIR MEN TO AWAIT THE RETURN OF THE LATEST VICTIM, **HERE** AT THE SUMMIT AS USUAL.
ALL THAT WILL STAND IN OUR WAY ARE THE WOMEN, CHILDREN, AND ELDERLY.
I ALSO WANT OUR FITTEST MEN OUT THERE. PARTICULARLY THOSE WITH FAMILIES OF THEIR OWN. NOTHING LIKE THE FEAR OF LEAVING YOUR LOVED ONES FATHERLESS TO MOTIVATE A SOLDIER.
AH, SUNN. PLEASE, HAVE A SEAT. WE'RE ALMOST FINISHED HERE.
AS I WAS SAYING, WE HIT THEM HARD. AND WITHOUT MERCY.

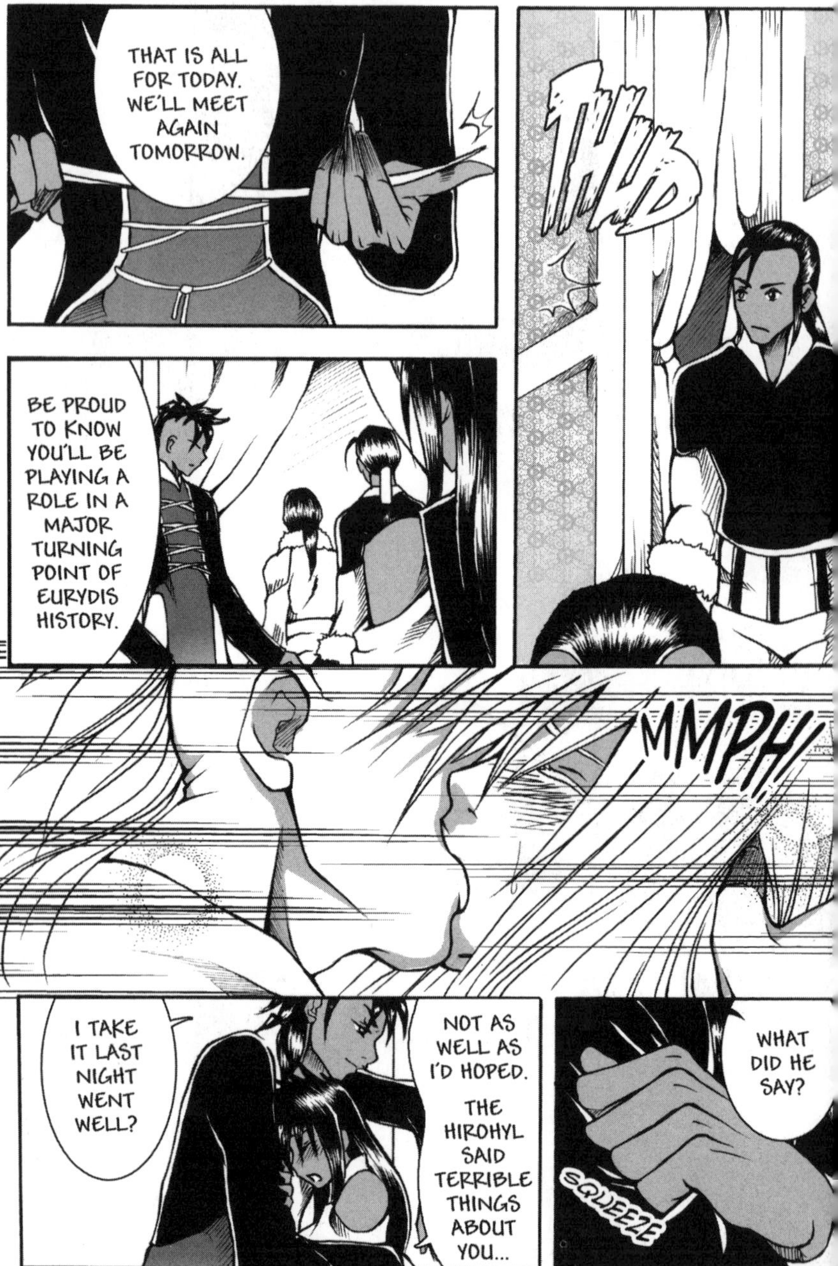
THAT IS ALL FOR TODAY. WE'LL MEET AGAIN TOMORROW.
THUD
BE PROUD TO KNOW YOU'LL BE PLAYING A ROLE IN A MAJOR TURNING POINT OF EURYDIS HISTORY.
MMPH!
I TAKE IT LAST NIGHT WENT WELL?
NOT AS WELL AS I'D HOPED.
THE HIROHYL SAID TERRIBLE THINGS ABOUT YOU...
WHAT DID HE SAY?
SQUEEZE

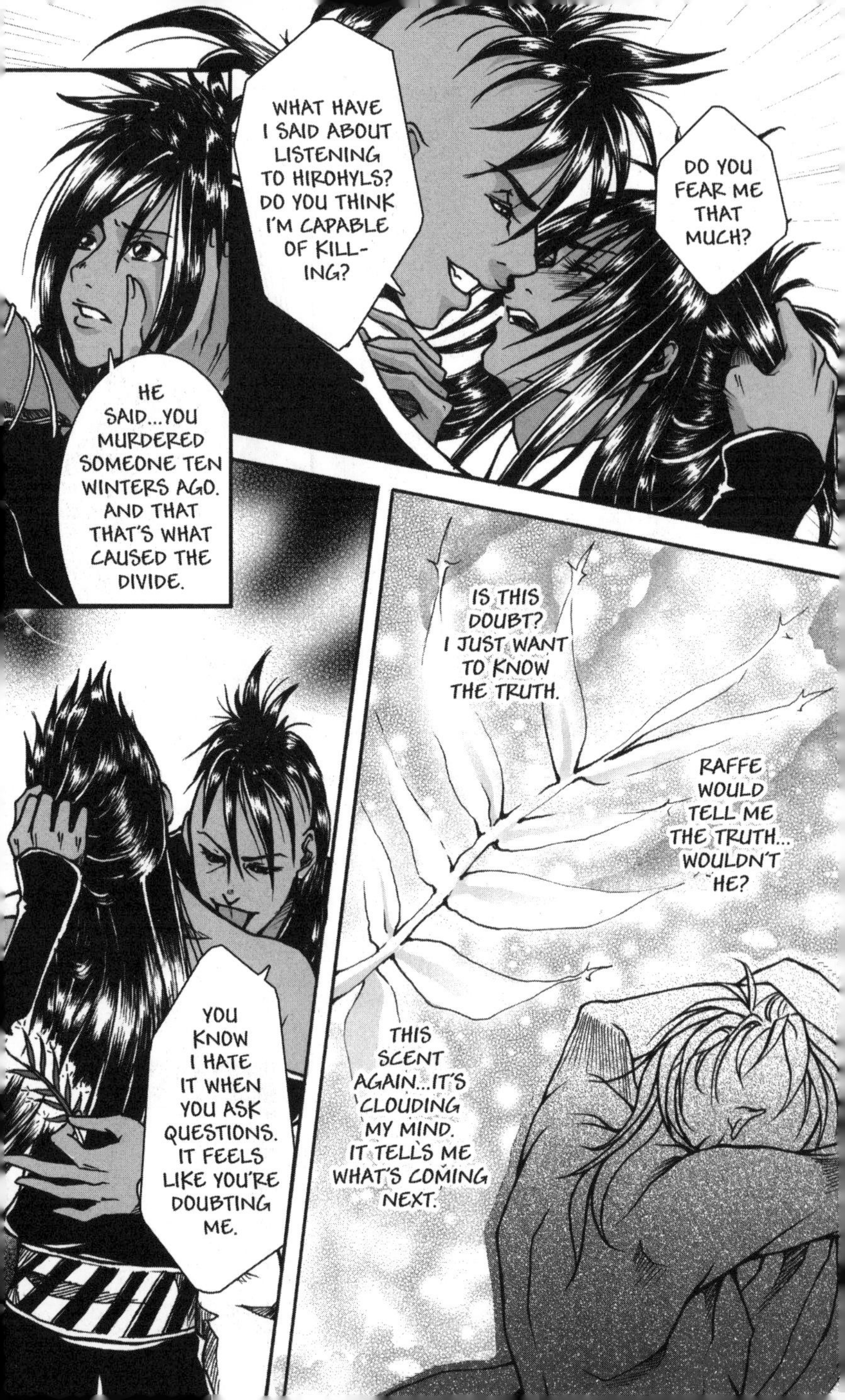

WHAT HAVE I SAID ABOUT LISTENING TO HIROHYLS? DO YOU THINK I'M CAPABLE OF KILL-ING?
DO YOU FEAR ME THAT MUCH?
HE SAID...YOU MURDERED SOMEONE TEN WINTERS AGO. AND THAT THAT'S WHAT CAUSED THE DIVIDE.
YOU KNOW I HATE IT WHEN YOU ASK QUESTIONS. IT FEELS LIKE YOU'RE DOUBTING ME.
IS THIS DOUBT? I JUST WANT TO KNOW THE TRUTH.
RAFFE WOULD TELL ME THE TRUTH... WOULDN'T HE?
THIS SCENT AGAIN...IT'S CLOUDING MY MIND. IT TELLS ME WHAT'S COMING NEXT.

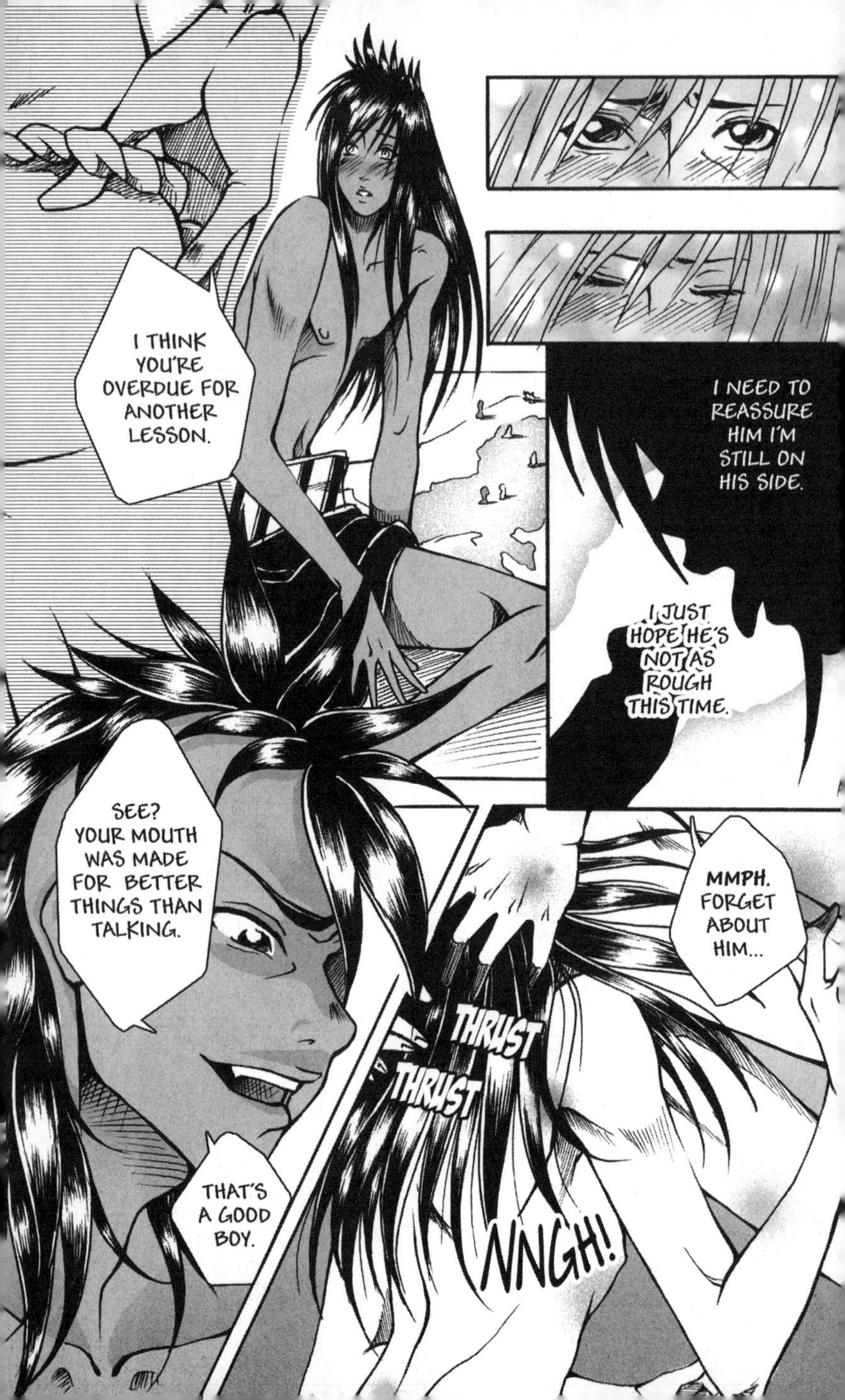
I NEED TO REASSURE HIM I'M STILL ON HIS SIDE.
I JUST HOPE HE'S NOT AS ROUGH THIS TIME.
I THINK YOU'RE OVERDUE FOR ANOTHER LESSON.
MMPH. FORGET ABOUT HIM...
THRUST
THRUST
NNGH!
SEE? YOUR MOUTH WAS MADE FOR BETTER THINGS THAN TALKING.
THAT'S A GOOD BOY.

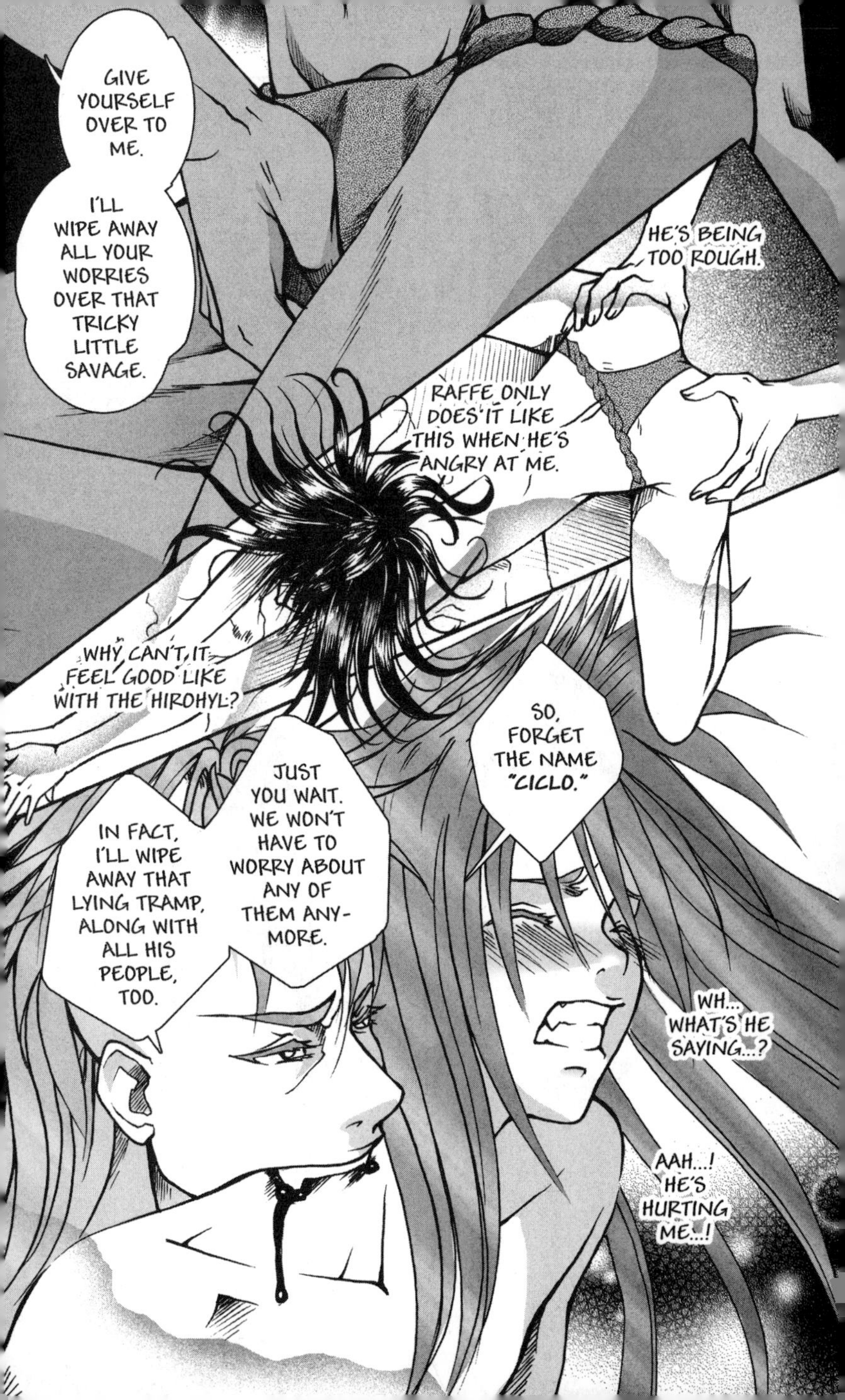
GIVE YOURSELF OVER TO ME.
I'LL WIPE AWAY ALL YOUR WORRIES OVER THAT TRICKY LITTLE SAVAGE.
HE'S BEING TOO ROUGH.
RAFFE ONLY DOES IT LIKE THIS WHEN HE'S ANGRY AT ME.
WHY CAN'T IT FEEL GOOD LIKE WITH THE HIROHYL?
SO, FORGET THE NAME "CICLO."
JUST YOU WAIT. WE WON'T HAVE TO WORRY ABOUT ANY OF THEM ANY-MORE.
IN FACT, I'LL WIPE AWAY THAT LYING TRAMP, ALONG WITH ALL HIS PEOPLE, TOO.
WH... WHAT'S HE SAYING...?
AAH...! HE'S HURTING ME...!

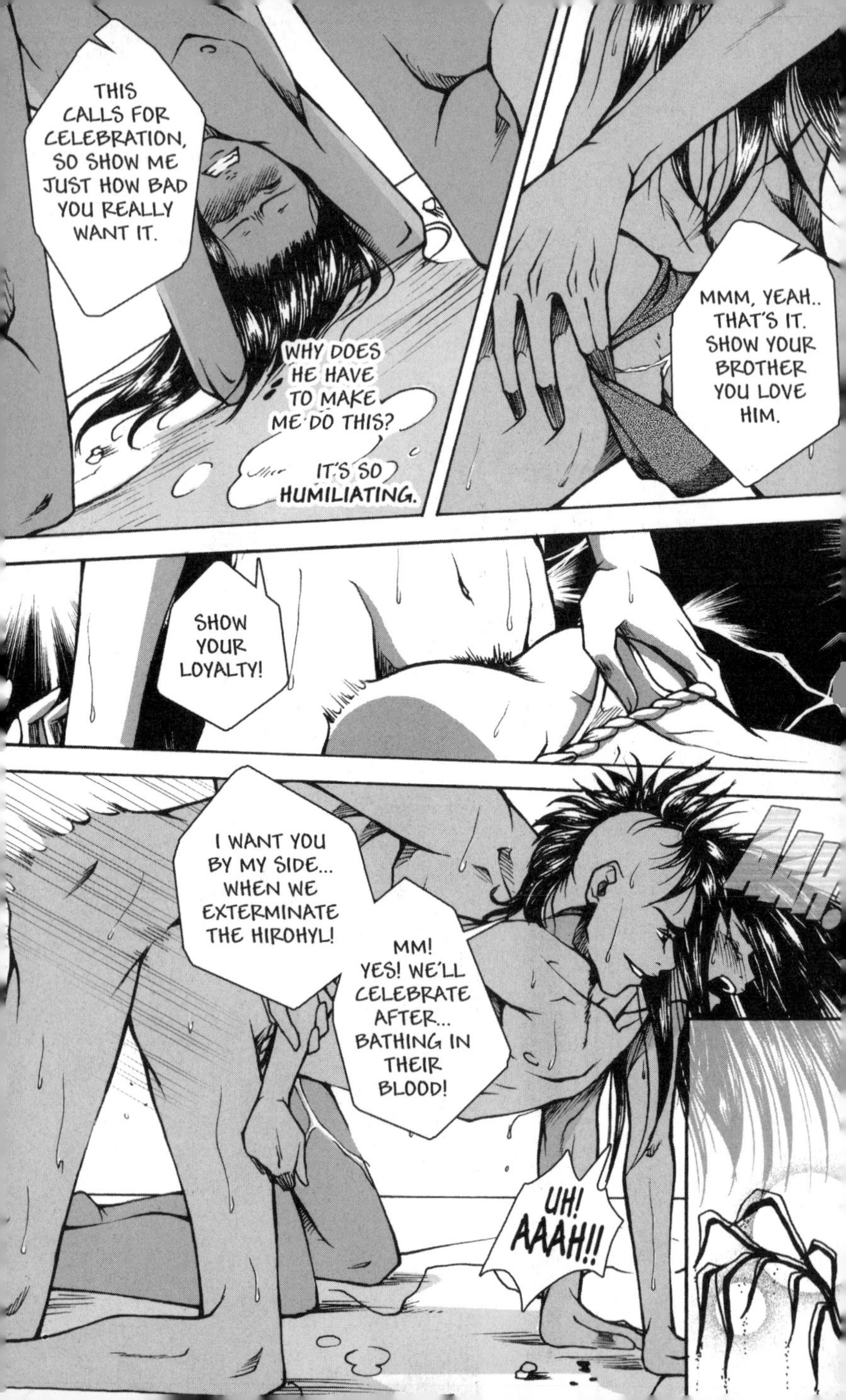
THIS CALLS FOR CELEBRATION, SO SHOW ME JUST HOW BAD YOU REALLY WANT IT.
WHY DOES HE HAVE TO MAKE ME DO THIS?
IT'S SO HUMILIATING.
MMM, YEAH.. THAT'S IT. SHOW YOUR BROTHER YOU LOVE HIM.
SHOW YOUR LOYALTY!
I WANT YOU BY MY SIDE... WHEN WE EXTERMINATE THE HIROHYL!
MM! YES! WE'LL CELEBRATE AFTER... BATHING IN THEIR BLOOD!
UH! AAAH!!

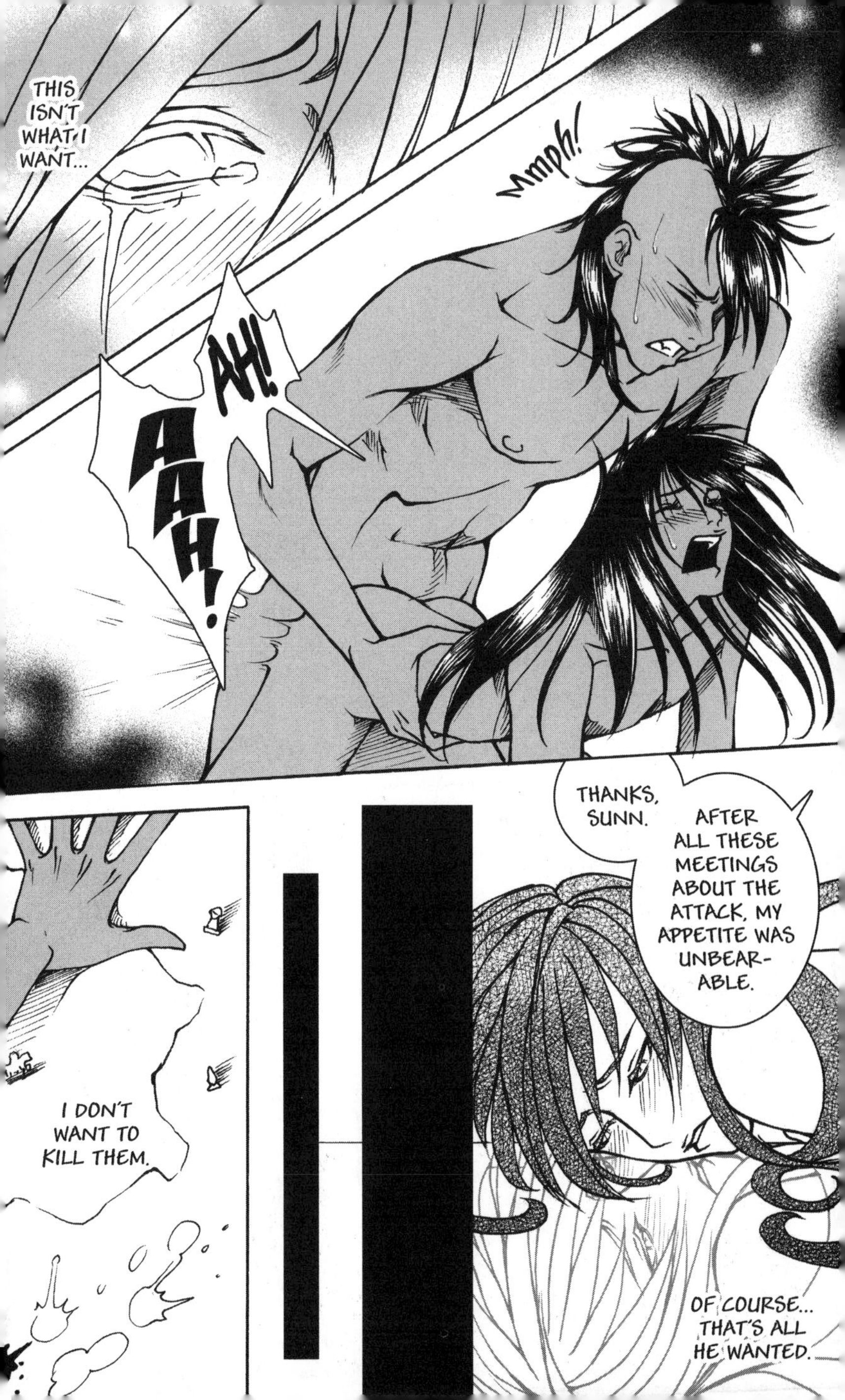
Mmph!
AH!
AAAH!
THIS ISN'T WHAT I WANT...
THANKS, SUNN.
AFTER ALL THESE MEETINGS ABOUT THE ATTACK, MY APPETITE WAS UNBEAR-ABLE.
OF COURSE... THAT'S ALL HE WANTED.
I DON'T WANT TO KILL THEM.

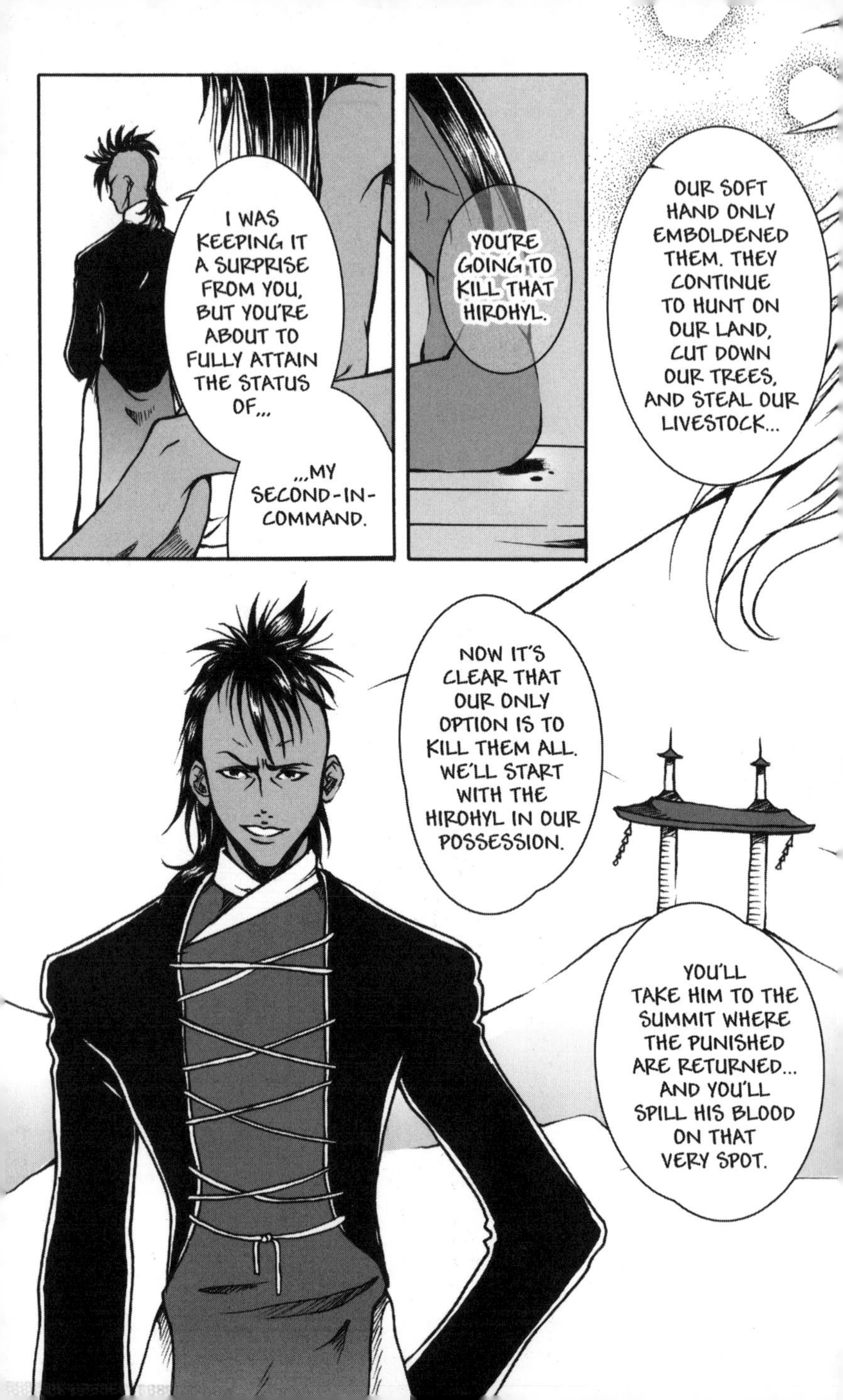
I WAS KEEPING IT A SURPRISE FROM YOU, BUT YOU'RE ABOUT TO FULLY ATTAIN THE STATUS OF...
...MY SECOND-IN-COMMAND.
YOU'RE GOING TO KILL THAT HIROHYL.
OUR SOFT HAND ONLY EMBOLDENED THEM. THEY CONTINUE TO HUNT ON OUR LAND, CUT DOWN OUR TREES, AND STEAL OUR LIVESTOCK...
NOW IT'S CLEAR THAT OUR ONLY OPTION IS TO KILL THEM ALL. WE'LL START WITH THE HIROHYL IN OUR POSSESSION.
YOU'LL TAKE HIM TO THE SUMMIT WHERE THE PUNISHED ARE RETURNED... AND YOU'LL SPILL HIS BLOOD ON THAT VERY SPOT.

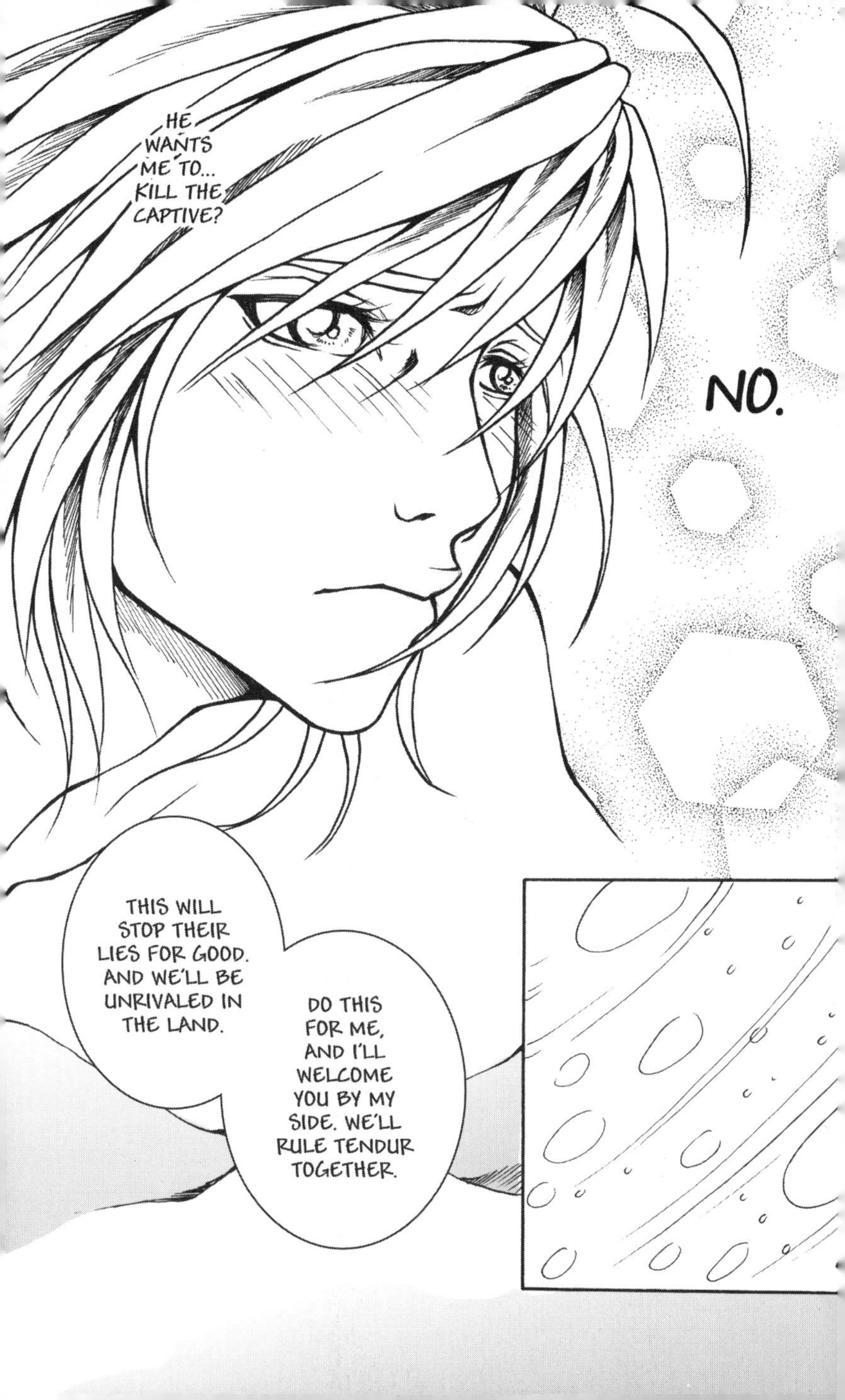
HE WANTS ME TO... KILL THE CAPTIVE?
NO.
THIS WILL STOP THEIR LIES FOR GOOD. AND WE'LL BE UNRIVALED IN THE LAND.
DO THIS FOR ME, AND I'LL WELCOME YOU BY MY SIDE. WE'LL RULE TENDUR TOGETHER.

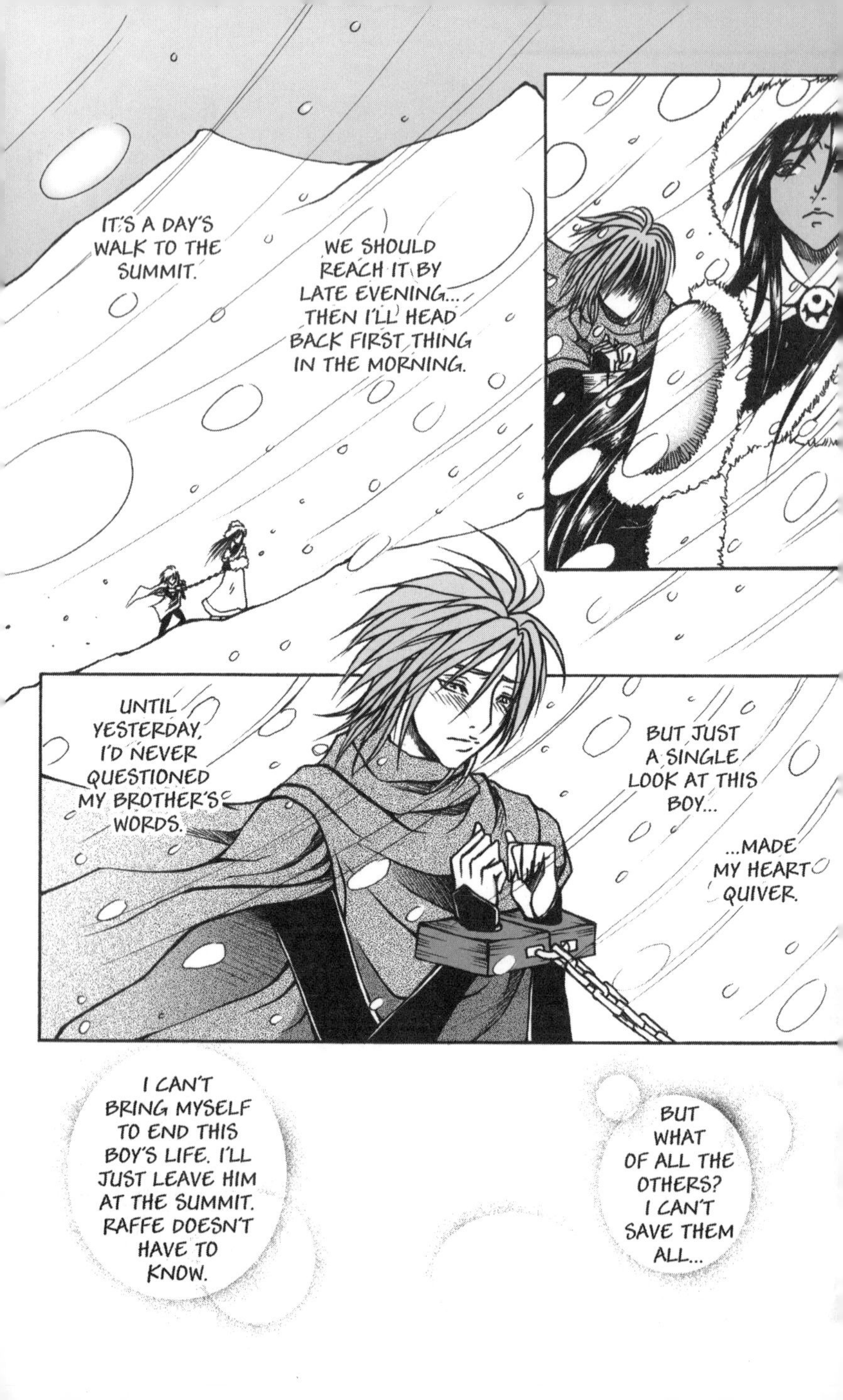
IT'S A DAY'S WALK TO THE SUMMIT.
WE SHOULD REACH IT BY LATE EVENING... THEN I'LL HEAD BACK FIRST THING IN THE MORNING.
UNTIL YESTERDAY, I'D NEVER QUESTIONED MY BROTHER'S WORDS.
BUT JUST A SINGLE LOOK AT THIS BOY...
...MADE MY HEART QUIVER.
I CAN'T BRING MYSELF TO END THIS BOY'S LIFE. I'LL JUST LEAVE HIM AT THE SUMMIT. RAFFE DOESN'T HAVE TO KNOW.
BUT WHAT OF ALL THE OTHERS? I CAN'T SAVE THEM ALL...

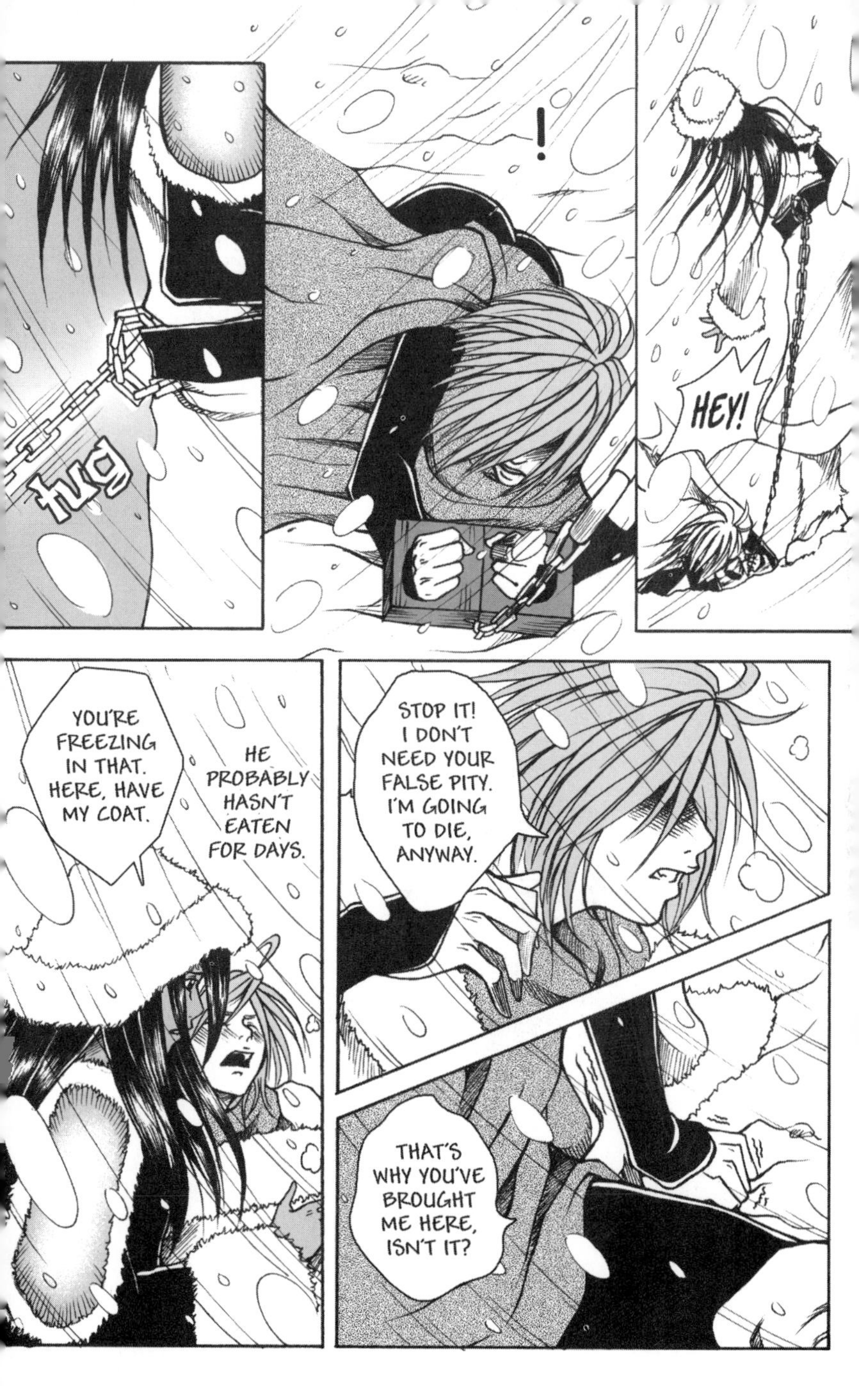
HEY!
!
tug
STOP IT! I DON'T NEED YOUR FALSE PITY. I'M GOING TO DIE, ANYWAY.
HE PROBABLY HASN'T EATEN FOR DAYS.
YOU'RE FREEZING IN THAT. HERE, HAVE MY COAT.
THAT'S WHY YOU'VE BROUGHT ME HERE, ISN'T IT?

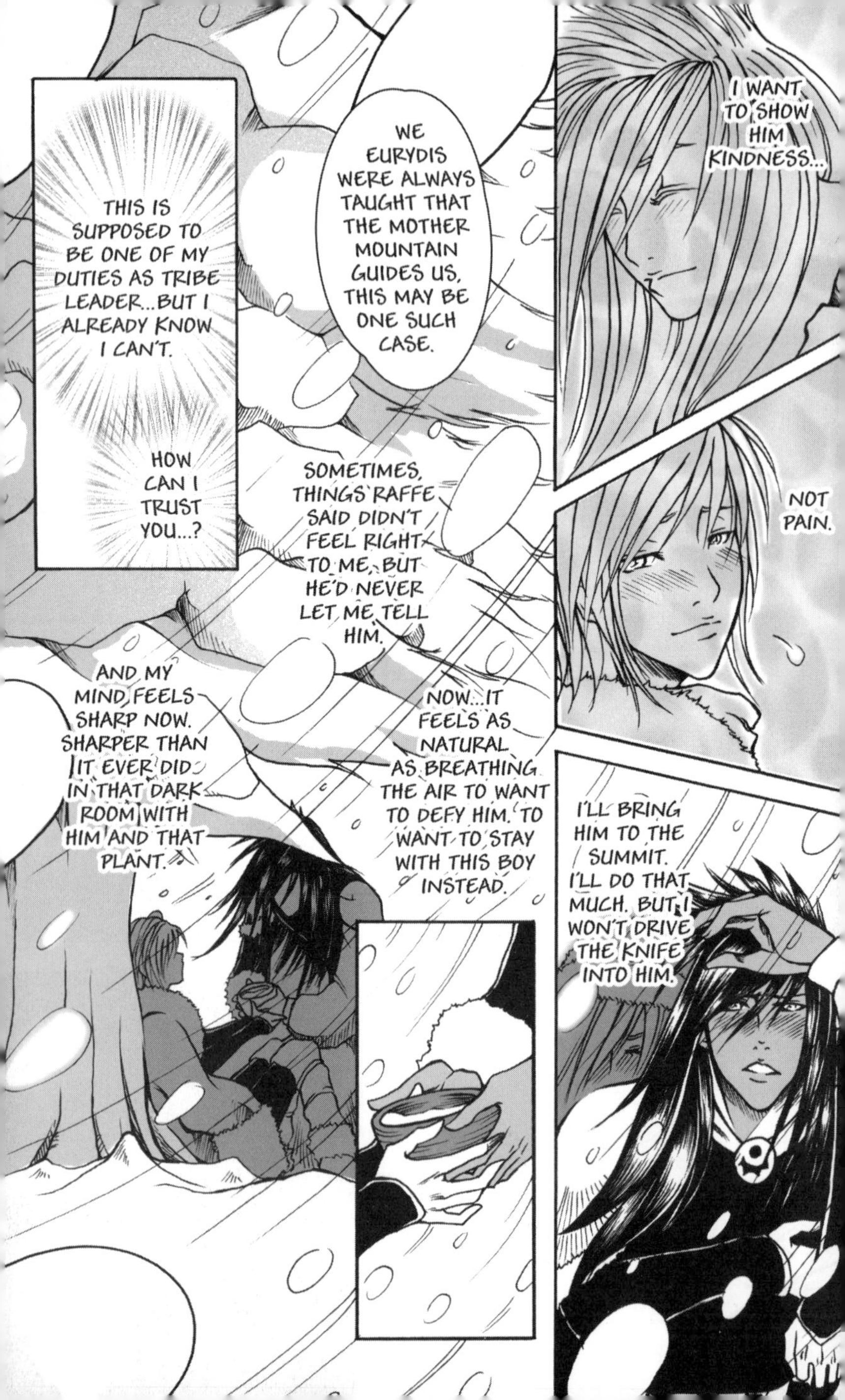
THIS IS SUPPOSED TO BE ONE OF MY DUTIES AS TRIBE LEADER...BUT I ALREADY KNOW I CAN'T.
WE EURYDIS WERE ALWAYS TAUGHT THAT THE MOTHER MOUNTAIN GUIDES US, THIS MAY BE ONE SUCH CASE.
I WANT TO SHOW HIM KINDNESS...
HOW CAN I TRUST YOU...?
SOMETIMES, THINGS RAFFE SAID DIDN'T FEEL RIGHT TO ME, BUT HE'D NEVER LET ME TELL HIM.
NOT PAIN.
AND MY MIND FEELS SHARP NOW. SHARPER THAN IT EVER DID IN THAT DARK ROOM WITH HIM AND THAT PLANT.
NOW...IT FEELS AS NATURAL AS BREATHING THE AIR TO WANT TO DEFY HIM. TO WANT TO STAY WITH THIS BOY INSTEAD.
I'LL BRING HIM TO THE SUMMIT. I'LL DO THAT MUCH. BUT I WON'T DRIVE THE KNIFE INTO HIM.

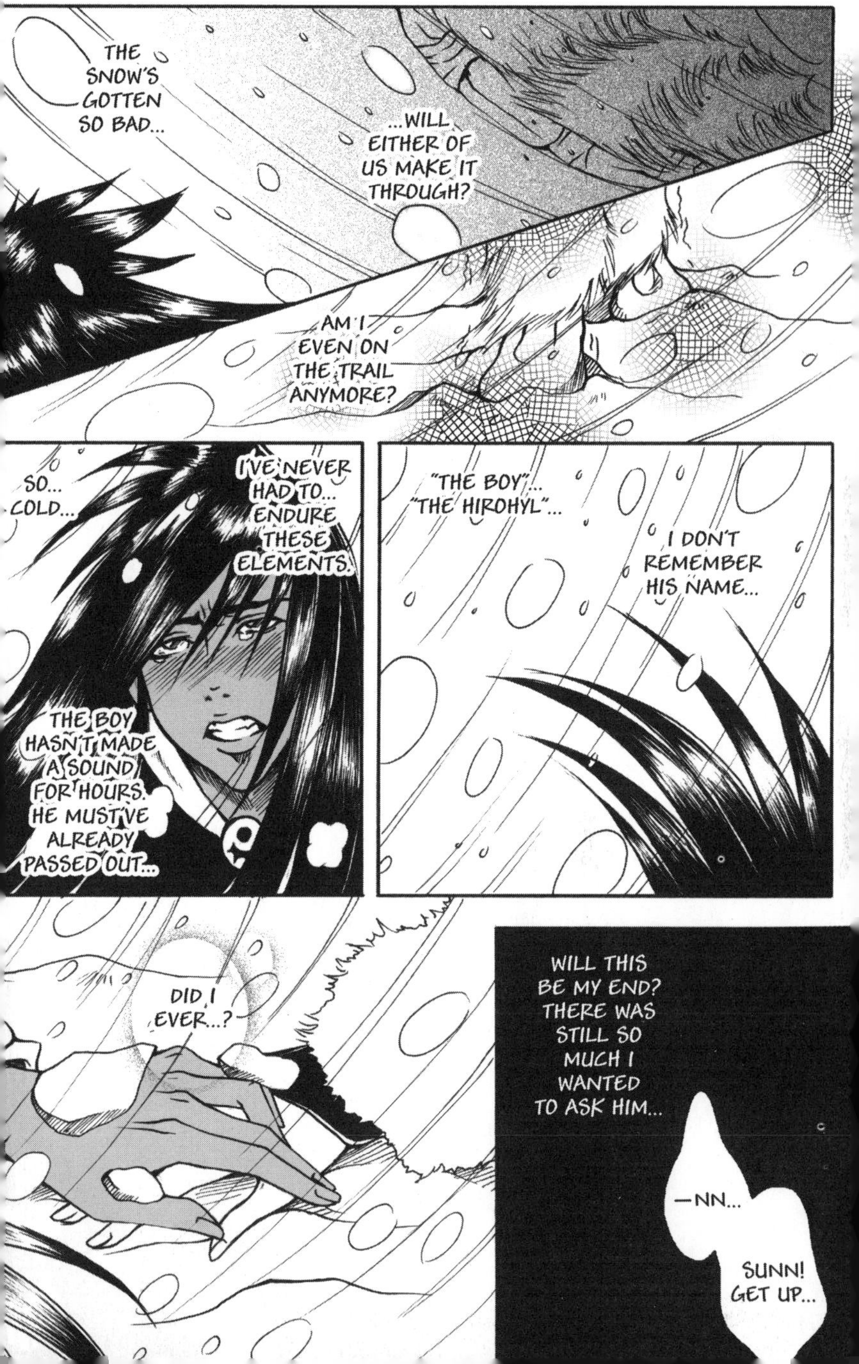
THE SNOW'S GOTTEN SO BAD...
...WILL EITHER OF US MAKE IT THROUGH?
AM I EVEN ON THE TRAIL ANYMORE?
SO... COLD...
I'VE NEVER HAD TO... ENDURE THESE ELEMENTS.
THE BOY HASN'T MADE A SOUND FOR HOURS. HE MUST'VE ALREADY PASSED OUT...
"THE BOY"... "THE HIROHYL"...
I DON'T REMEMBER HIS NAME...
DID I EVER...?
WILL THIS BE MY END? THERE WAS STILL SO MUCH I WANTED TO ASK HIM...
—NN...
SUNN! GET UP...

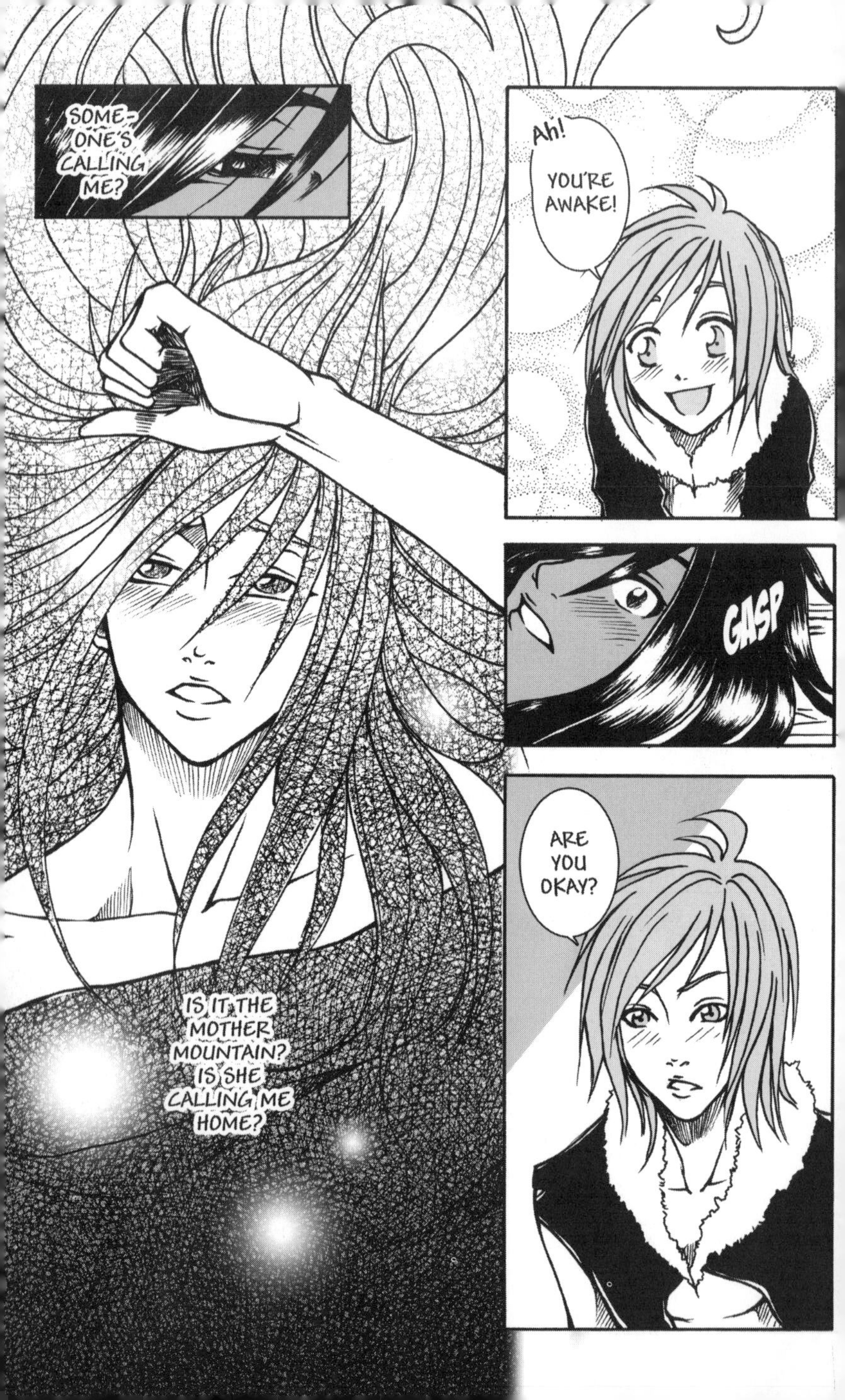
SOME-ONE'S CALLING ME?
IS IT THE MOTHER MOUNTAIN? IS SHE CALLING ME HOME?
Ah!
YOU'RE AWAKE!
GASP
ARE YOU OKAY?

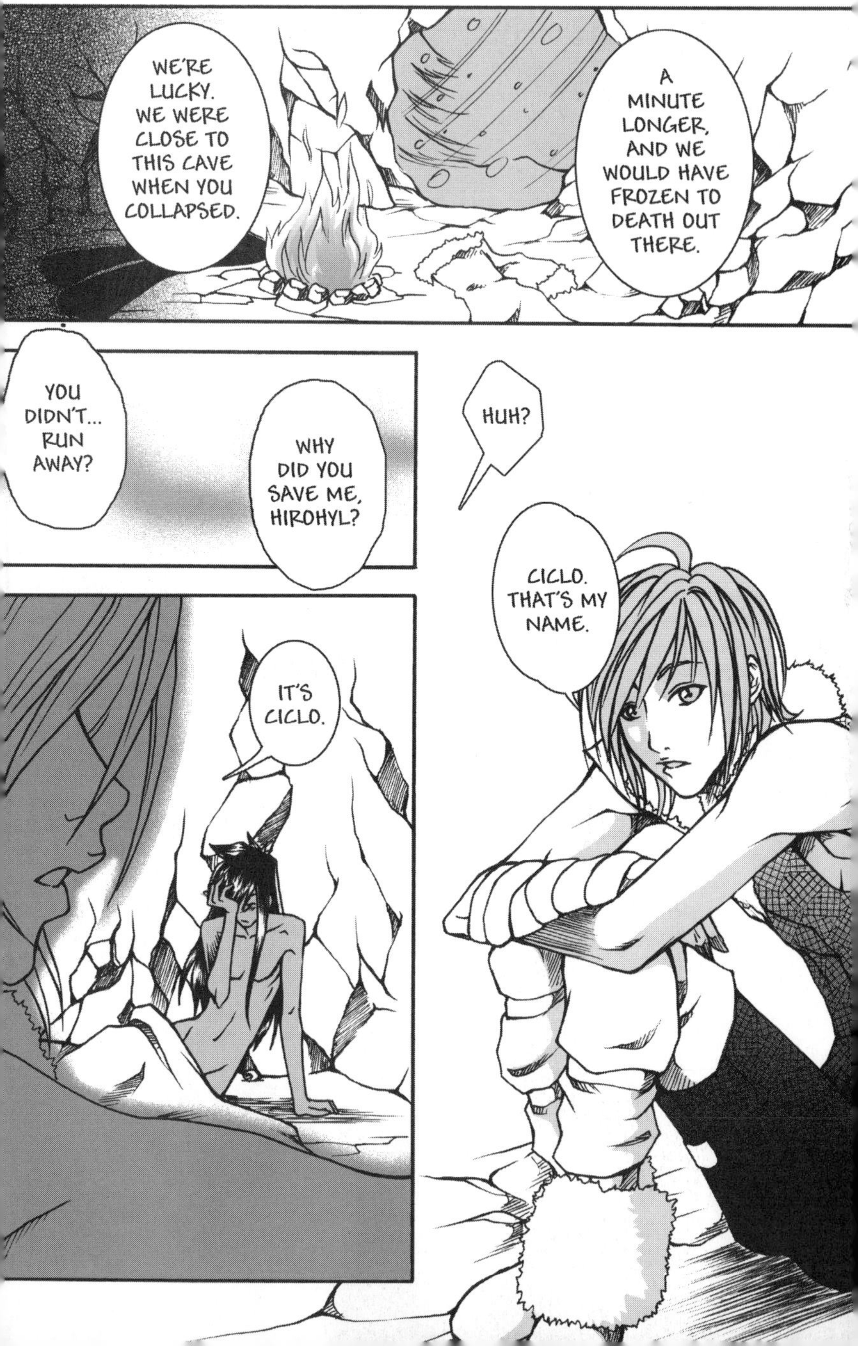
WE'RE LUCKY. WE WERE CLOSE TO THIS CAVE WHEN YOU COLLAPSED.
A MINUTE LONGER, AND WE WOULD HAVE FROZEN TO DEATH OUT THERE.
YOU DIDN'T... RUN AWAY?
WHY DID YOU SAVE ME, HIROHYL?
HUH?
IT'S CICLO.
CICLO. THAT'S MY NAME.

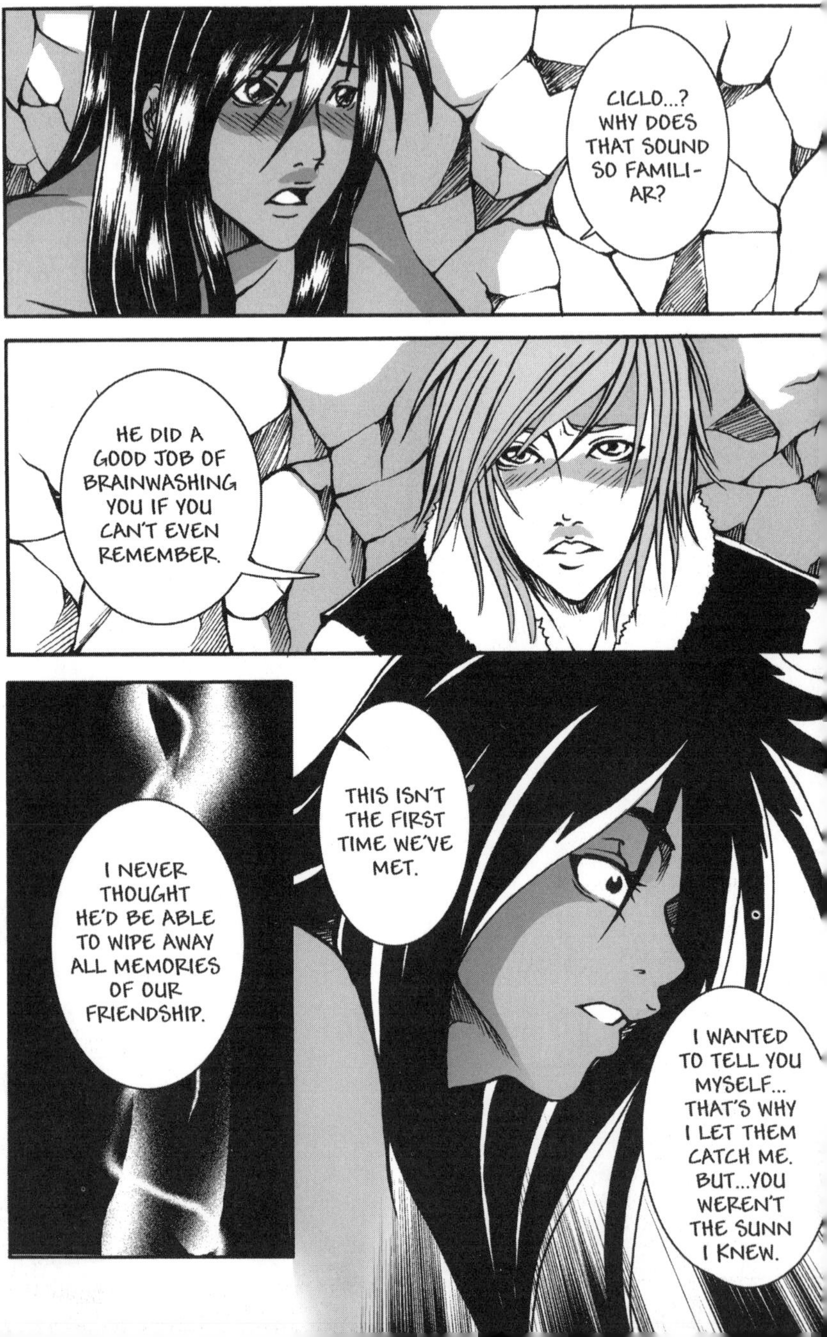
CICLO...? WHY DOES THAT SOUND SO FAMILI-AR?
HE DID A GOOD JOB OF BRAINWASHING YOU IF YOU CAN'T EVEN REMEMBER.
THIS ISN'T THE FIRST TIME WE'VE MET.
I NEVER THOUGHT HE'D BE ABLE TO WIPE AWAY ALL MEMORIES OF OUR FRIENDSHIP.
I WANTED TO TELL YOU MYSELF... THAT'S WHY I LET THEM CATCH ME. BUT...YOU WEREN'T THE SUNN I KNEW.

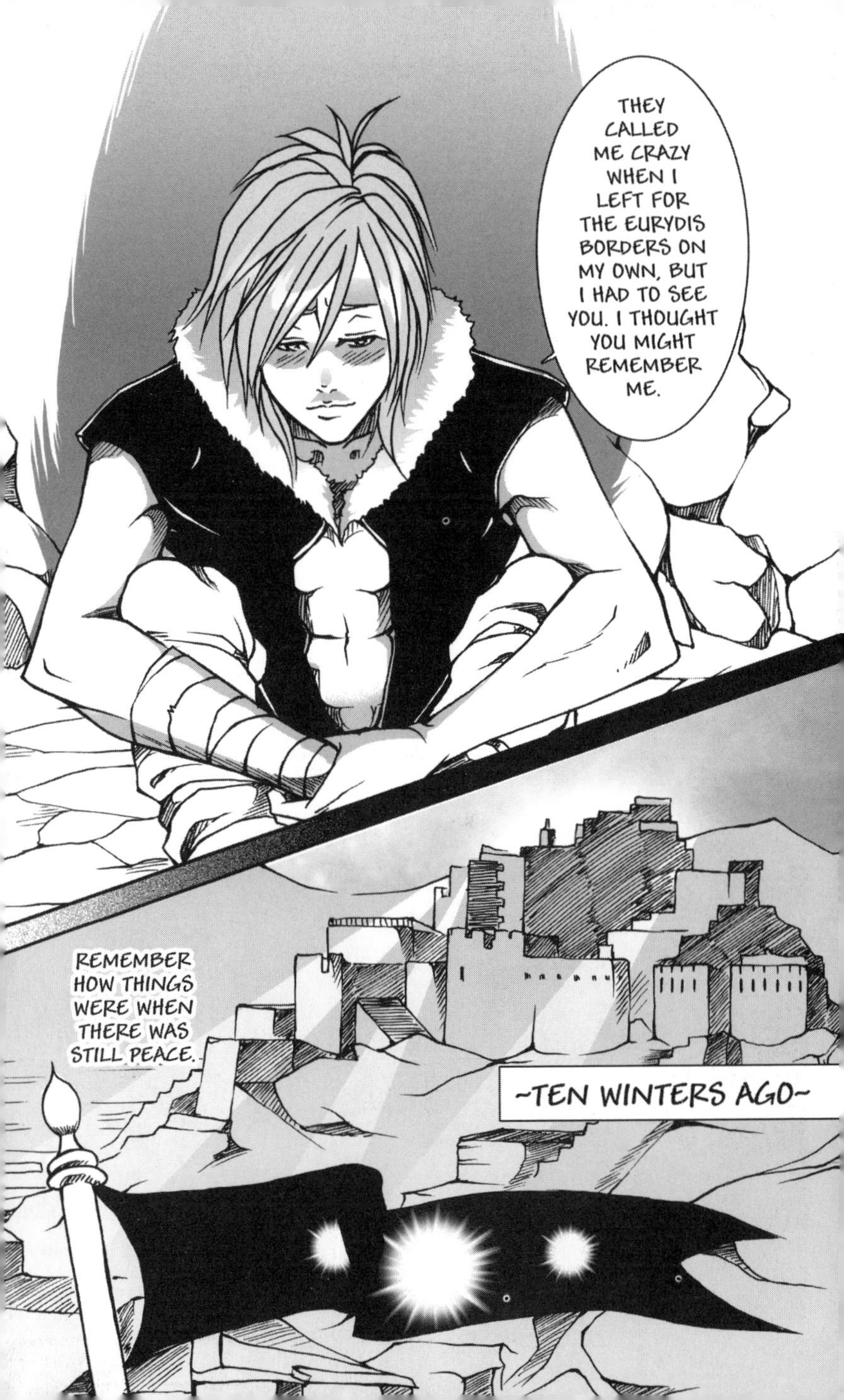
THEY CALLED ME CRAZY WHEN I LEFT FOR THE EURYDIS BORDERS ON MY OWN, BUT I HAD TO SEE YOU. I THOUGHT YOU MIGHT REMEMBER ME.
REMEMBER HOW THINGS WERE WHEN THERE WAS STILL PEACE.
~TEN WINTERS AGO~

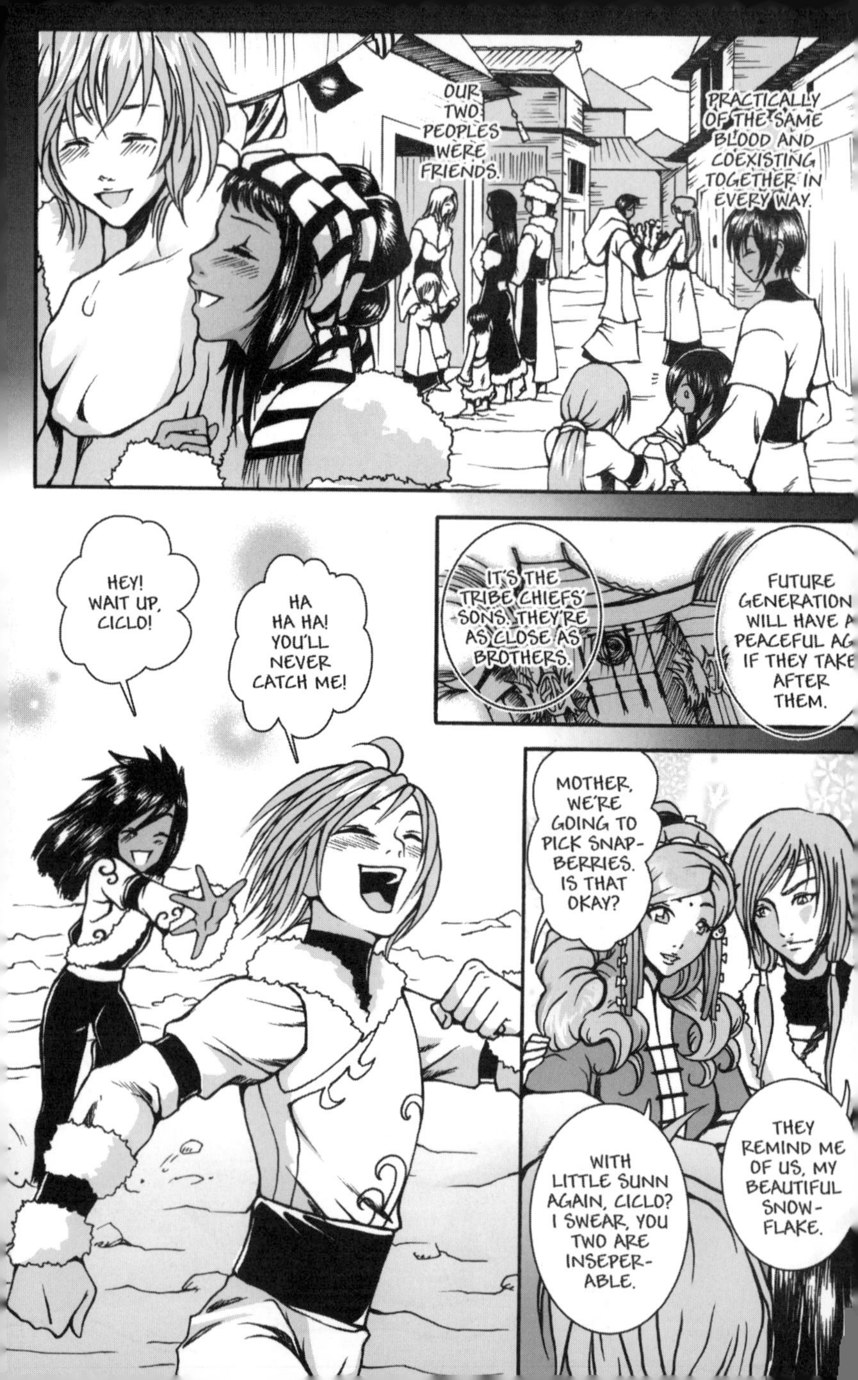
OUR TWO PEOPLES WERE FRIENDS.
PRACTICALLY OF THE SAME BLOOD AND COEXISTING TOGETHER IN EVERY WAY.
IT'S THE TRIBE CHIEFS' SONS. THEY'RE AS CLOSE AS BROTHERS.
FUTURE GENERATION WILL HAVE A PEACEFUL AG IF THEY TAKE AFTER THEM.
HEY! WAIT UP, CICLO!
HA HA HA! YOU'LL NEVER CATCH ME!
MOTHER, WE'RE GOING TO PICK SNAP-BERRIES. IS THAT OKAY?
WITH LITTLE SUNN AGAIN, CICLO? I SWEAR, YOU TWO ARE INSEPER-ABLE.
THEY REMIND ME OF US, MY BEAUTIFUL SNOW-FLAKE.

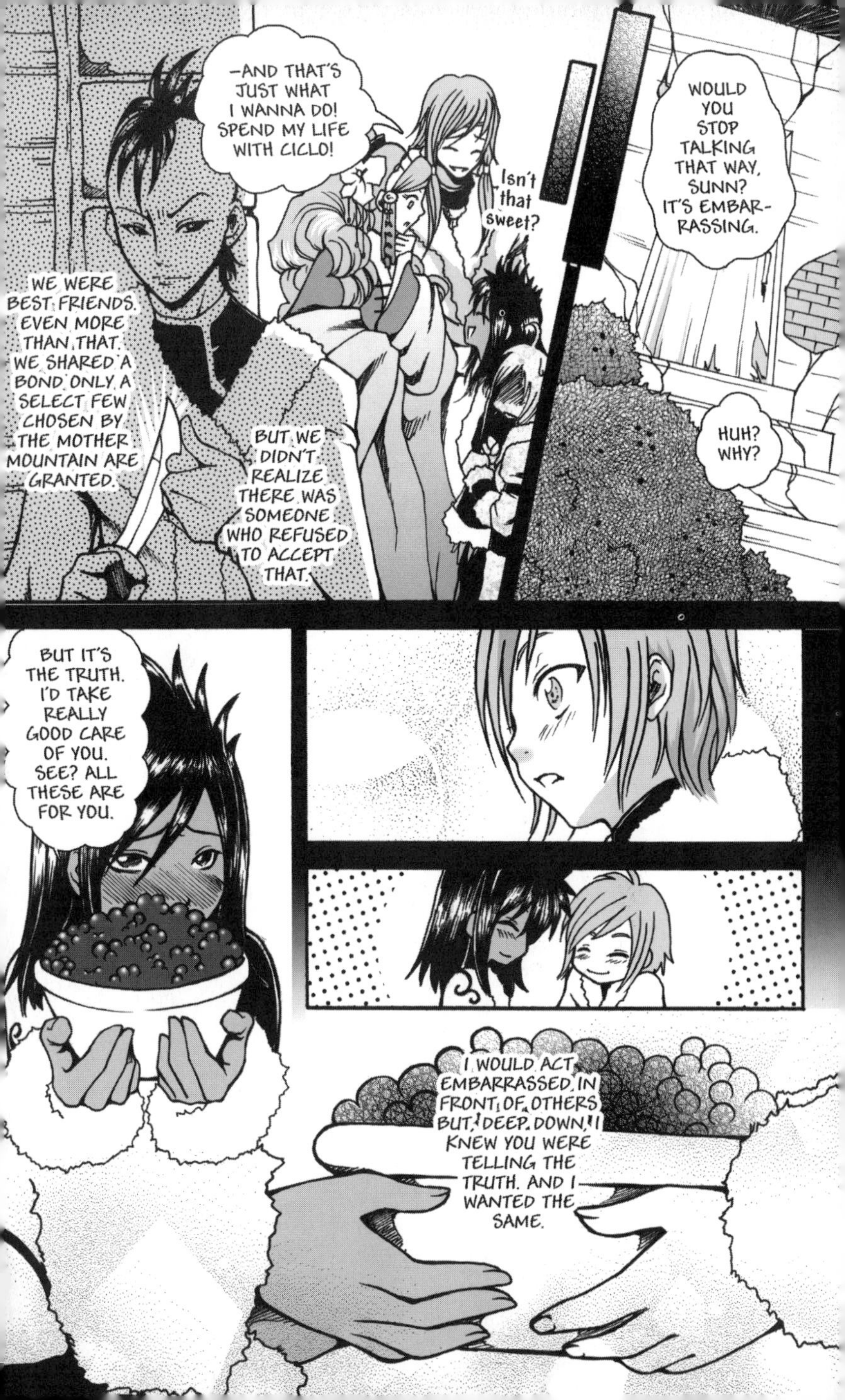

-AND THAT'S JUST WHAT I WANNA DO! SPEND MY LIFE WITH CICLO!
Isn't that sweet?
WE WERE BEST FRIENDS. EVEN MORE THAN THAT. WE SHARED A BOND ONLY A SELECT FEW CHOSEN BY THE MOTHER MOUNTAIN ARE GRANTED.
BUT WE DIDN'T REALIZE THERE WAS SOMEONE WHO REFUSED TO ACCEPT THAT.
WOULD YOU STOP TALKING THAT WAY, SUNN? IT'S EMBARRASSING.
HUH? WHY?
BUT IT'S THE TRUTH. I'D TAKE REALLY GOOD CARE OF YOU. SEE? ALL THESE ARE FOR YOU.
I WOULD ACT EMBARRASSED IN FRONT OF OTHERS BUT, DEEP DOWN, I KNEW YOU WERE TELLING THE TRUTH. AND I WANTED THE SAME.

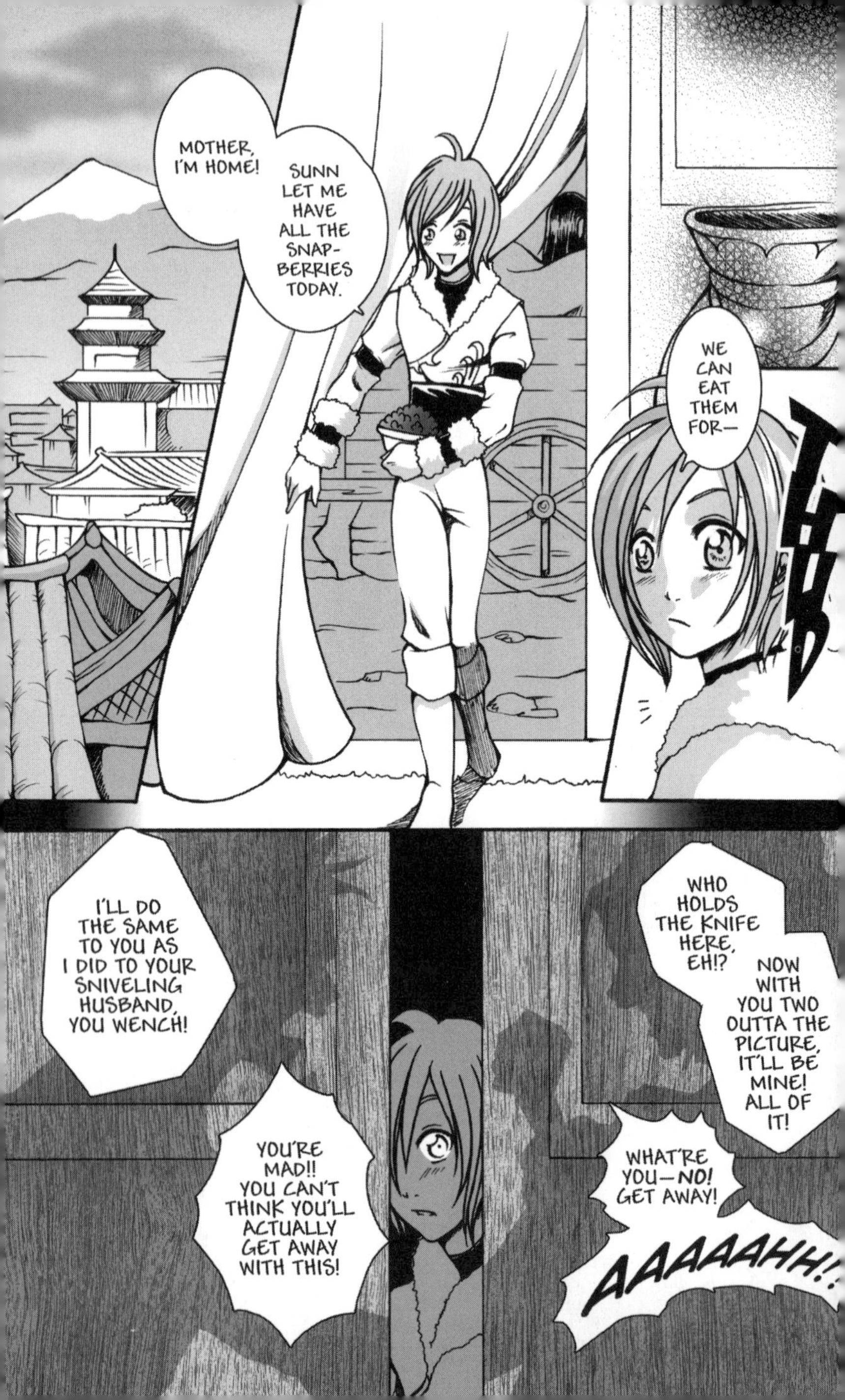
MOTHER, I'M HOME!
SUNN LET ME HAVE ALL THE SNAP-BERRIES TODAY.
WE CAN EAT THEM FOR—
I'LL DO THE SAME TO YOU AS I DID TO YOUR SNIVELING HUSBAND, YOU WENCH!
WHO HOLDS THE KNIFE HERE, EH!?
NOW WITH YOU TWO OUTTA THE PICTURE, IT'LL BE MINE! ALL OF IT!
YOU'RE MAD!! YOU CAN'T THINK YOU'LL ACTUALLY GET AWAY WITH THIS!
WHAT'RE YOU—NO! GET AWAY!
AAAAAHH!!

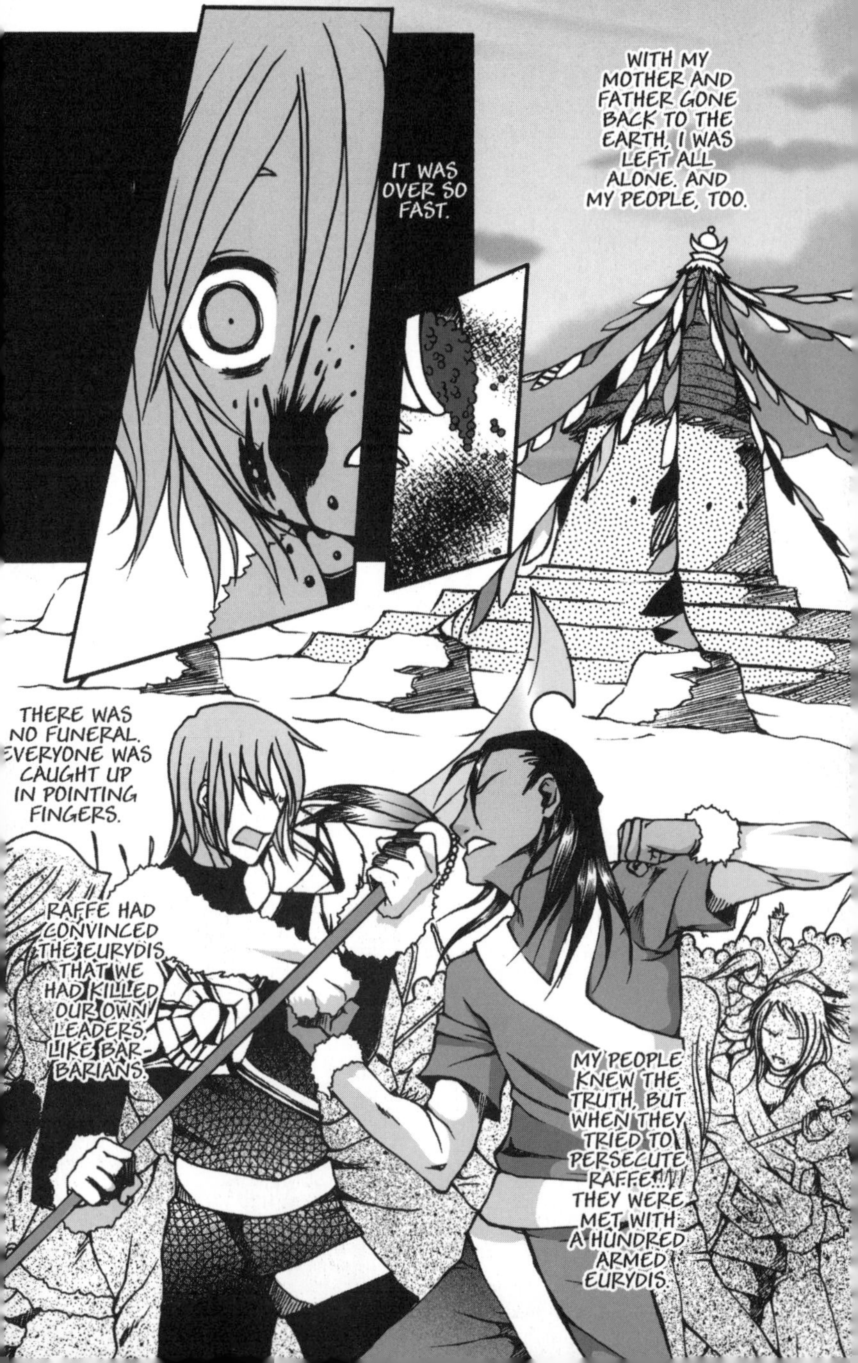
WITH MY MOTHER AND FATHER GONE BACK TO THE EARTH, I WAS LEFT ALL ALONE. AND MY PEOPLE, TOO.
IT WAS OVER SO FAST.
THERE WAS NO FUNERAL. EVERYONE WAS CAUGHT UP IN POINTING FINGERS.
RAFFE HAD CONVINCED THE EURYDIS THAT WE HAD KILLED OUR OWN LEADERS, LIKE BAR-BARIANS.
MY PEOPLE KNEW THE TRUTH, BUT WHEN THEY TRIED TO PERSECUTE RAFFE, THEY WERE MET WITH A HUNDRED ARMED EURYDIS.

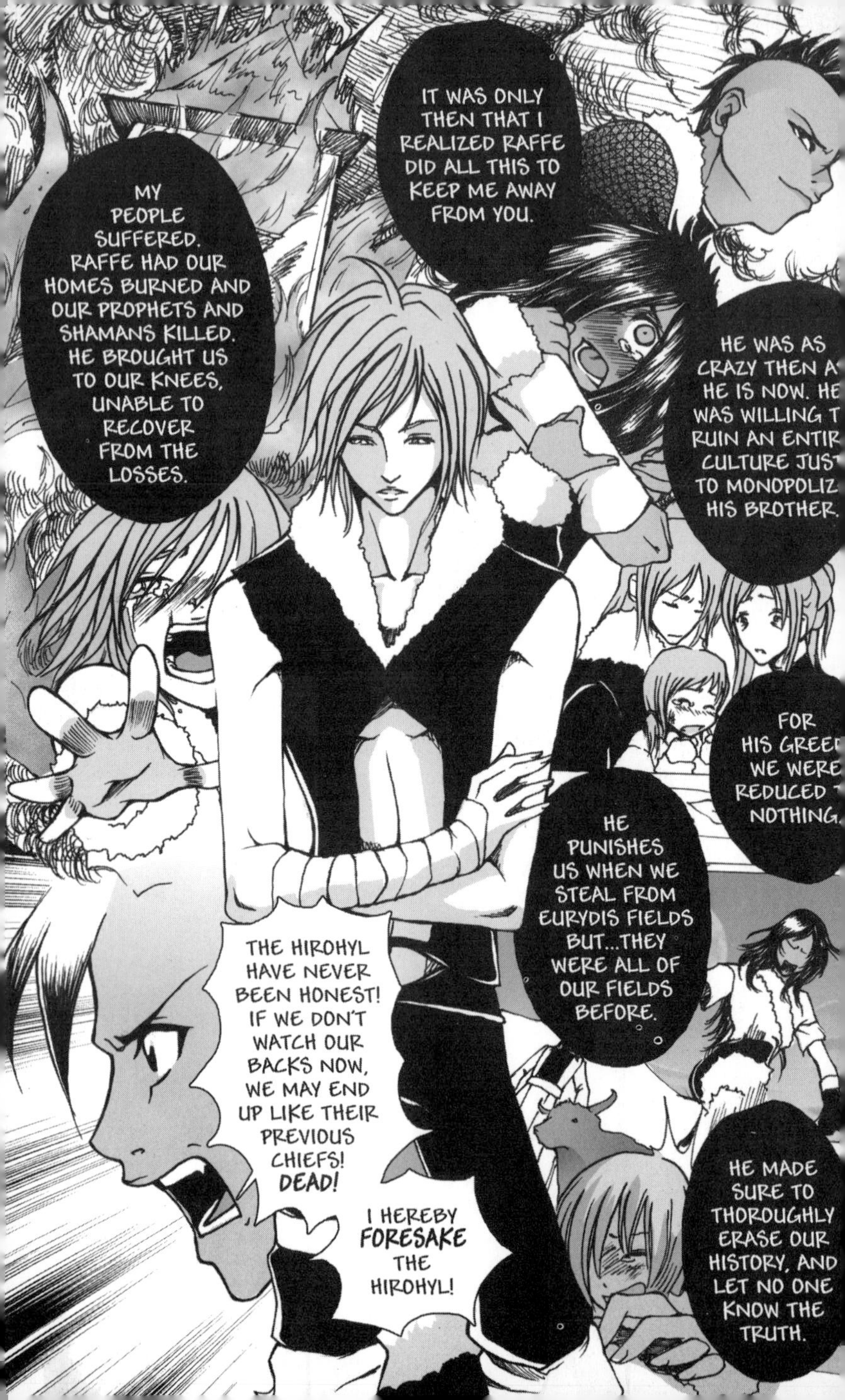
MY PEOPLE SUFFERED. RAFFE HAD OUR HOMES BURNED AND OUR PROPHETS AND SHAMANS KILLED. HE BROUGHT US TO OUR KNEES, UNABLE TO RECOVER FROM THE LOSSES.
IT WAS ONLY THEN THAT I REALIZED RAFFE DID ALL THIS TO KEEP ME AWAY FROM YOU.
HE WAS AS CRAZY THEN A HE IS NOW. HE WAS WILLING T RUIN AN ENTIR CULTURE JUST TO MONOPOLIZ HIS BROTHER.
FOR HIS GREED WE WERE REDUCED T NOTHING.
HE PUNISHES US WHEN WE STEAL FROM EURYDIS FIELDS BUT...THEY WERE ALL OF OUR FIELDS BEFORE.
THE HIROHYL HAVE NEVER BEEN HONEST! IF WE DON'T WATCH OUR BACKS NOW, WE MAY END UP LIKE THEIR PREVIOUS CHIEFS! DEAD!
I HEREBY FORESAKE THE HIROHYL!
HE MADE SURE TO THOROUGHLY ERASE OUR HISTORY, AND LET NO ONE KNOW THE TRUTH.

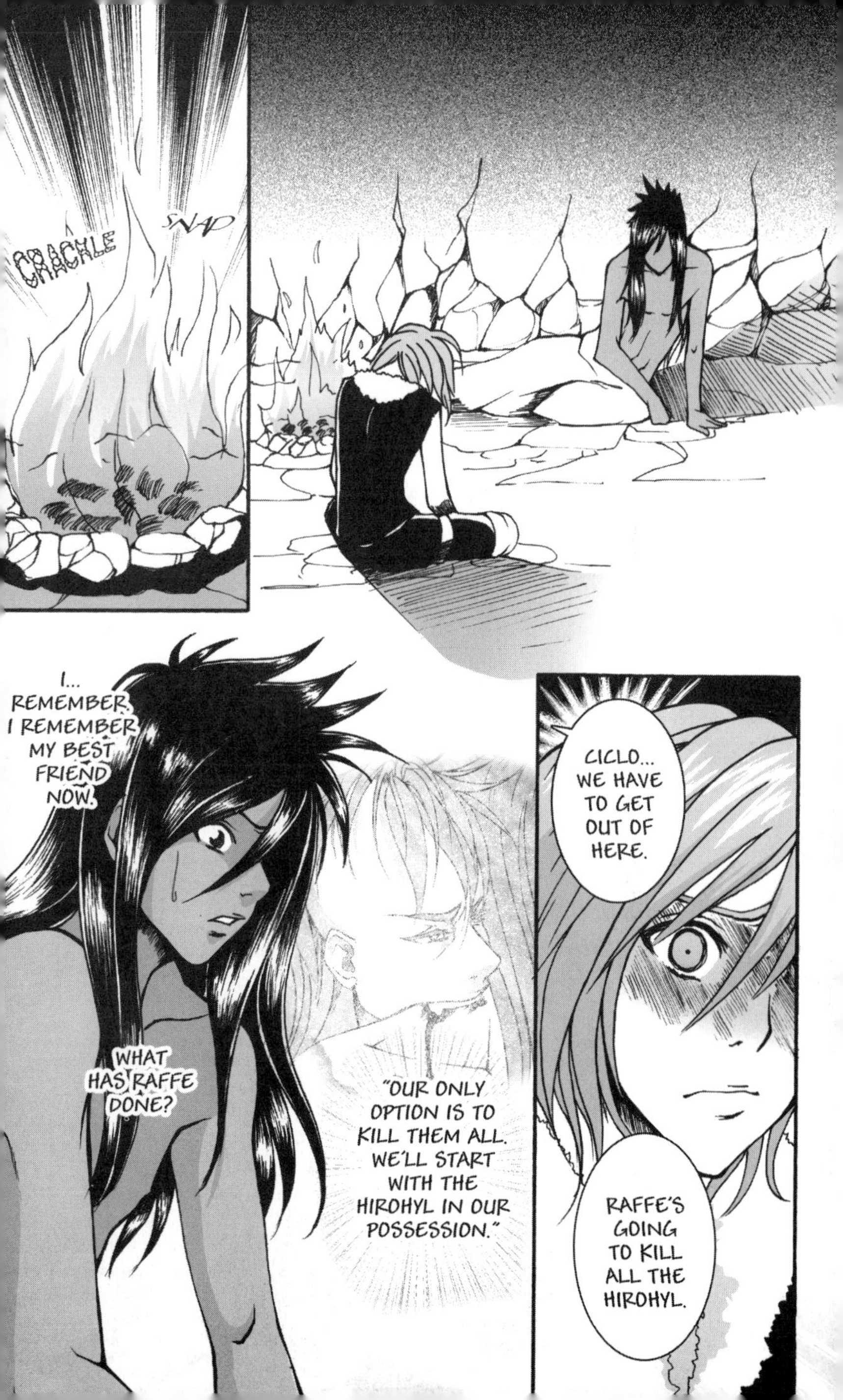
CRACKLE
SNAP
I... REMEMBER. I REMEMBER MY BEST FRIEND NOW.
CICLO... WE HAVE TO GET OUT OF HERE.
WHAT HAS RAFFE DONE?
"OUR ONLY OPTION IS TO KILL THEM ALL. WE'LL START WITH THE HIROHYL IN OUR POSSESSION."
RAFFE'S GOING TO KILL ALL THE HIROHYL.

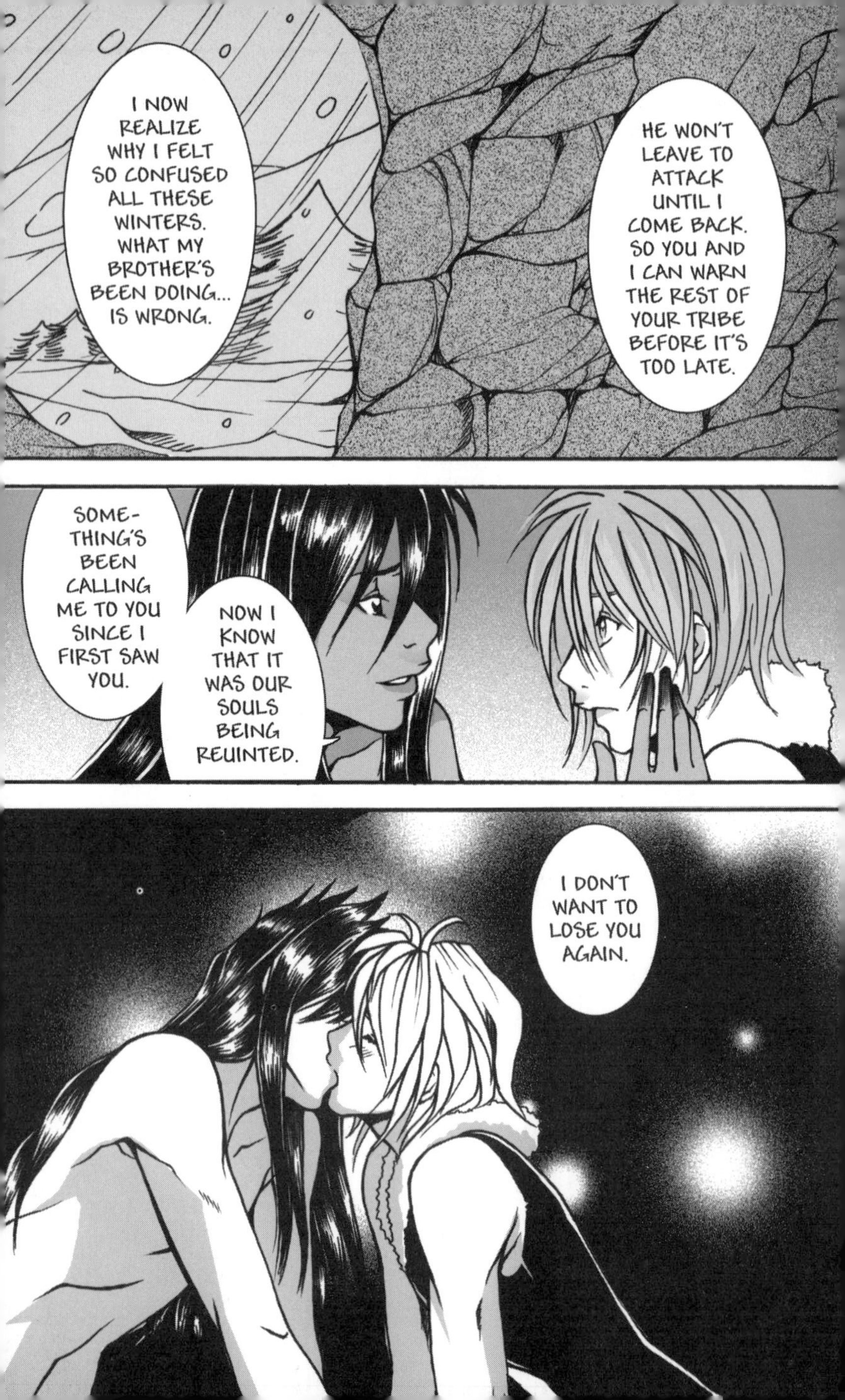
I NOW REALIZE WHY I FELT SO CONFUSED ALL THESE WINTERS. WHAT MY BROTHER'S BEEN DOING... IS WRONG.
HE WON'T LEAVE TO ATTACK UNTIL I COME BACK. SO YOU AND I CAN WARN THE REST OF YOUR TRIBE BEFORE IT'S TOO LATE.
SOME-THING'S BEEN CALLING ME TO YOU SINCE I FIRST SAW YOU.
NOW I KNOW THAT IT WAS OUR SOULS BEING REUINTED.
I DON'T WANT TO LOSE YOU AGAIN.

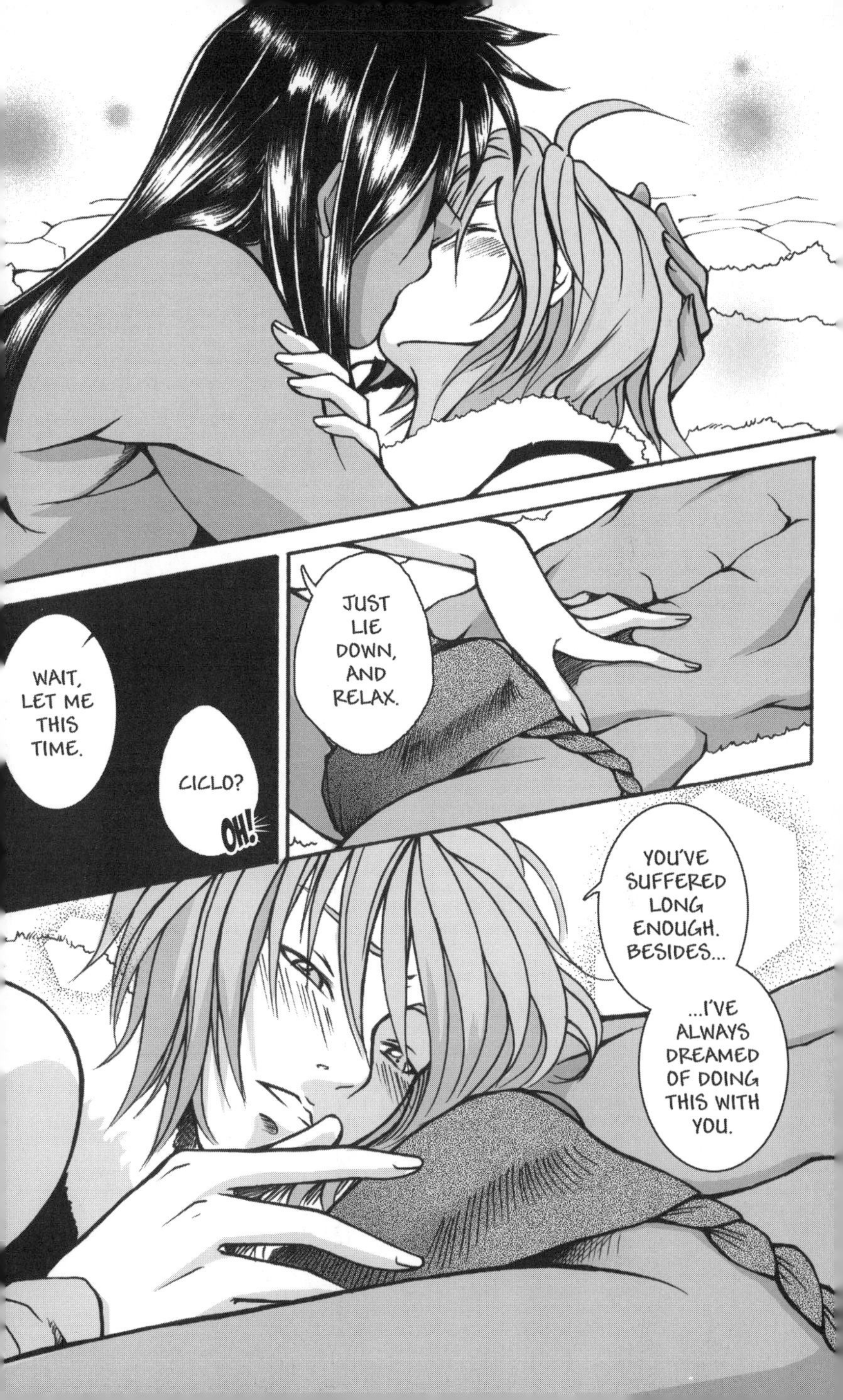
JUST LIE DOWN, AND RELAX.
WAIT, LET ME THIS TIME.
CICLO?
OH!
YOU'VE SUFFERED LONG ENOUGH. BESIDES...
...I'VE ALWAYS DREAMED OF DOING THIS WITH YOU.

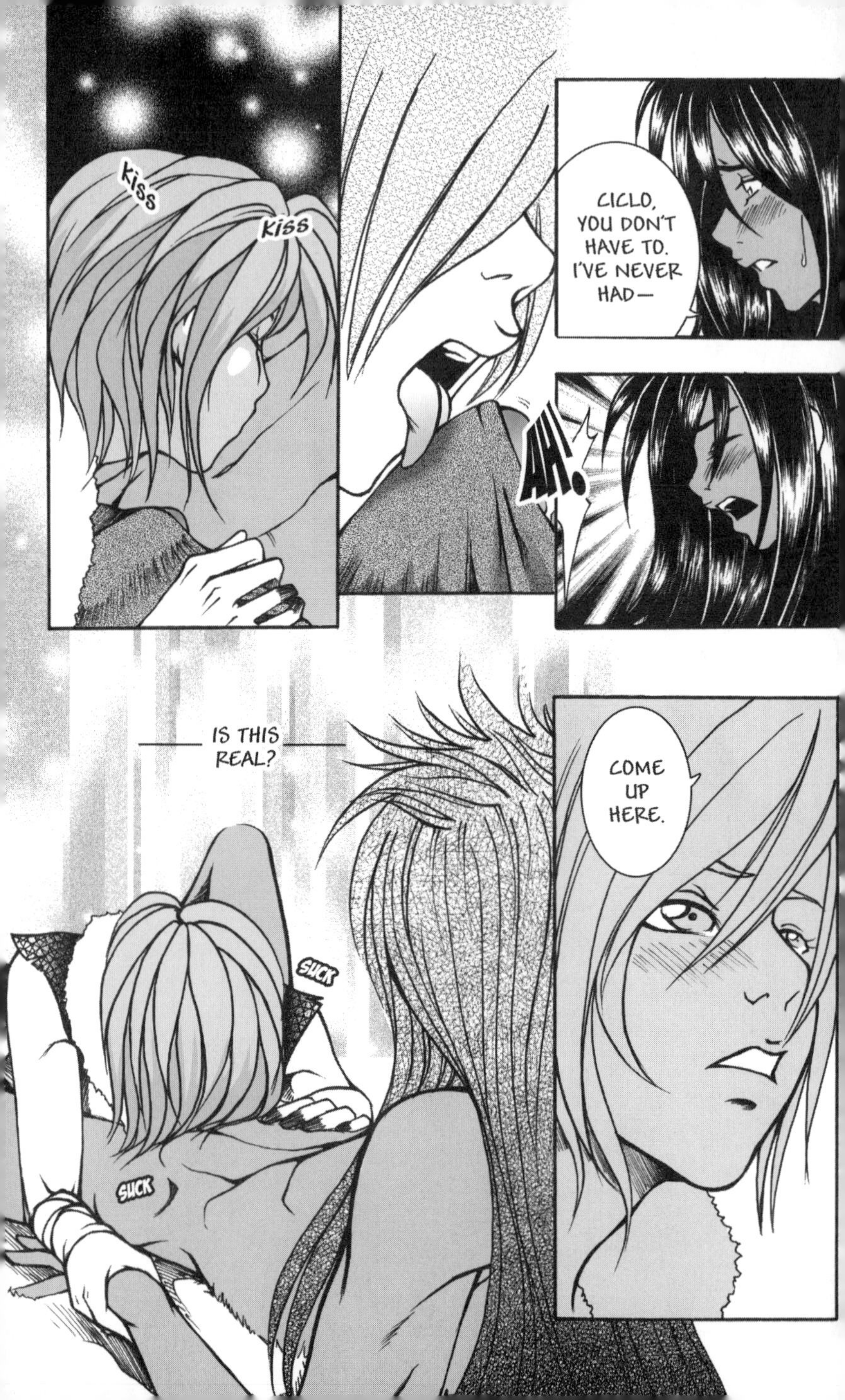

KISS
KISS
CICLO, YOU DON'T HAVE TO. I'VE NEVER HAD—
AH!
—— IS THIS REAL? ——
SUCK
SUCK
COME UP HERE.

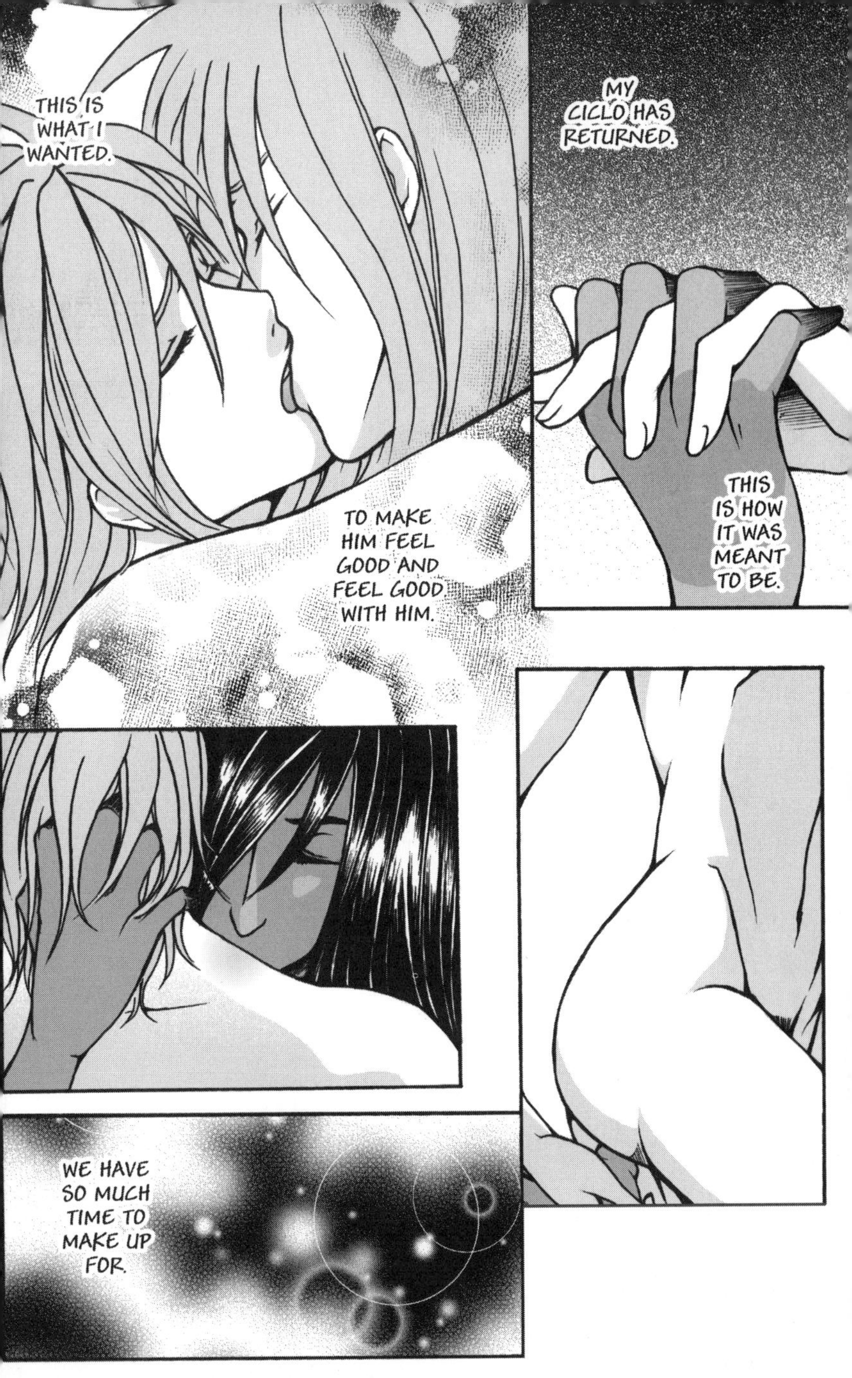
MY CICLO HAS RETURNED.
THIS IS HOW IT WAS MEANT TO BE.
THIS IS WHAT I WANTED.
TO MAKE HIM FEEL GOOD AND FEEL GOOD WITH HIM.
WE HAVE SO MUCH TIME TO MAKE UP FOR.

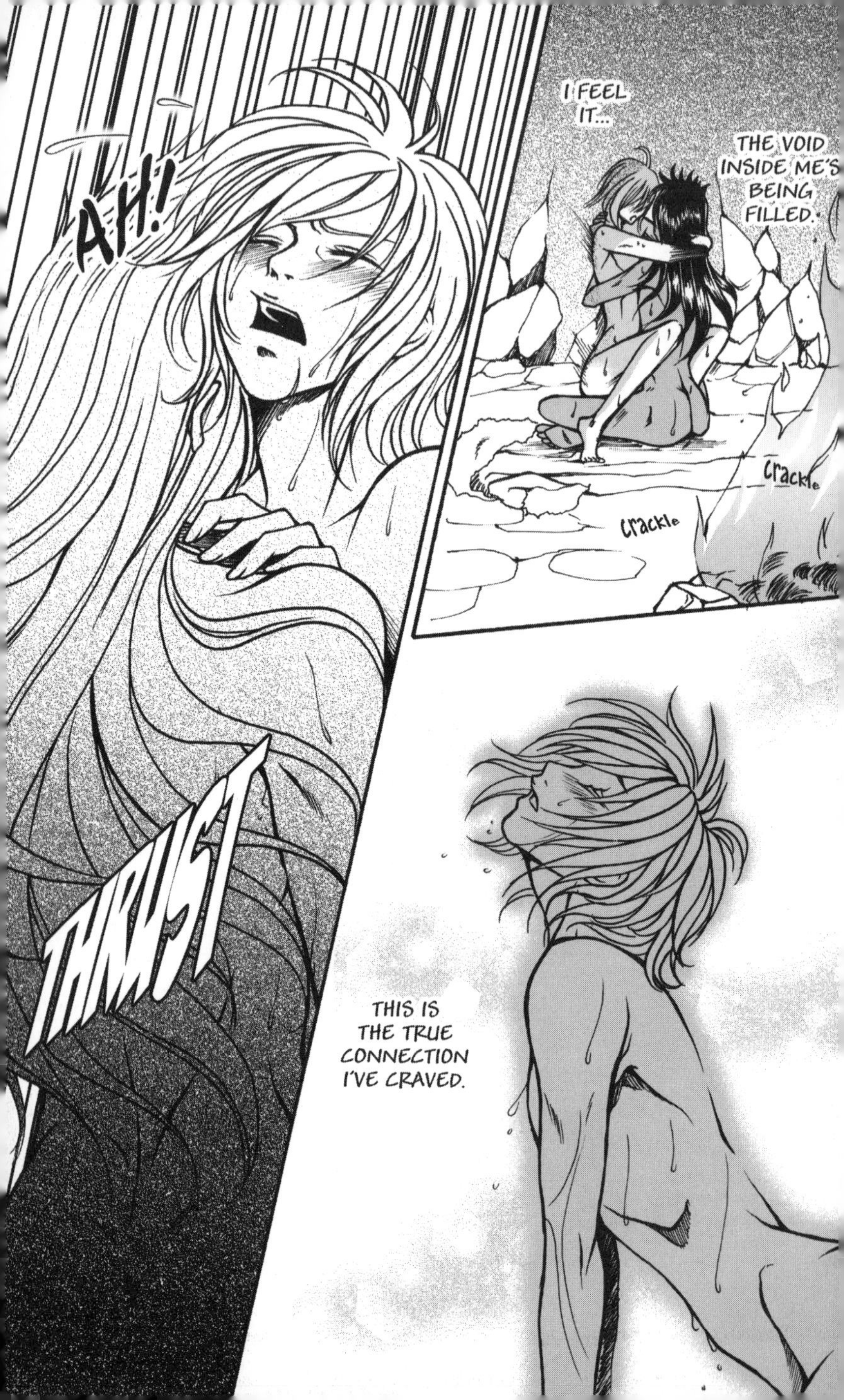
I FEEL IT...
THE VOID INSIDE ME'S BEING FILLED.
crackle
crackle
AH!
THRUST
THIS IS THE TRUE CONNECTION I'VE CRAVED.

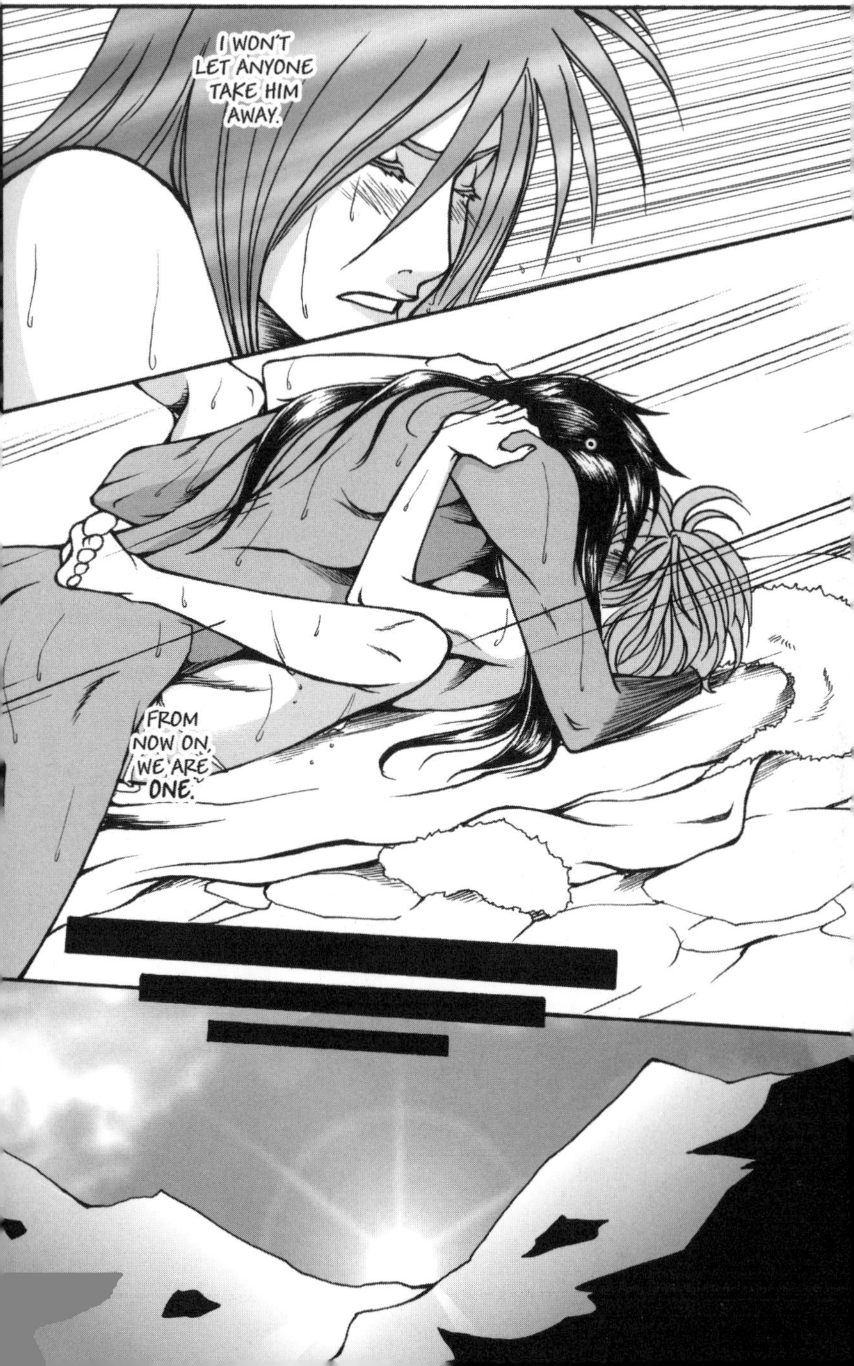
I WON'T LET ANYONE TAKE HIM AWAY.
FROM NOW ON, WE ARE ONE.
[redacted]

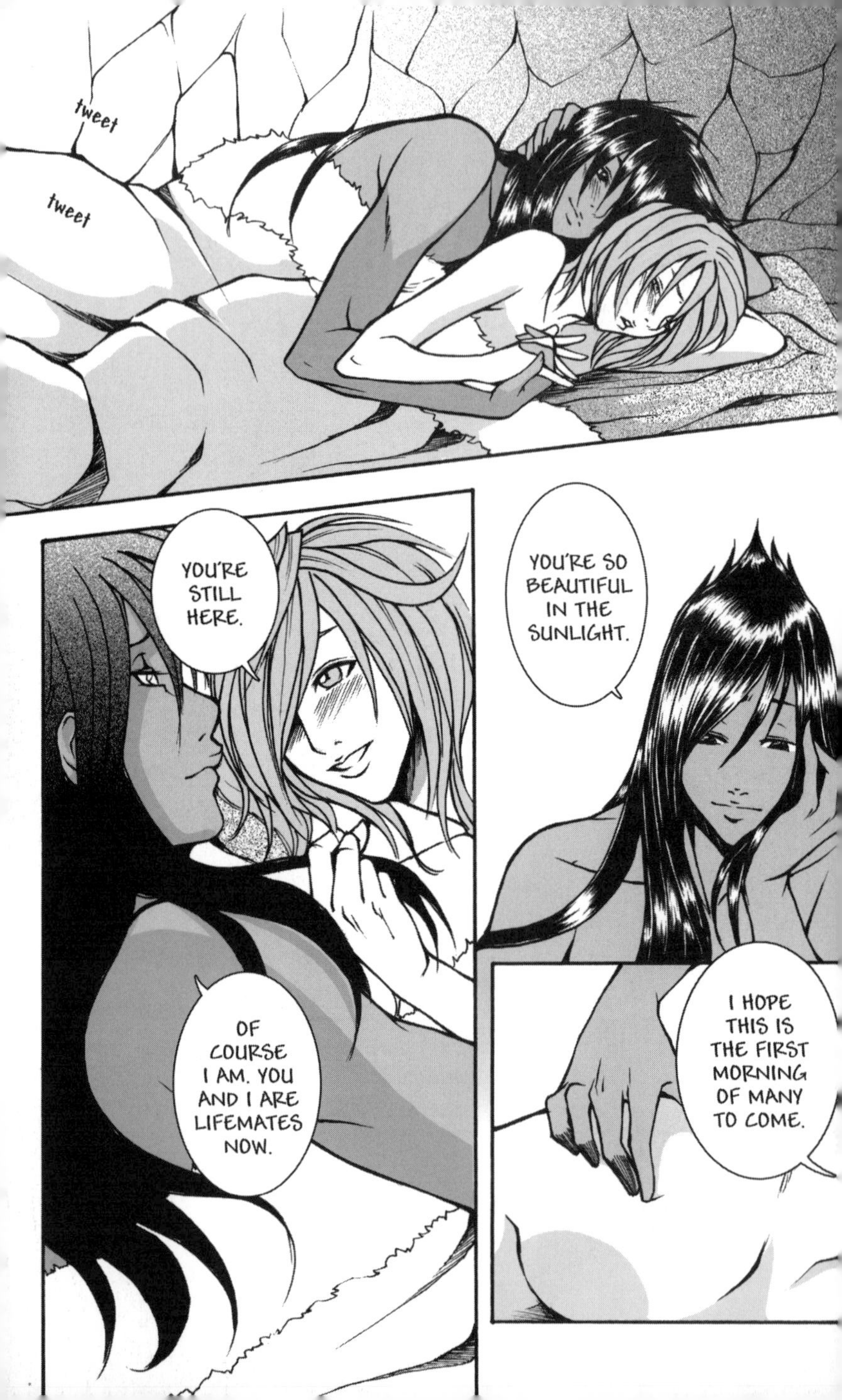
tweet
tweet
YOU'RE SO BEAUTIFUL IN THE SUNLIGHT.
YOU'RE STILL HERE.
OF COURSE I AM. YOU AND I ARE LIFEMATES NOW.
I HOPE THIS IS THE FIRST MORNING OF MANY TO COME.

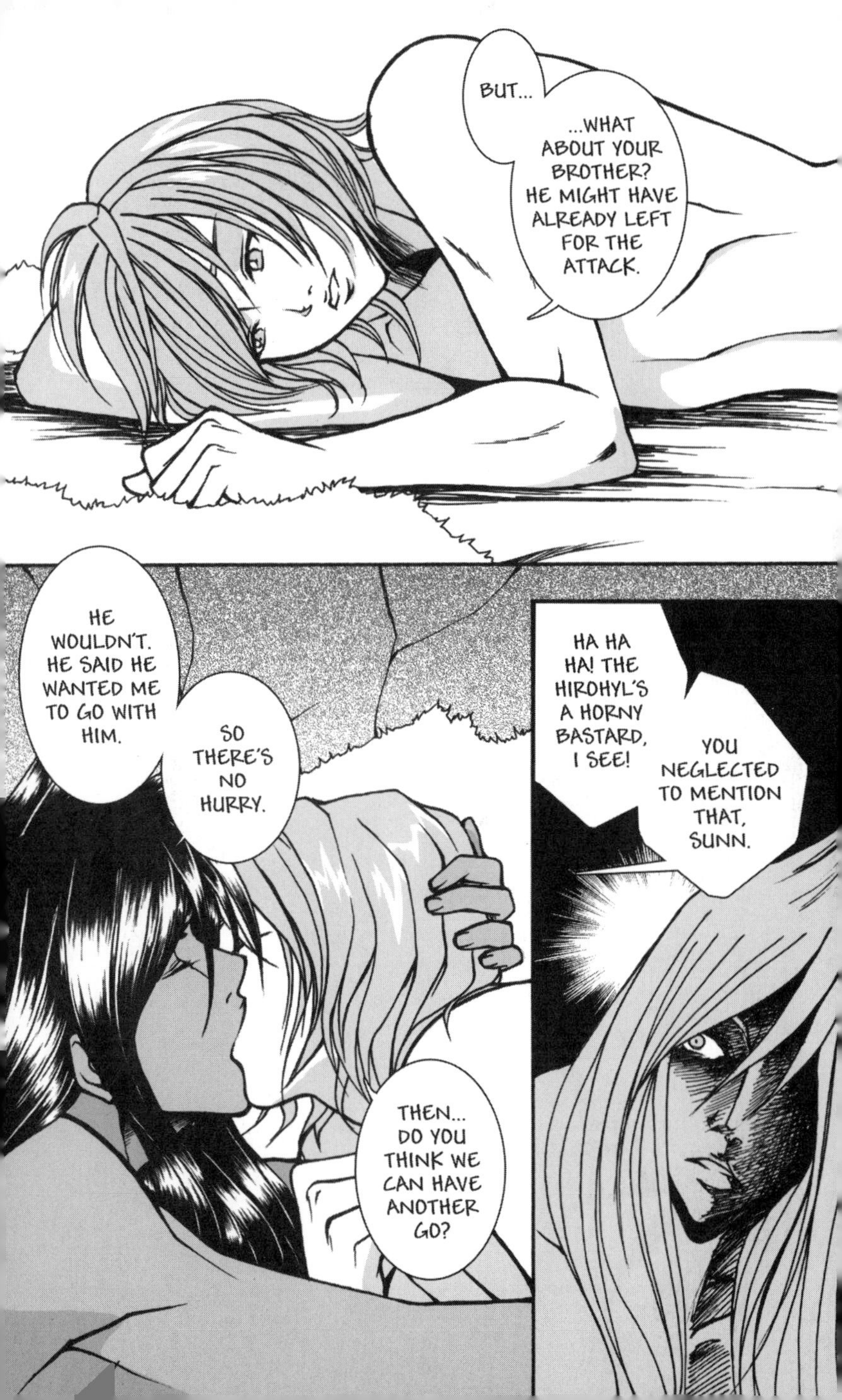

BUT...
...WHAT ABOUT YOUR BROTHER? HE MIGHT HAVE ALREADY LEFT FOR THE ATTACK.
HE WOULDN'T. HE SAID HE WANTED ME TO GO WITH HIM.
SO THERE'S NO HURRY.
THEN... DO YOU THINK WE CAN HAVE ANOTHER GO?
HA HA HA! THE HIROHYL'S A HORNY BASTARD, I SEE!
YOU NEGLECTED TO MENTION THAT, SUNN.

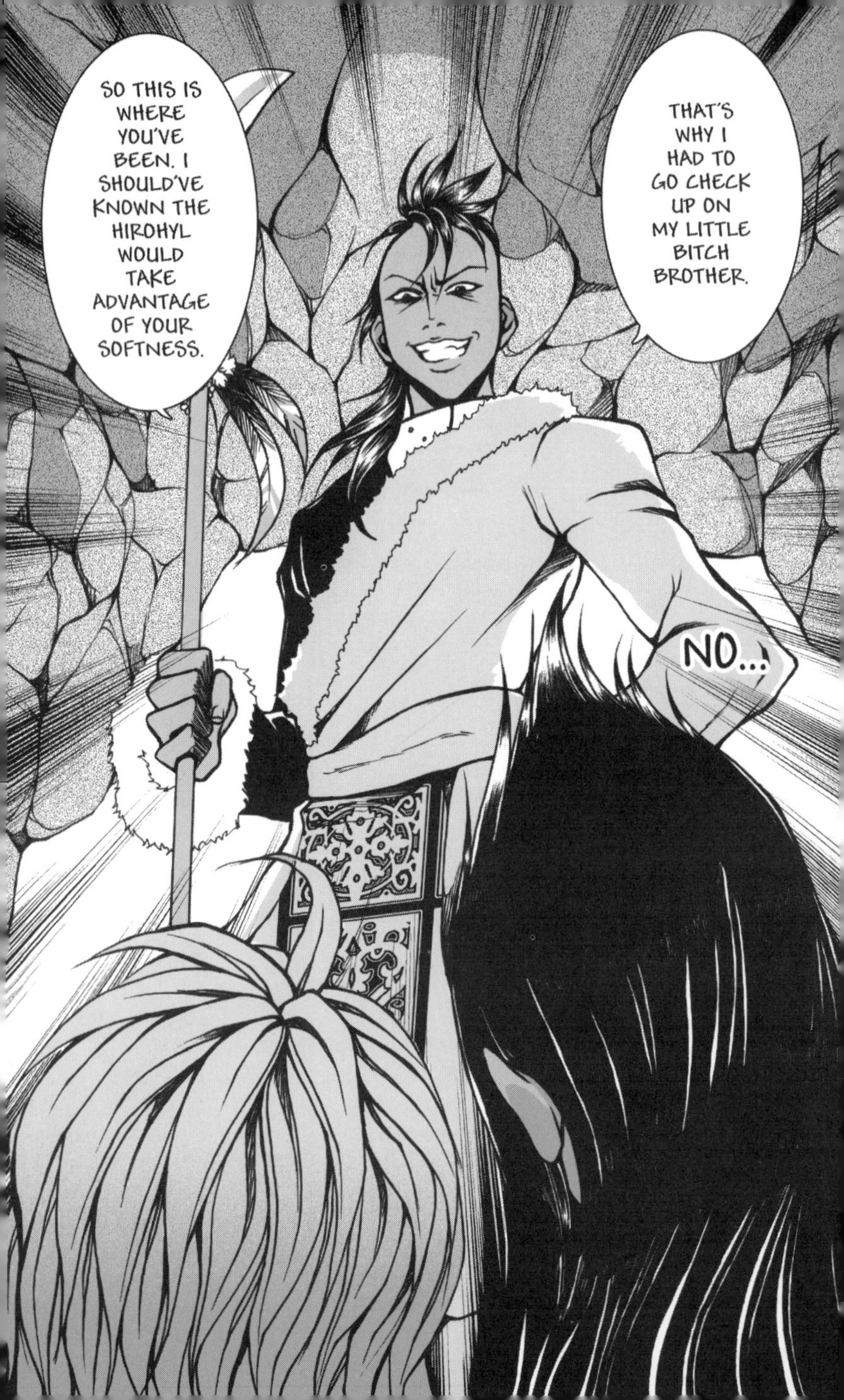
SO THIS IS WHERE YOU'VE BEEN. I SHOULD'VE KNOWN THE HIROHYL WOULD TAKE ADVANTAGE OF YOUR SOFTNESS.
THAT'S WHY I HAD TO GO CHECK UP ON MY LITTLE BITCH BROTHER.
NO...

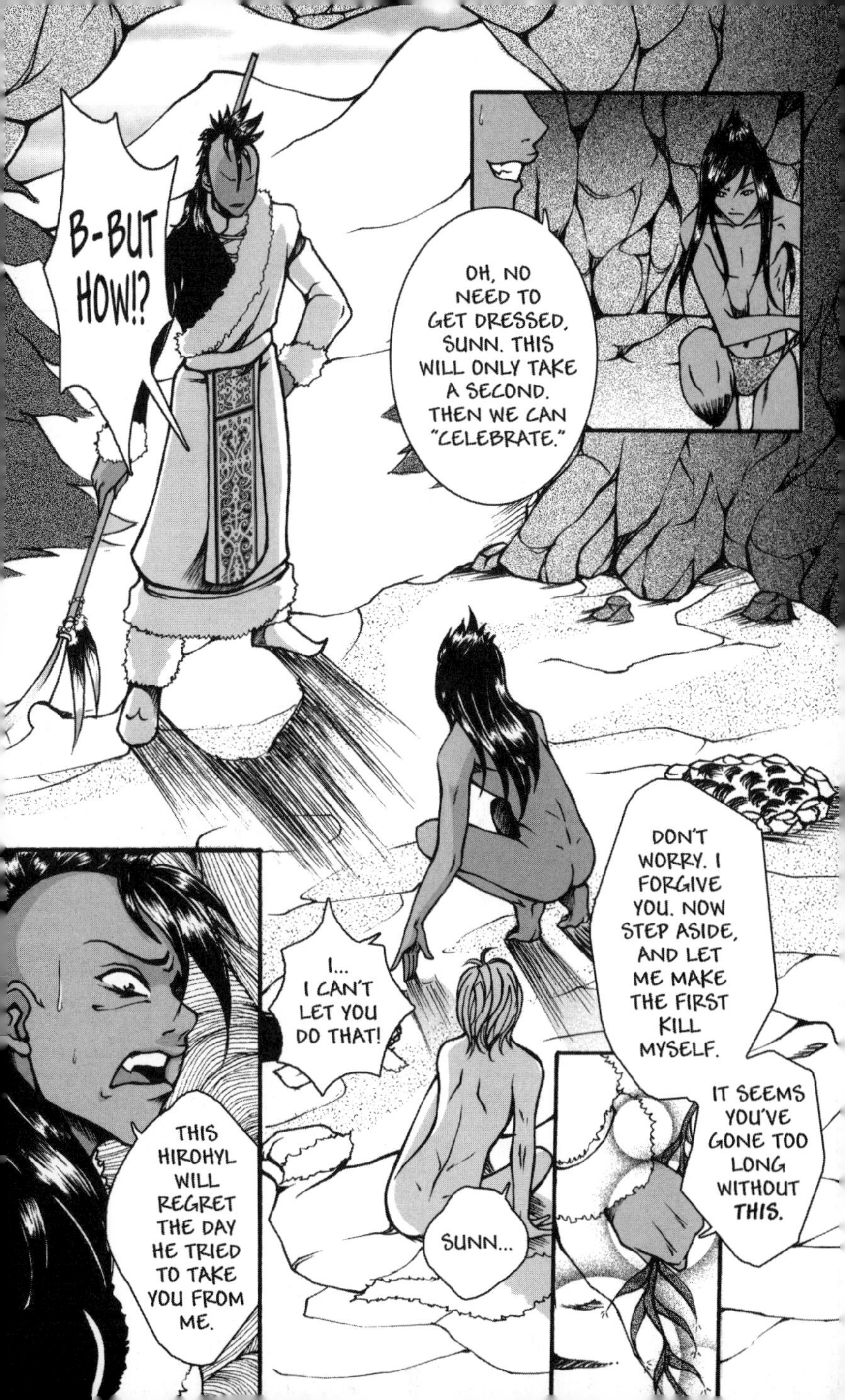
B-BUT HOW!?
OH, NO NEED TO GET DRESSED, SUNN. THIS WILL ONLY TAKE A SECOND. THEN WE CAN "CELEBRATE."
DON'T WORRY. I FORGIVE YOU. NOW STEP ASIDE, AND LET ME MAKE THE FIRST KILL MYSELF.
I... I CAN'T LET YOU DO THAT!
THIS HIROHYL WILL REGRET THE DAY HE TRIED TO TAKE YOU FROM ME.
SUNN...
IT SEEMS YOU'VE GONE TOO LONG WITHOUT THIS.

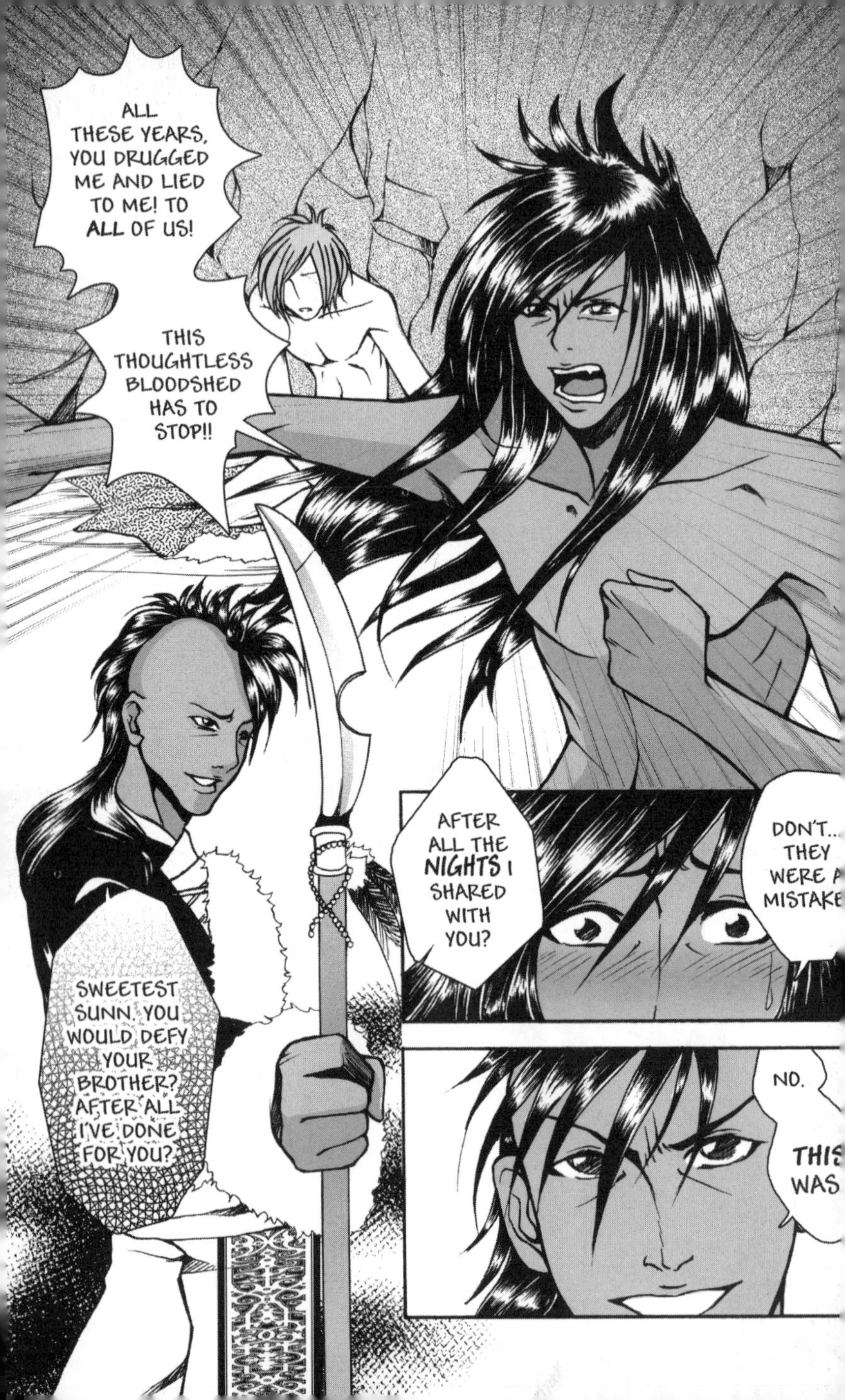
ALL THESE YEARS, YOU DRUGGED ME AND LIED TO ME! TO ALL OF US!
THIS THOUGHTLESS BLOODSHED HAS TO STOP!!
SWEETEST SUNN. YOU WOULD DEFY YOUR BROTHER? AFTER ALL I'VE DONE FOR YOU?
AFTER ALL THE NIGHTS I SHARED WITH YOU?
DON'T... THEY WERE A MISTAKE
NO.
THIS WAS

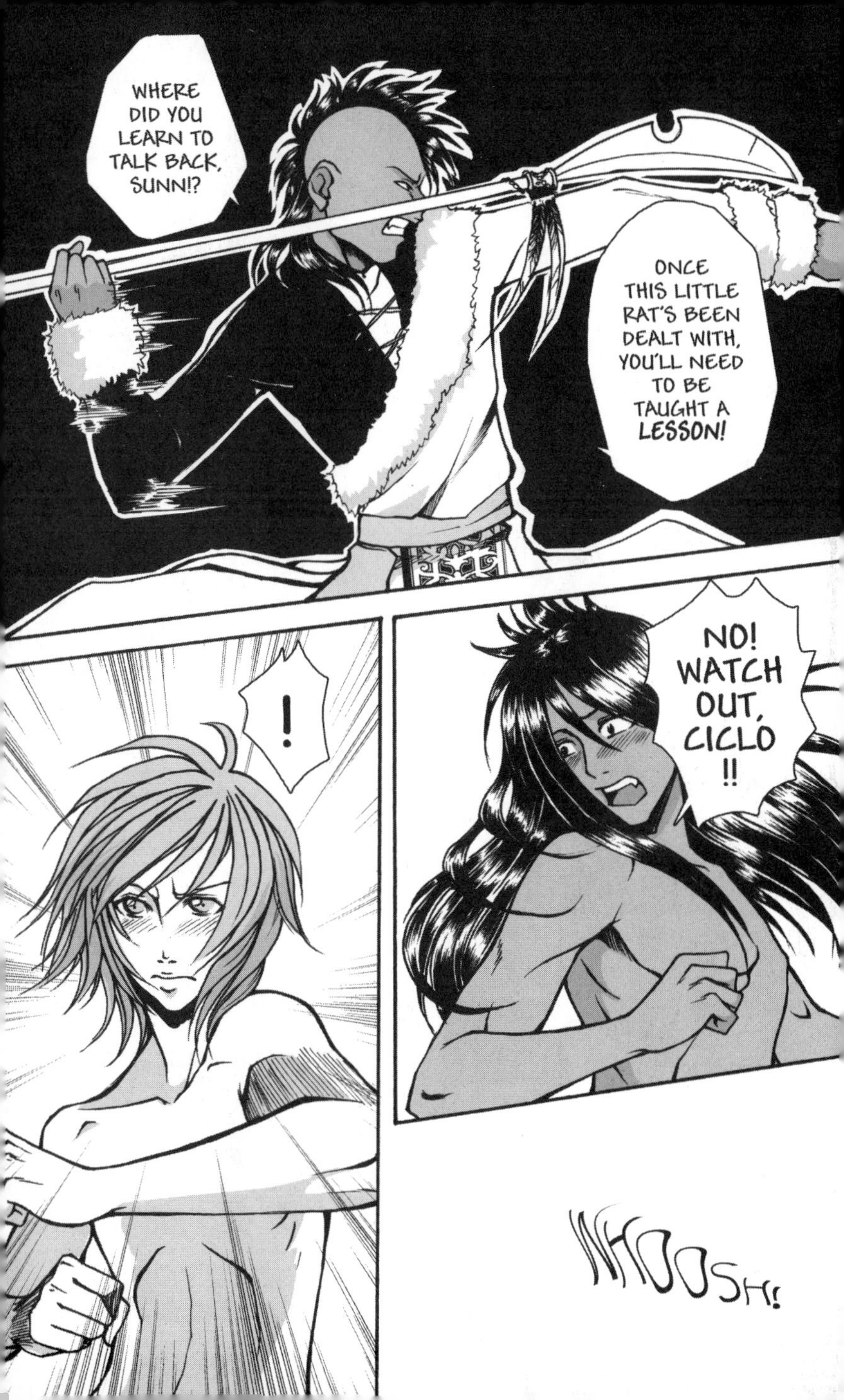
WHERE DID YOU LEARN TO TALK BACK, SUNN!?
ONCE THIS LITTLE RAT'S BEEN DEALT WITH, YOU'LL NEED TO BE TAUGHT A LESSON!
NO! WATCH OUT, CICLO !!
!
WHOOSH!

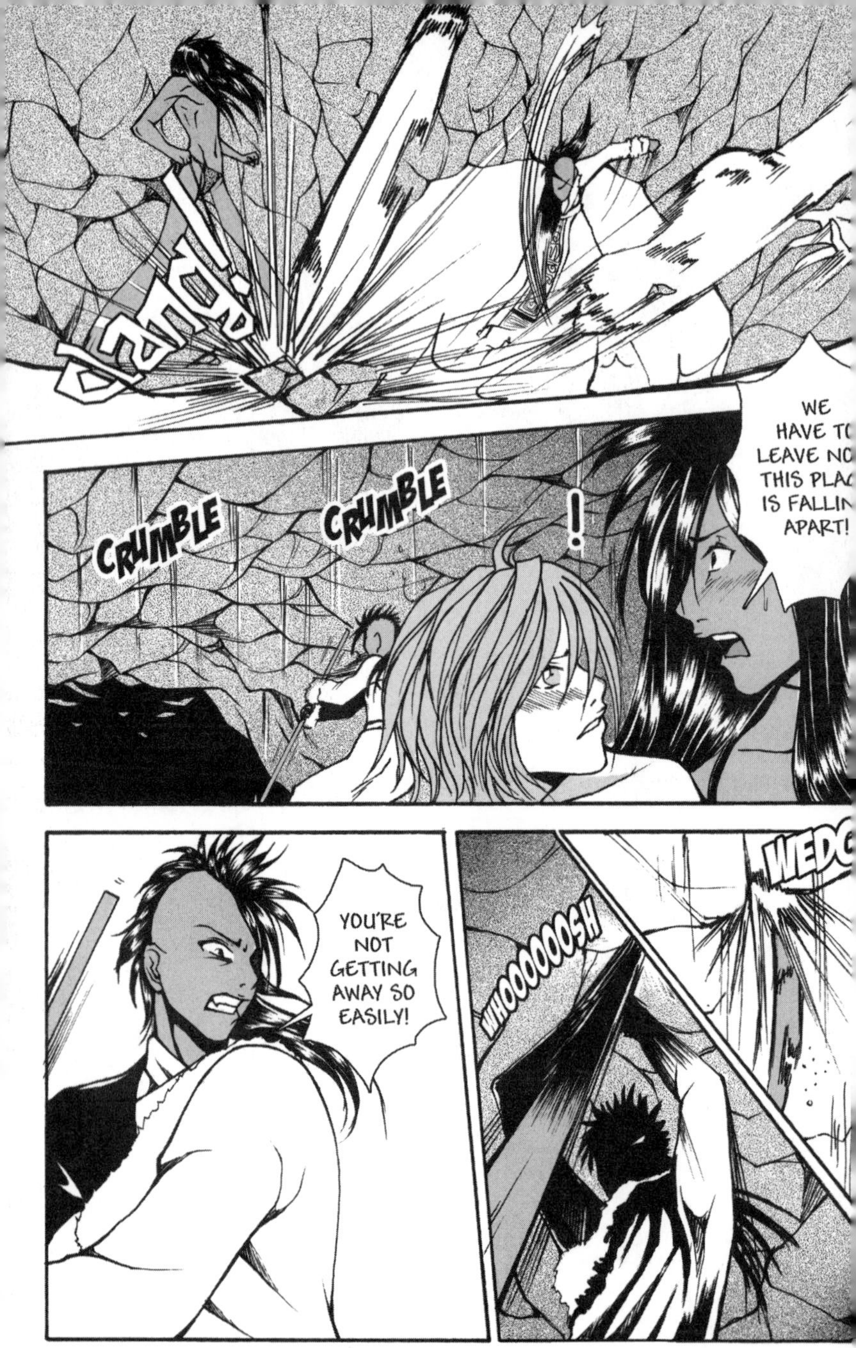
CRUMBLE
CRUMBLE
!
WE HAVE TO LEAVE NO THIS PLAC IS FALLIN APART!
YOU'RE NOT GETTING AWAY SO EASILY!
WHOOOOOOSH
WEDG

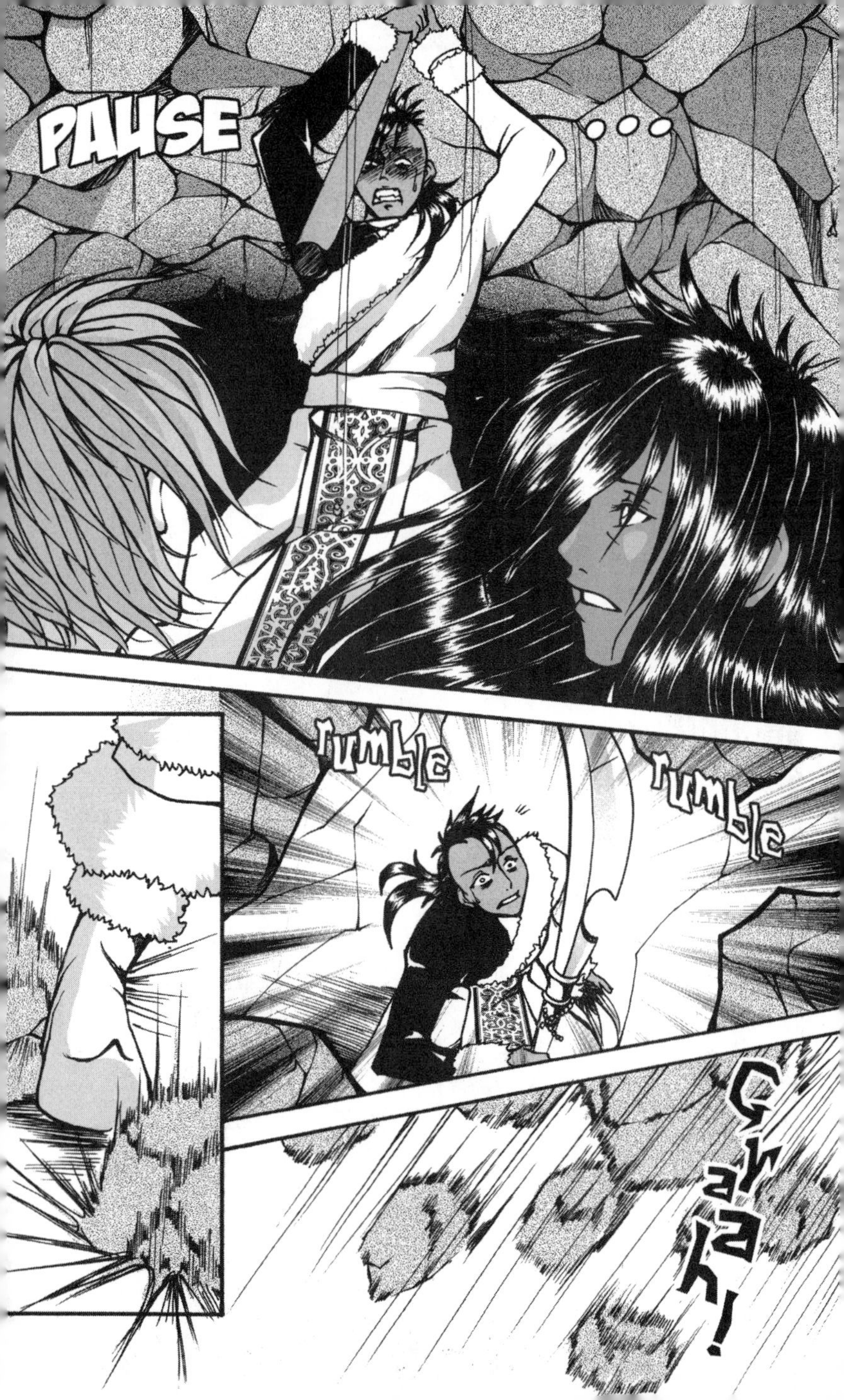
PAUSE
...
rumble
rumble
Gyaah!

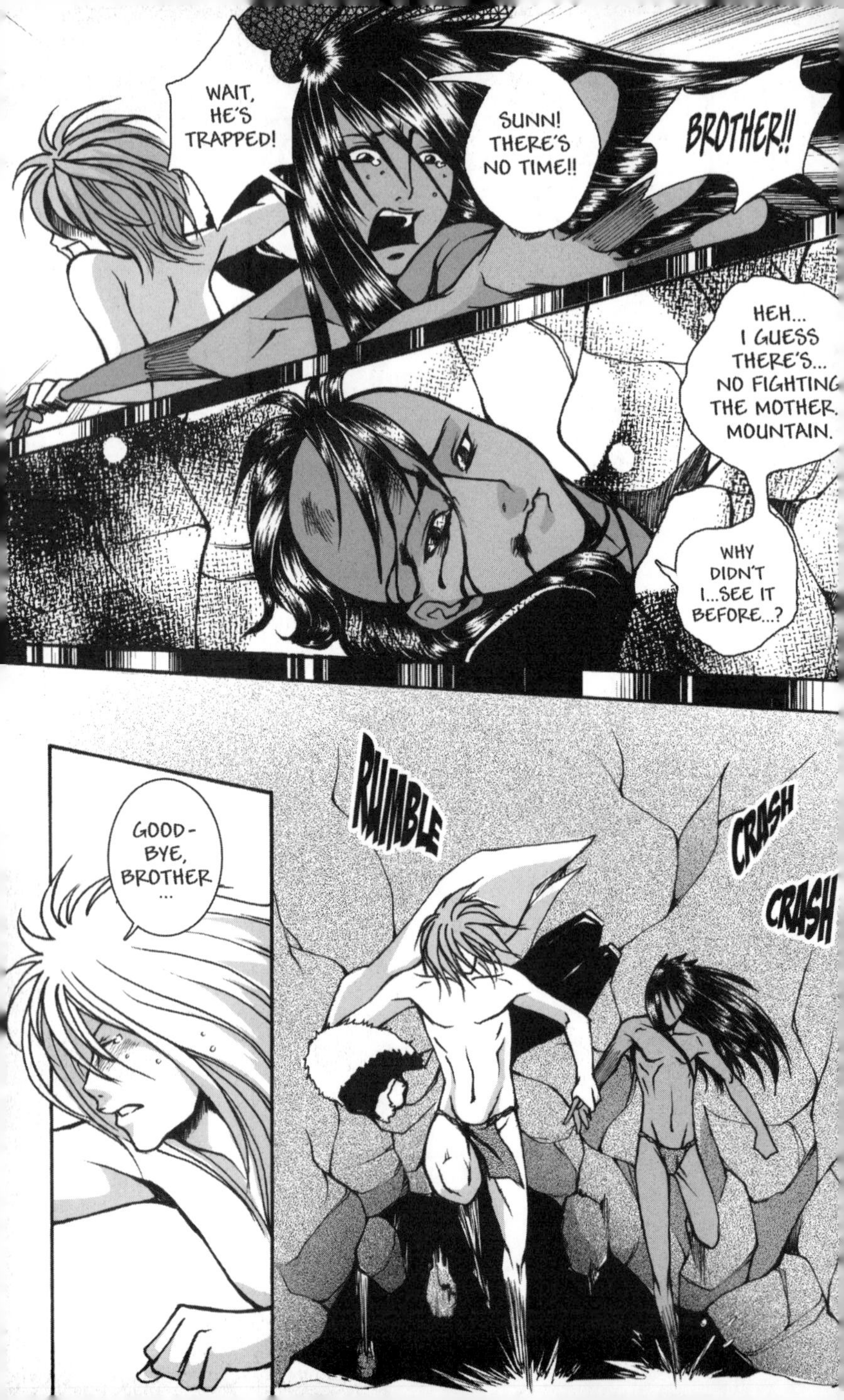
BROTHER!!
SUNN! THERE'S NO TIME!!
WAIT, HE'S TRAPPED!
HEH... I GUESS THERE'S... NO FIGHTING THE MOTHER MOUNTAIN.
WHY DIDN'T I...SEE IT BEFORE...?
RUMBLE
CRASH
CRASH
GOOD-BYE, BROTHER ...

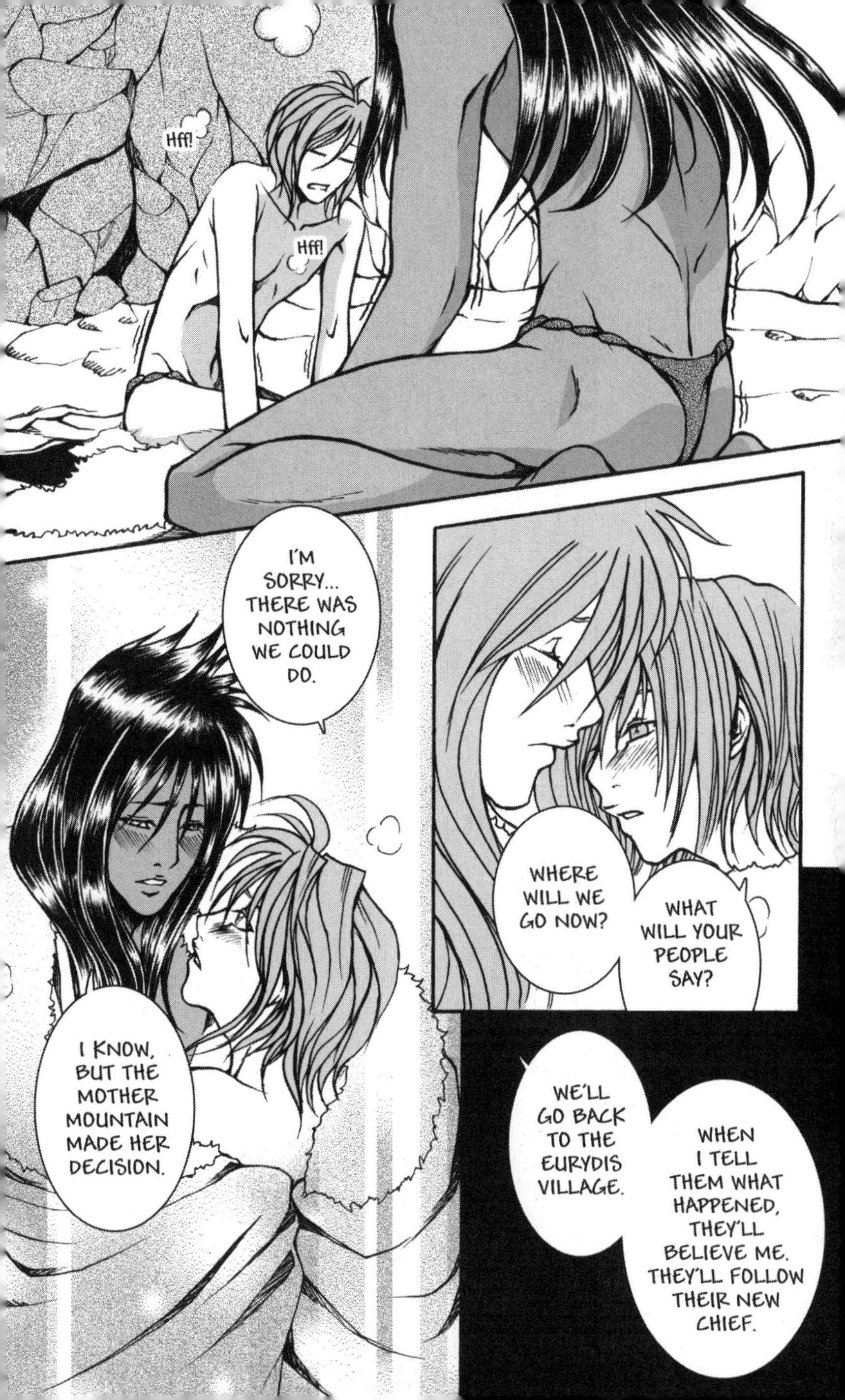
Hff!
Hff!
I'M SORRY... THERE WAS NOTHING WE COULD DO.
I KNOW, BUT THE MOTHER MOUNTAIN MADE HER DECISION.
WHERE WILL WE GO NOW?
WHAT WILL YOUR PEOPLE SAY?
WE'LL GO BACK TO THE EURYDIS VILLAGE.
WHEN I TELL THEM WHAT HAPPENED, THEY'LL BELIEVE ME. THEY'LL FOLLOW THEIR NEW CHIEF.

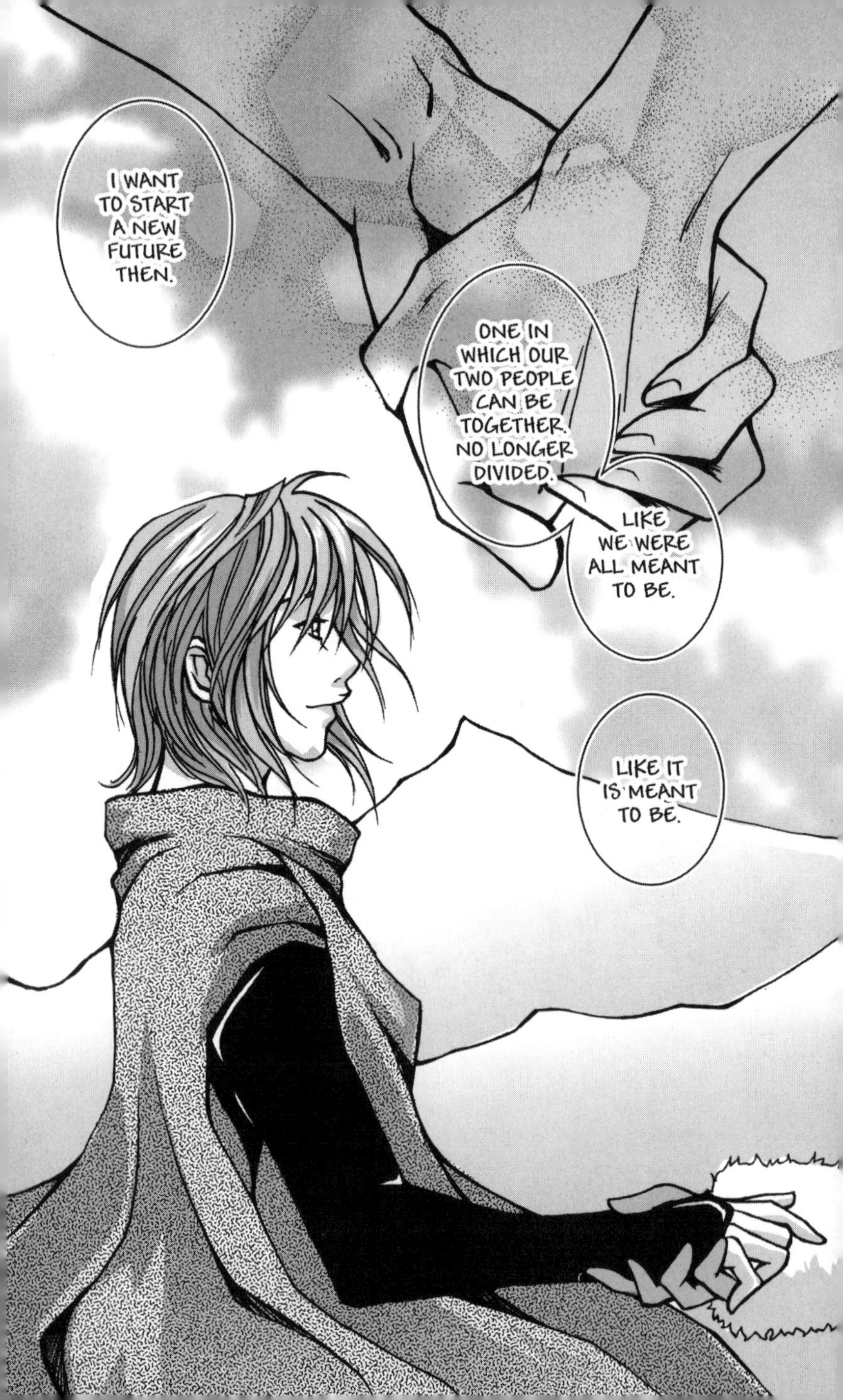
I WANT TO START A NEW FUTURE THEN.
ONE IN WHICH OUR TWO PEOPLE CAN BE TOGETHER. NO LONGER DIVIDED.
LIKE WE WERE ALL MEANT TO BE.
LIKE IT IS MEANT TO BE.

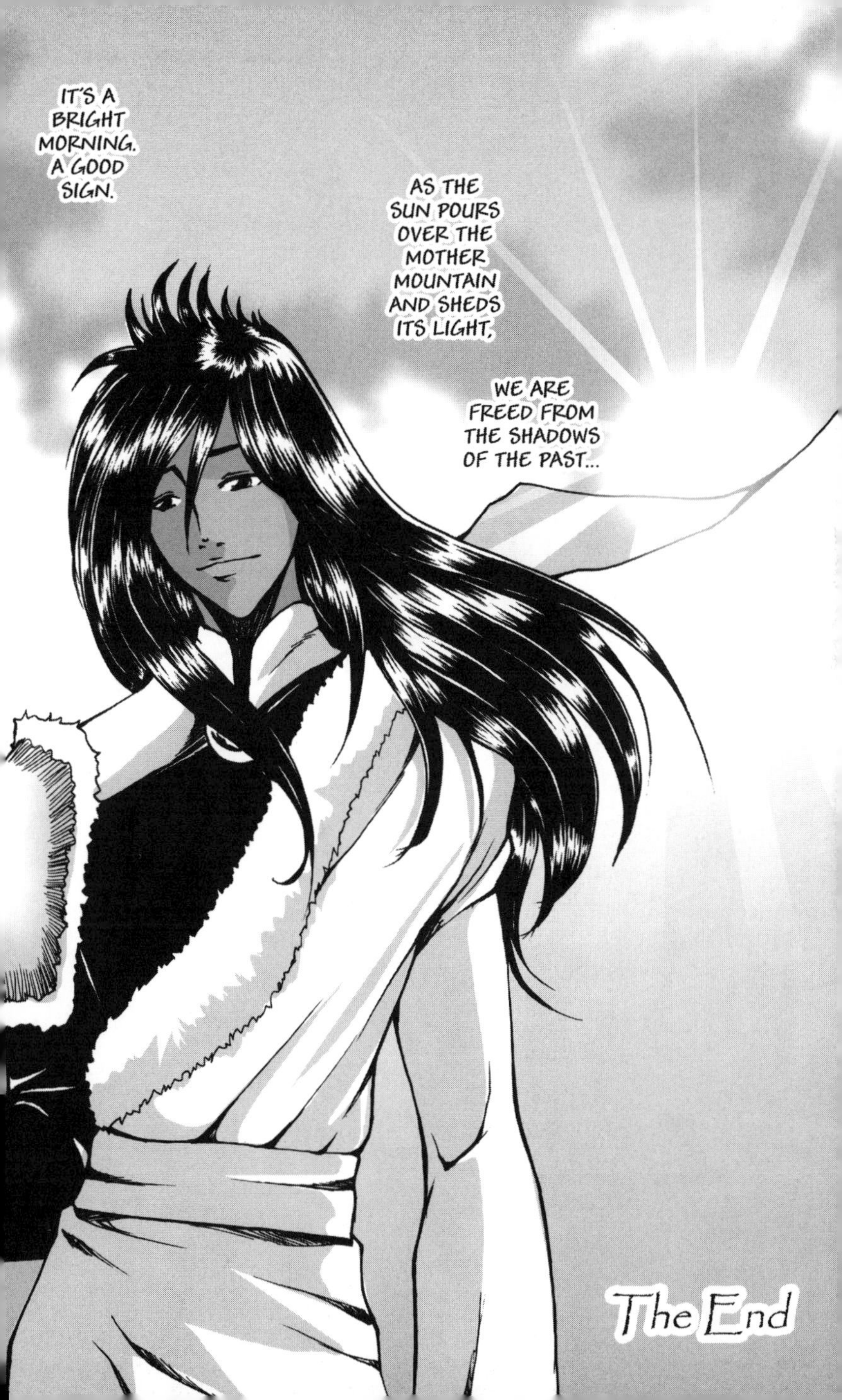
IT'S A BRIGHT MORNING. A GOOD SIGN.
AS THE SUN POURS OVER THE MOTHER MOUNTAIN AND SHEDS ITS LIGHT,
WE ARE FREED FROM THE SHADOWS OF THE PAST...
The End

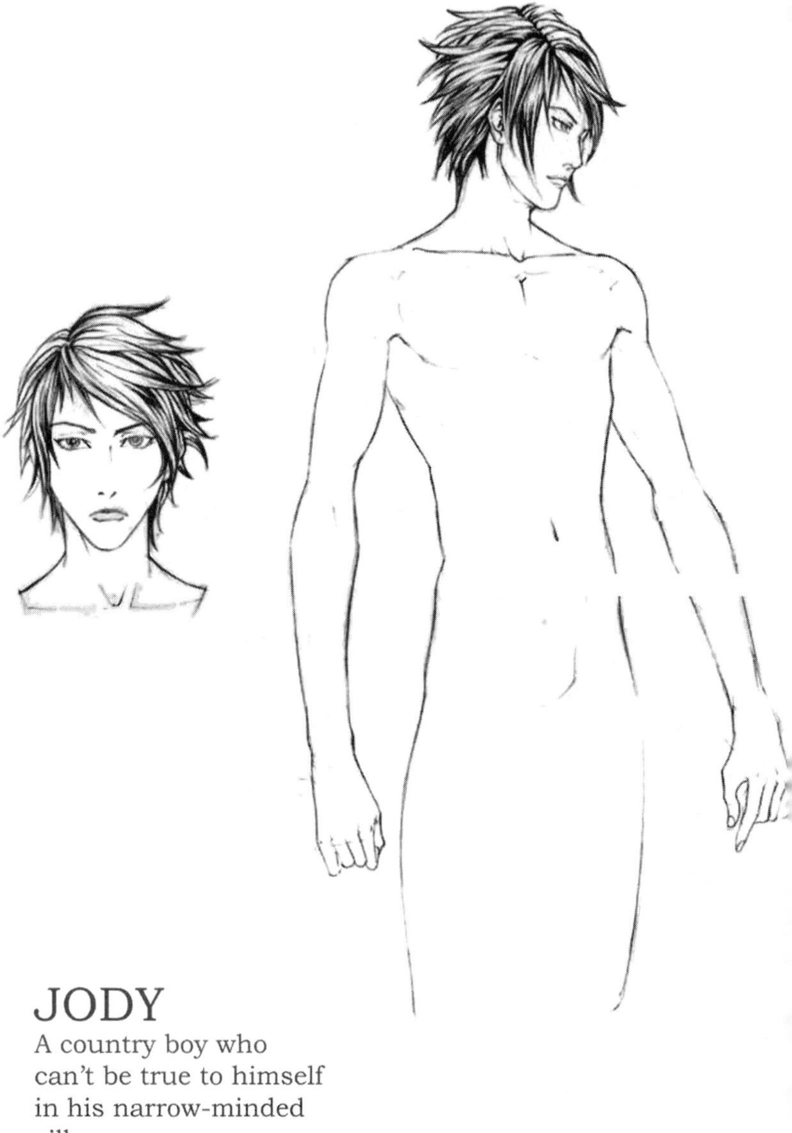

JODY

A country boy who can't be true to himself in his narrow-minded village.

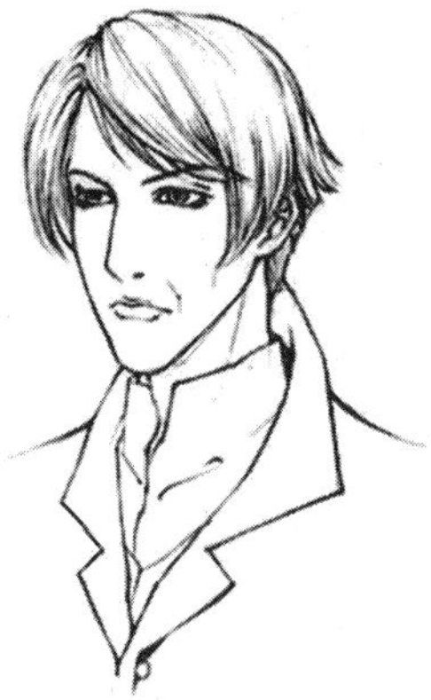

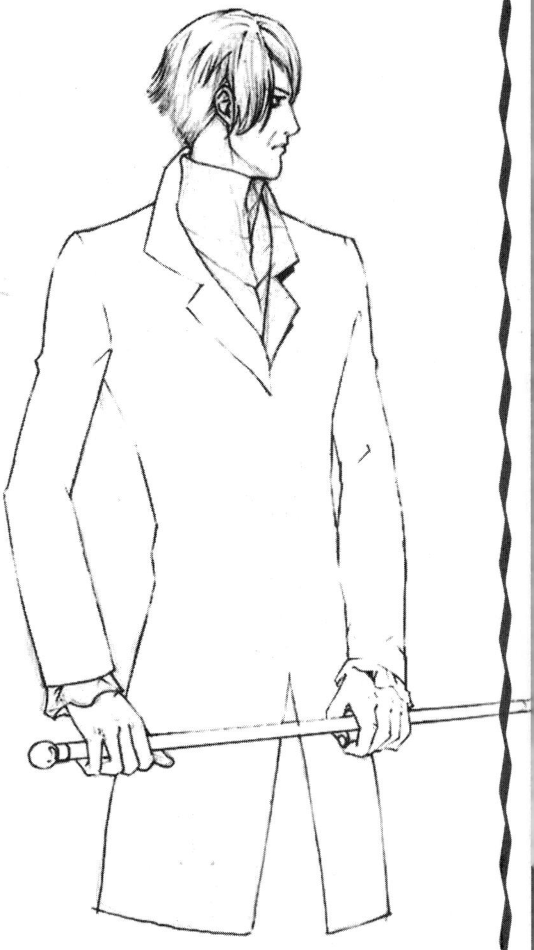

ALATORE

The owner of the factory nearly every man in the village works at. Despite that, he's ostracized by the community for never hiding his homosexuality.

Servant

Story by Yamila Abraham
Art by Jablay Studios
Letters by April FitzGerald

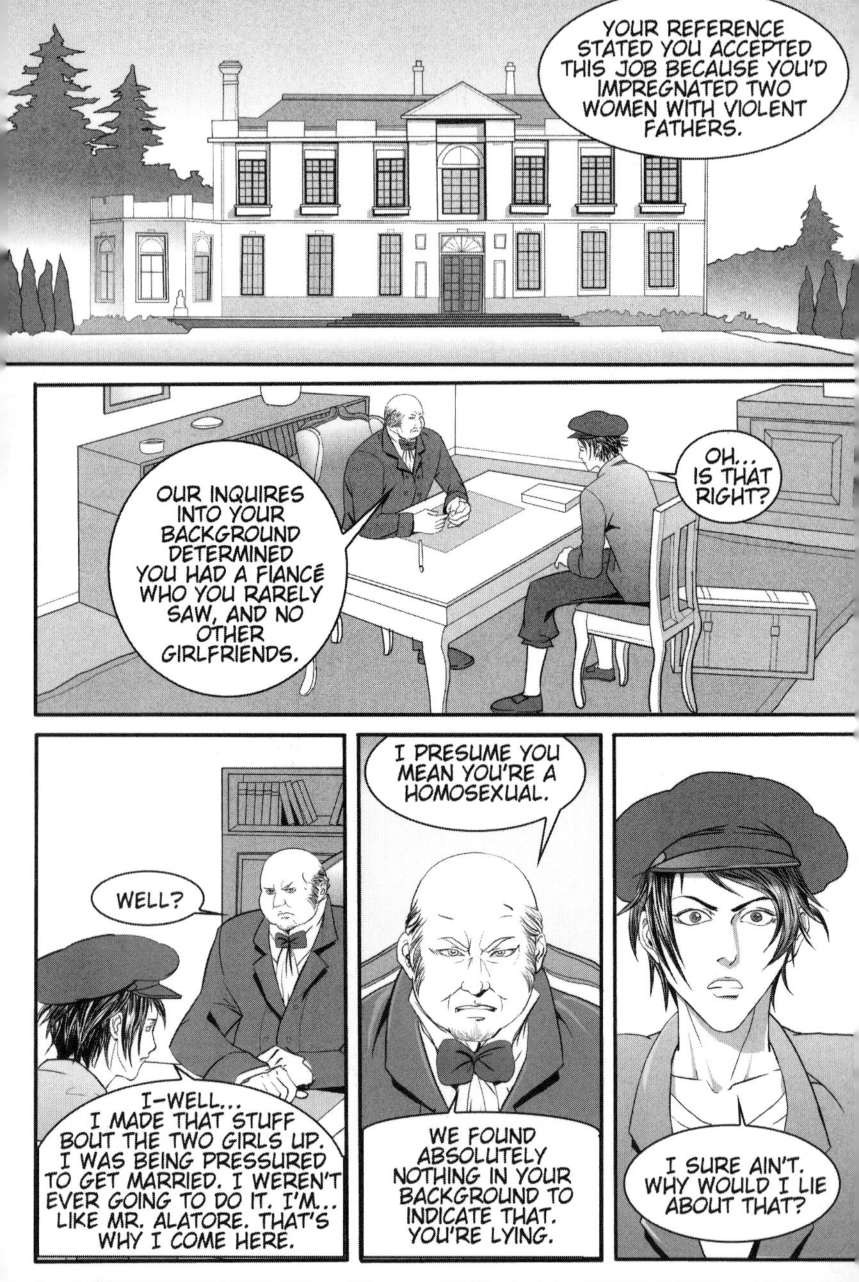
YOUR REFERENCE STATED YOU ACCEPTED THIS JOB BECAUSE YOU'D IMPREGNATED TWO WOMEN WITH VIOLENT FATHERS.
OUR INQUIRES INTO YOUR BACKGROUND DETERMINED YOU HAD A FIANCÉ WHO YOU RARELY SAW, AND NO OTHER GIRLFRIENDS.
OH... IS THAT RIGHT?
WELL?
I-WELL... I MADE THAT STUFF BOUT THE TWO GIRLS UP. I WAS BEING PRESSURED TO GET MARRIED. I WEREN'T EVER GOING TO DO IT. I'M... LIKE MR. ALATORE. THAT'S WHY I COME HERE.
I PRESUME YOU MEAN YOU'RE A HOMOSEXUAL.
WE FOUND ABSOLUTELY NOTHING IN YOUR BACKGROUND TO INDICATE THAT. YOU'RE LYING.
I SURE AIN'T. WHY WOULD I LIE ABOUT THAT?

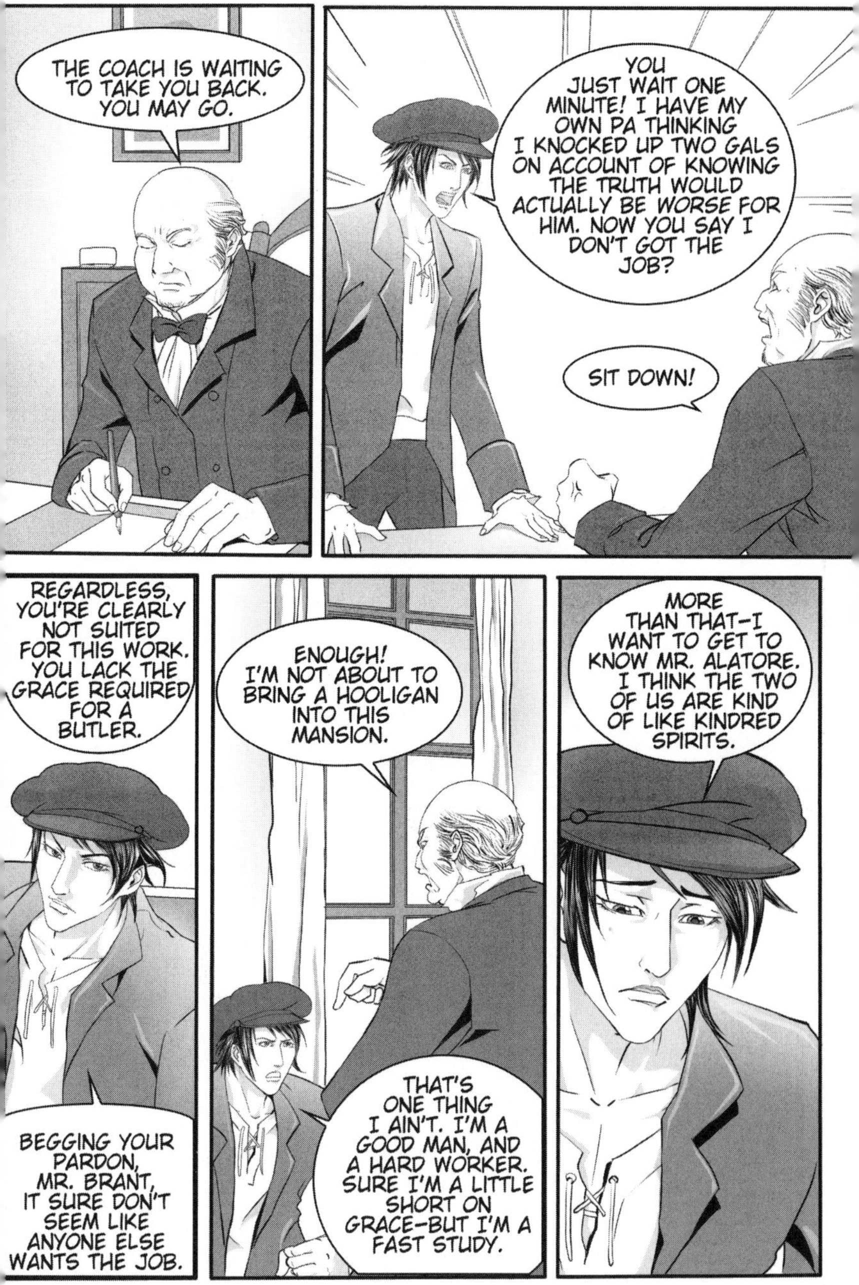
THE COACH IS WAITING TO TAKE YOU BACK. YOU MAY GO.
YOU JUST WAIT ONE MINUTE! I HAVE MY OWN PA THINKING I KNOCKED UP TWO GALS ON ACCOUNT OF KNOWING THE TRUTH WOULD ACTUALLY BE WORSE FOR HIM. NOW YOU SAY I DON'T GOT THE JOB?
SIT DOWN!
REGARDLESS, YOU'RE CLEARLY NOT SUITED FOR THIS WORK. YOU LACK THE GRACE REQUIRED FOR A BUTLER.
BEGGING YOUR PARDON, MR. BRANT, IT SURE DON'T SEEM LIKE ANYONE ELSE WANTS THE JOB.
ENOUGH! I'M NOT ABOUT TO BRING A HOOLIGAN INTO THIS MANSION.
THAT'S ONE THING I AIN'T. I'M A GOOD MAN, AND A HARD WORKER. SURE I'M A LITTLE SHORT ON GRACE—BUT I'M A FAST STUDY.
MORE THAN THAT—I WANT TO GET TO KNOW MR. ALATORE. I THINK THE TWO OF US ARE KIND OF LIKE KINDRED SPIRITS.

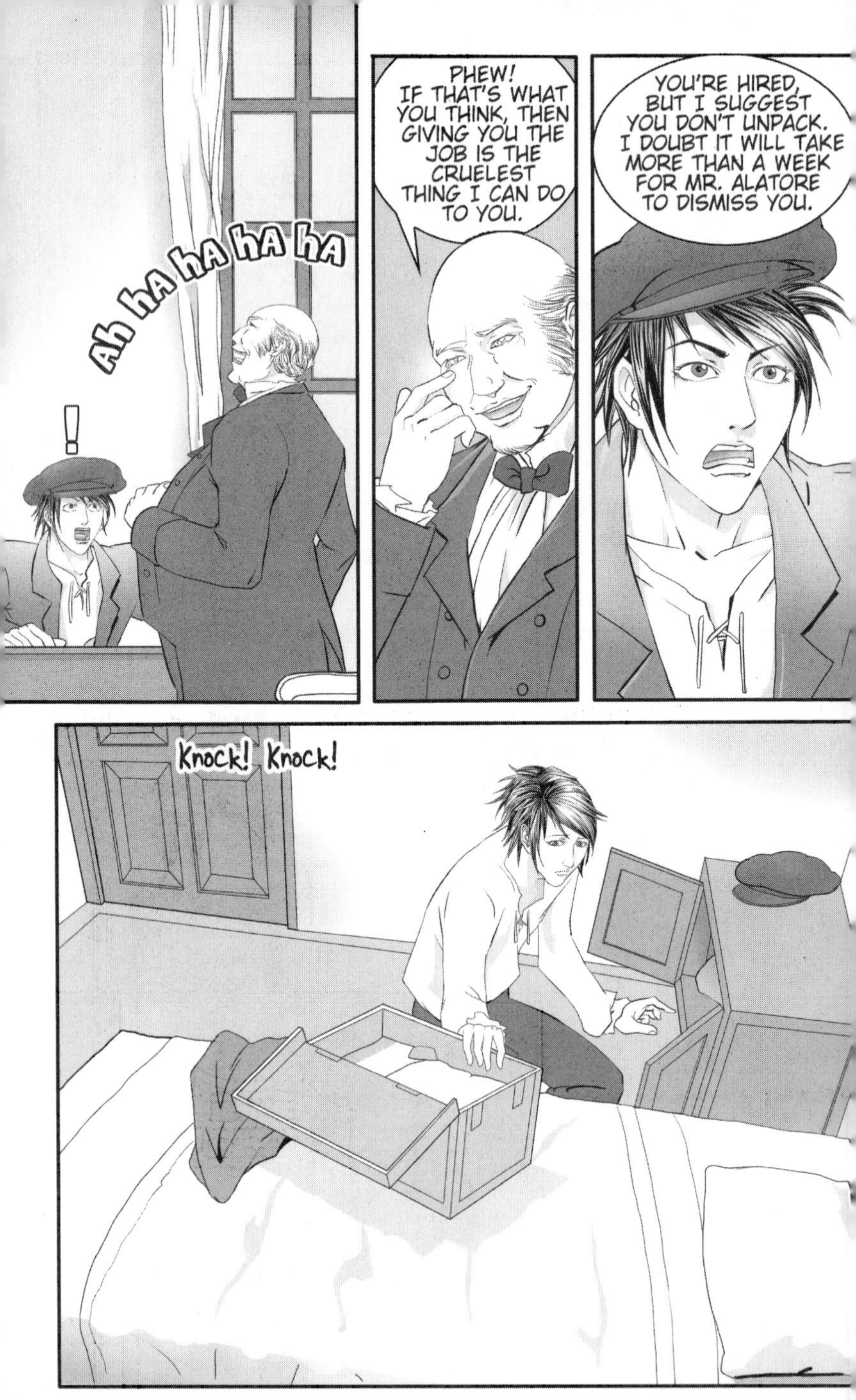
Ah ha ha ha ha
!
PHEW! IF THAT'S WHAT YOU THINK, THEN GIVING YOU THE JOB IS THE CRUELEST THING I CAN DO TO YOU.
YOU'RE HIRED, BUT I SUGGEST YOU DON'T UNPACK. I DOUBT IT WILL TAKE MORE THAN A WEEK FOR MR. ALATORE TO DISMISS YOU.
Knock! Knock!

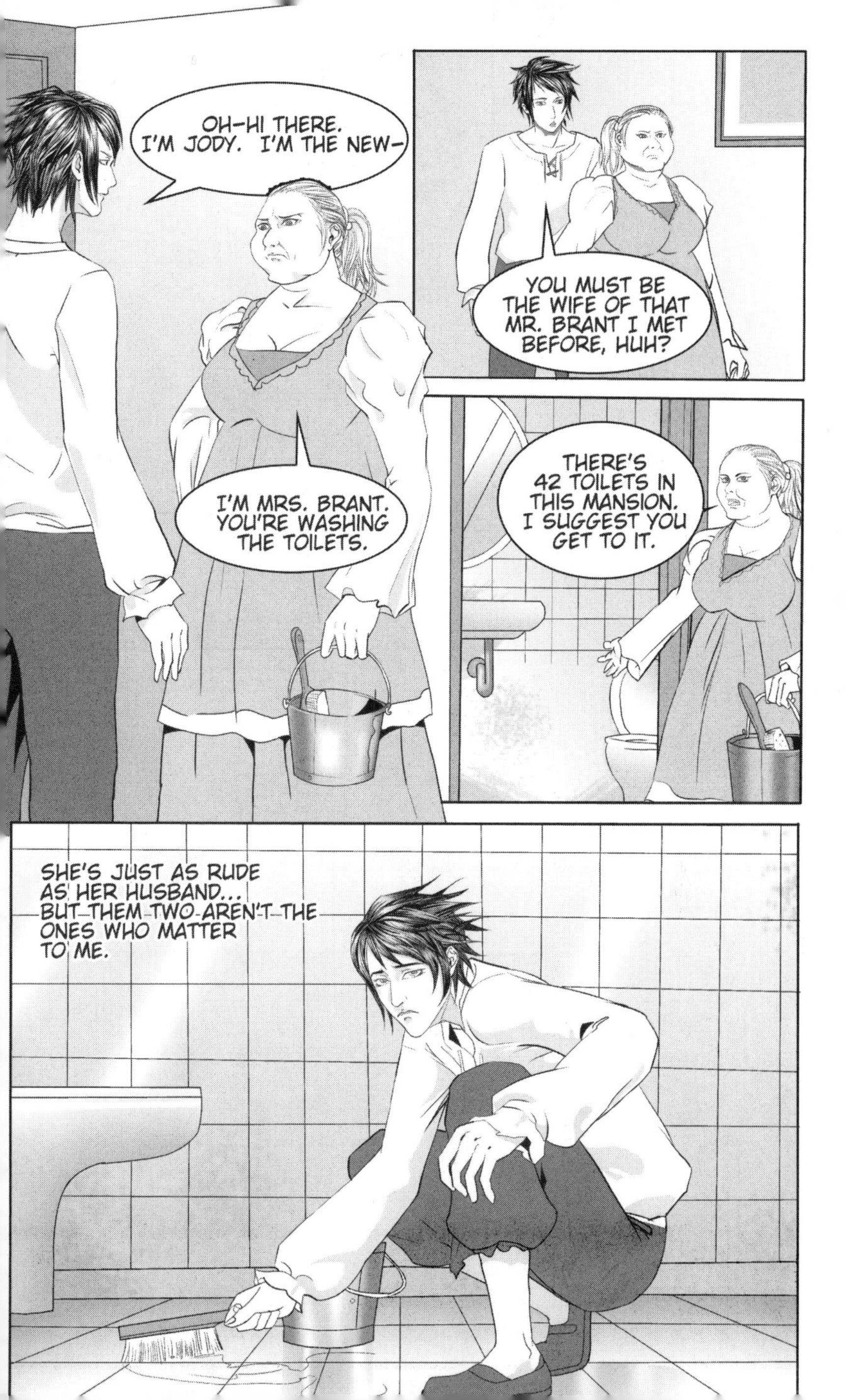
OH–HI THERE. I'M JODY. I'M THE NEW–
YOU MUST BE THE WIFE OF THAT MR. BRANT I MET BEFORE, HUH?
I'M MRS. BRANT. YOU'RE WASHING THE TOILETS.
THERE'S 42 TOILETS IN THIS MANSION. I SUGGEST YOU GET TO IT.
SHE'S JUST AS RUDE AS HER HUSBAND... BUT THEM TWO AREN'T THE ONES WHO MATTER TO ME.

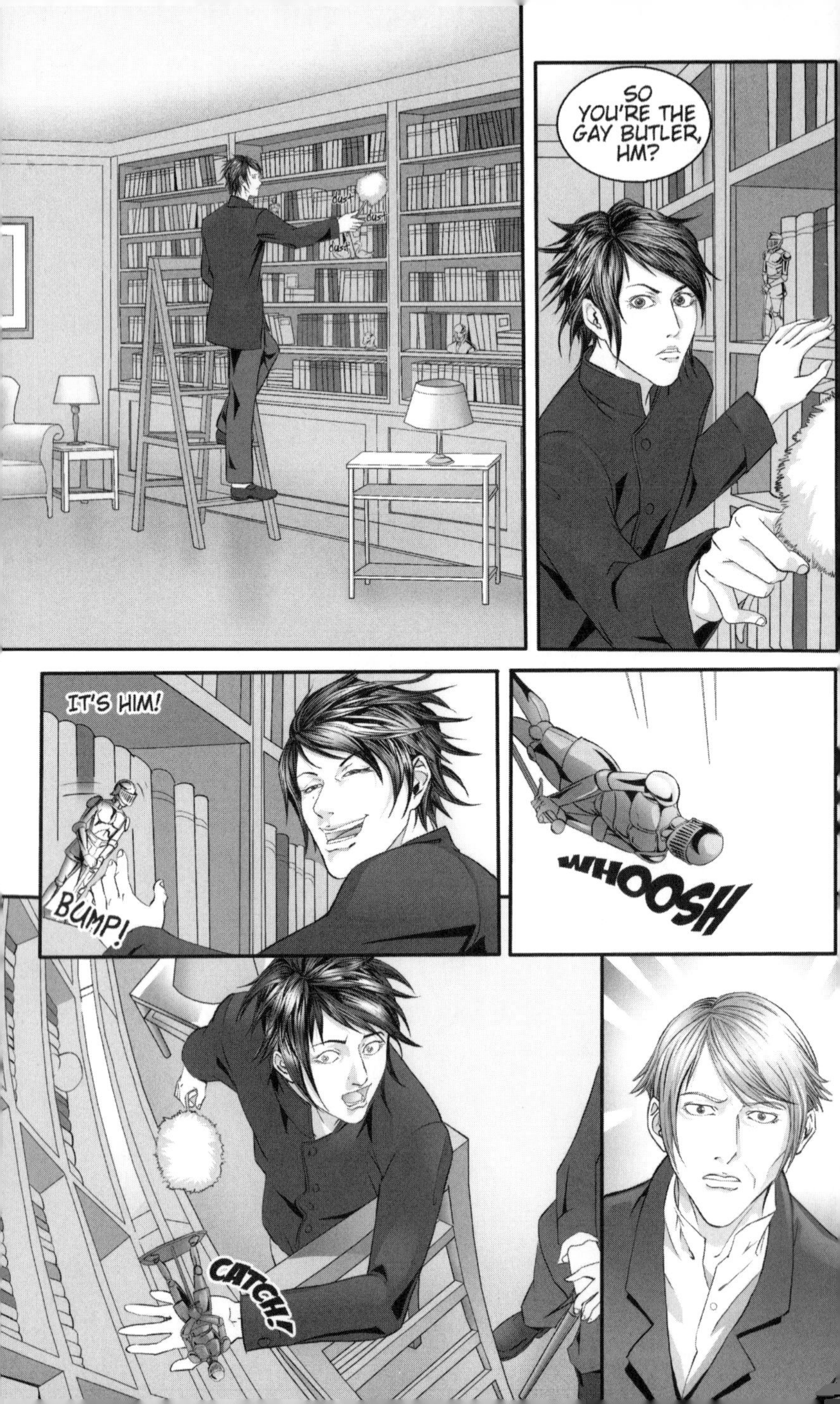
dust
dust
dust
SO YOU'RE THE GAY BUTLER, HM?
IT'S HIM!
BUMP!
WHOOSH
CATCH!

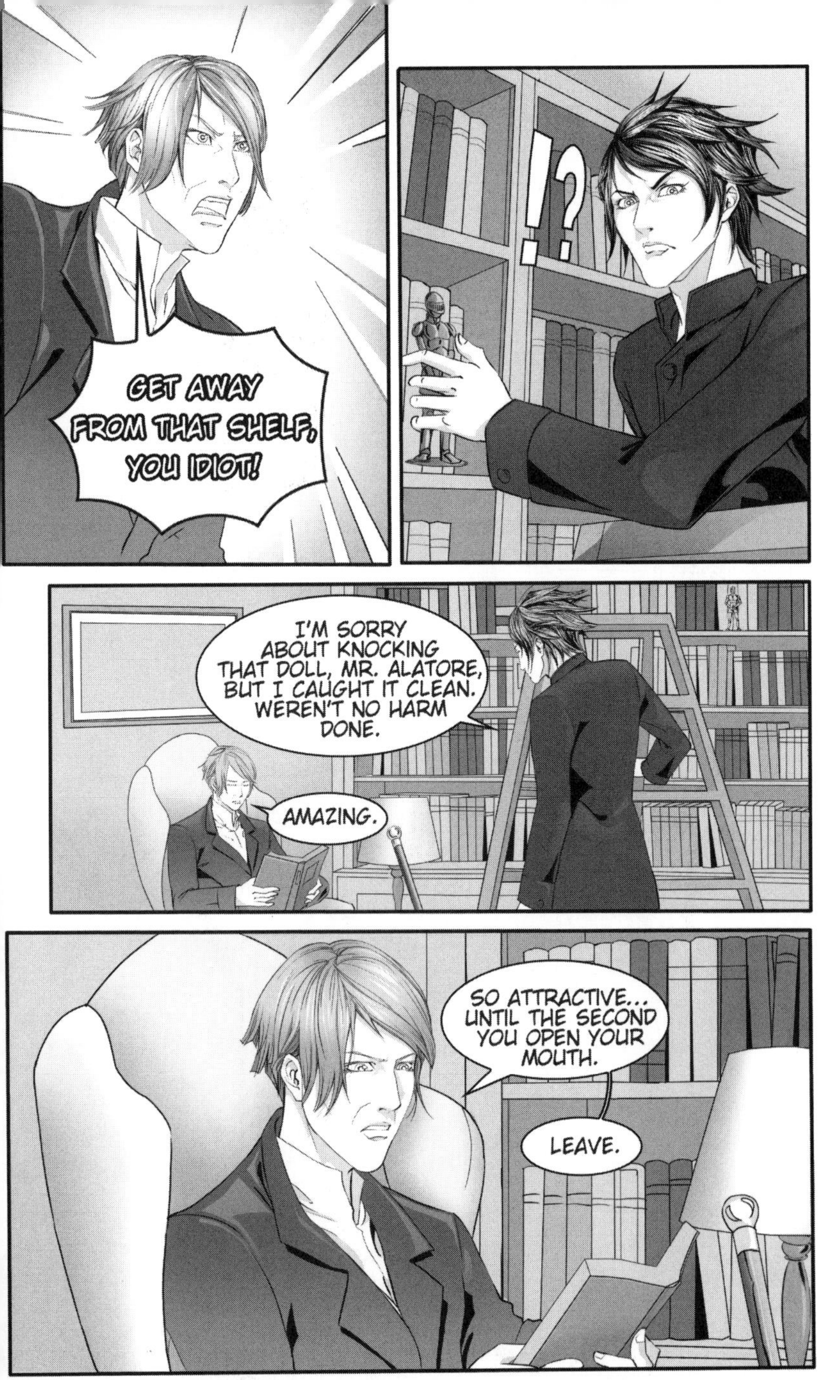
GET AWAY FROM THAT SHELF, YOU IDIOT!
!?
I'M SORRY ABOUT KNOCKING THAT DOLL, MR. ALATORE, BUT I CAUGHT IT CLEAN. WEREN'T NO HARM DONE.
AMAZING.
SO ATTRACTIVE... UNTIL THE SECOND YOU OPEN YOUR MOUTH.
LEAVE.

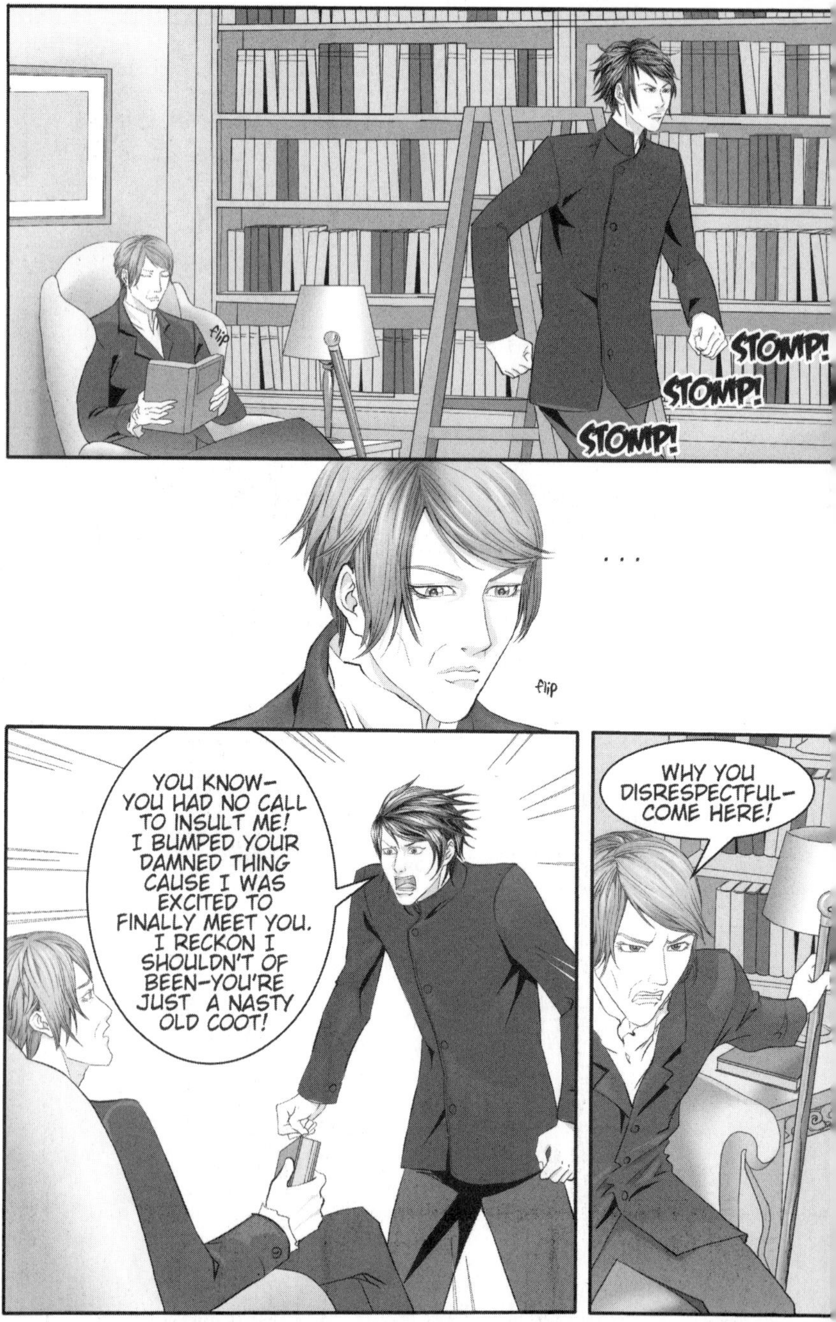
flip
STOMP!
STOMP!
STOMP!
. . .
flip
YOU KNOW- YOU HAD NO CALL TO INSULT ME! I BUMPED YOUR DAMNED THING CAUSE I WAS EXCITED TO FINALLY MEET YOU. I RECKON I SHOULDN'T OF BEEN-YOU'RE JUST A NASTY OLD COOT!
WHY YOU DISRESPECTFUL- COME HERE!

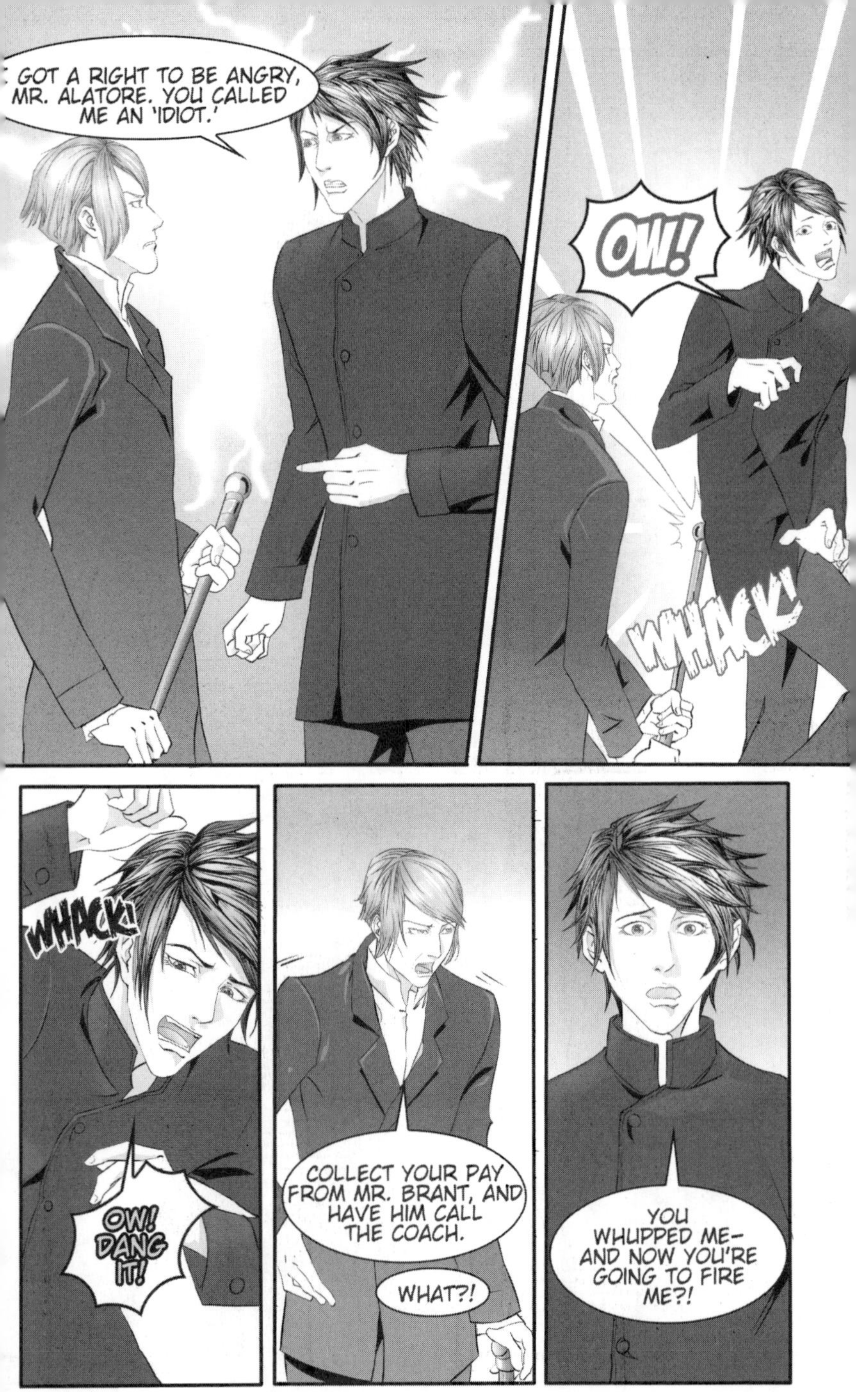
GOT A RIGHT TO BE ANGRY, MR. ALATORE. YOU CALLED ME AN 'IDIOT.'
OW!
WHACK!
WHACK!
OW! DANG IT!
COLLECT YOUR PAY FROM MR. BRANT, AND HAVE HIM CALL THE COACH.
WHAT?!
YOU WHUPPED ME— AND NOW YOU'RE GOING TO FIRE ME?!

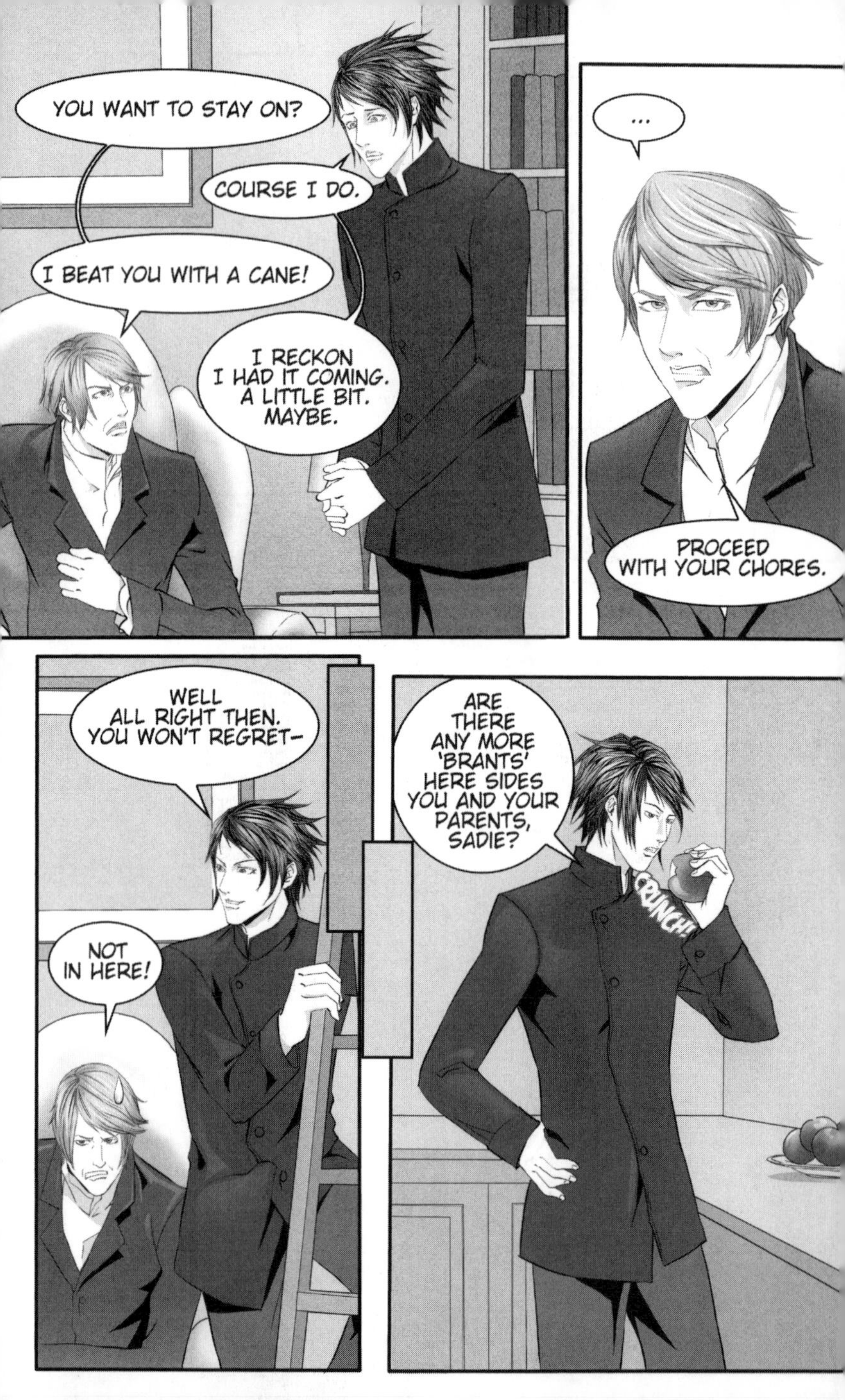

YOU WANT TO STAY ON?
COURSE I DO.
I BEAT YOU WITH A CANE!
I RECKON I HAD IT COMING. A LITTLE BIT. MAYBE.
...
PROCEED WITH YOUR CHORES.
WELL ALL RIGHT THEN. YOU WON'T REGRET-
NOT IN HERE!
ARE THERE ANY MORE 'BRANTS' HERE SIDES YOU AND YOUR PARENTS, SADIE?
CRUNCH!

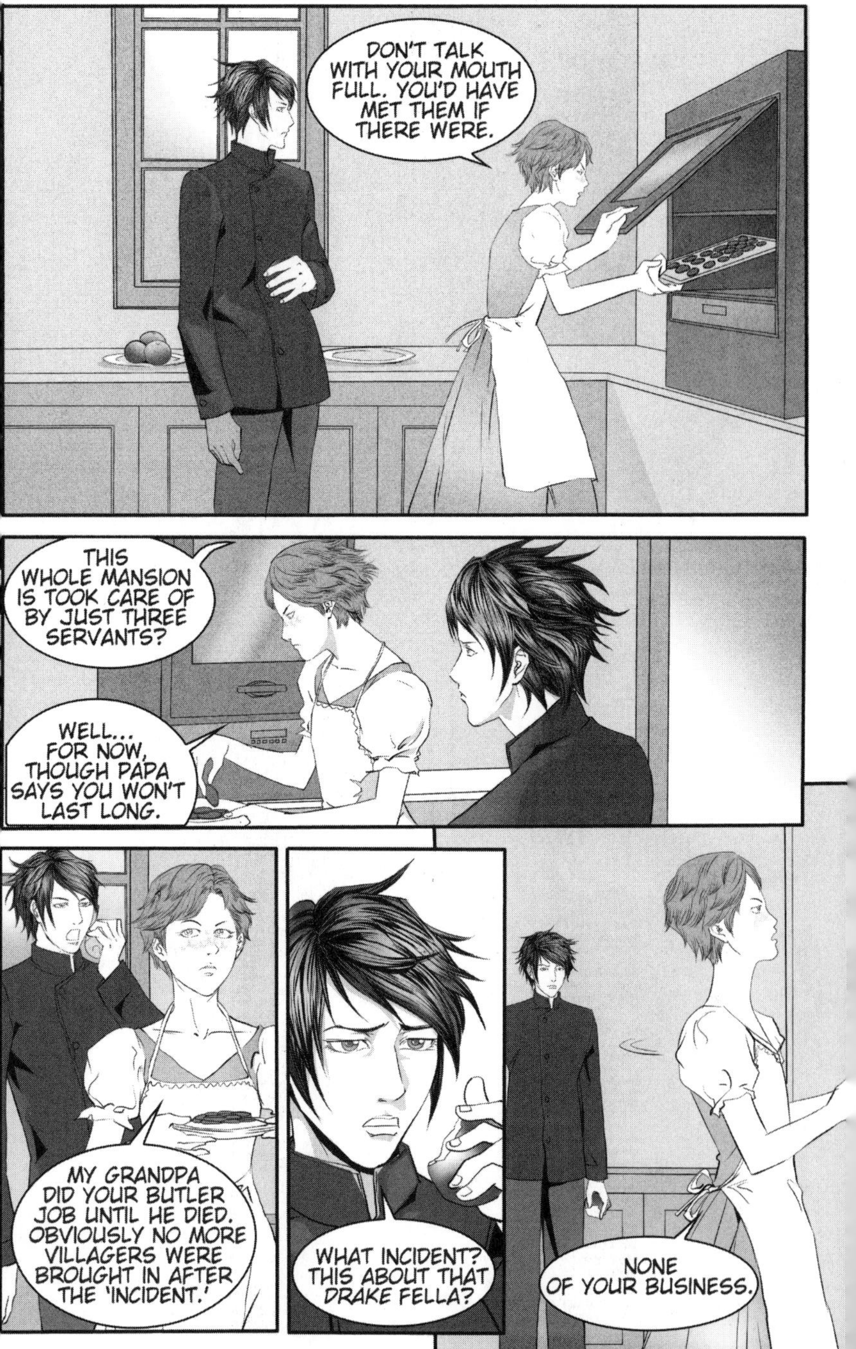
DON'T TALK WITH YOUR MOUTH FULL. YOU'D HAVE MET THEM IF THERE WERE.
THIS WHOLE MANSION IS TOOK CARE OF BY JUST THREE SERVANTS?
WELL... FOR NOW, THOUGH PAPA SAYS YOU WON'T LAST LONG.
MY GRANDPA DID YOUR BUTLER JOB UNTIL HE DIED. OBVIOUSLY NO MORE VILLAGERS WERE BROUGHT IN AFTER THE 'INCIDENT.'
WHAT INCIDENT? THIS ABOUT THAT DRAKE FELLA?
NONE OF YOUR BUSINESS.

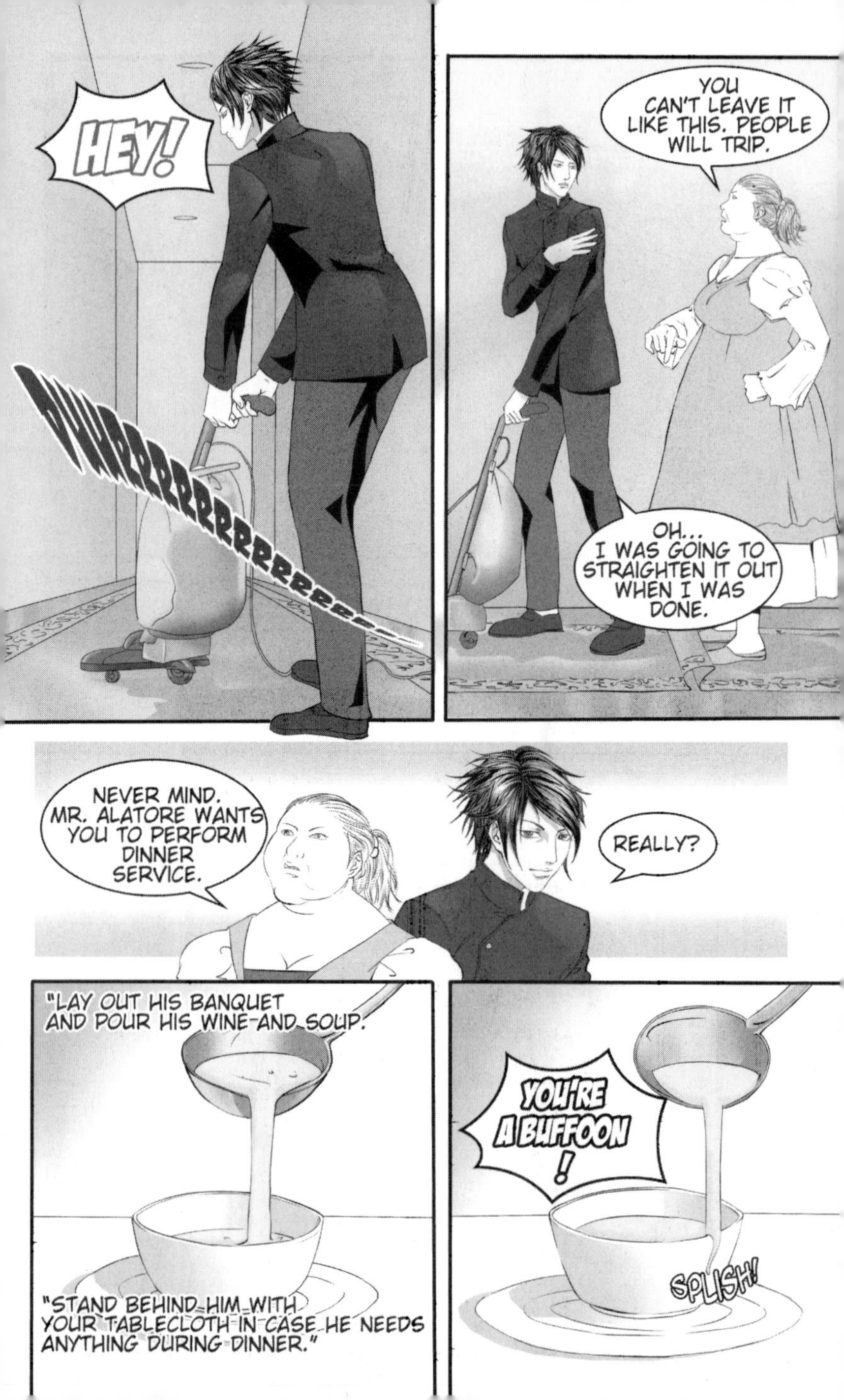
HEY!
YOU CAN'T LEAVE IT LIKE THIS. PEOPLE WILL TRIP.
OH... I WAS GOING TO STRAIGHTEN IT OUT WHEN I WAS DONE.
NEVER MIND. MR. ALATORE WANTS YOU TO PERFORM DINNER SERVICE.
REALLY?
"LAY OUT HIS BANQUET AND POUR HIS WINE AND SOUP.
"STAND BEHIND HIM WITH YOUR TABLECLOTH IN CASE HE NEEDS ANYTHING DURING DINNER."
YOU'RE A BUFFOON!
SPLISH!

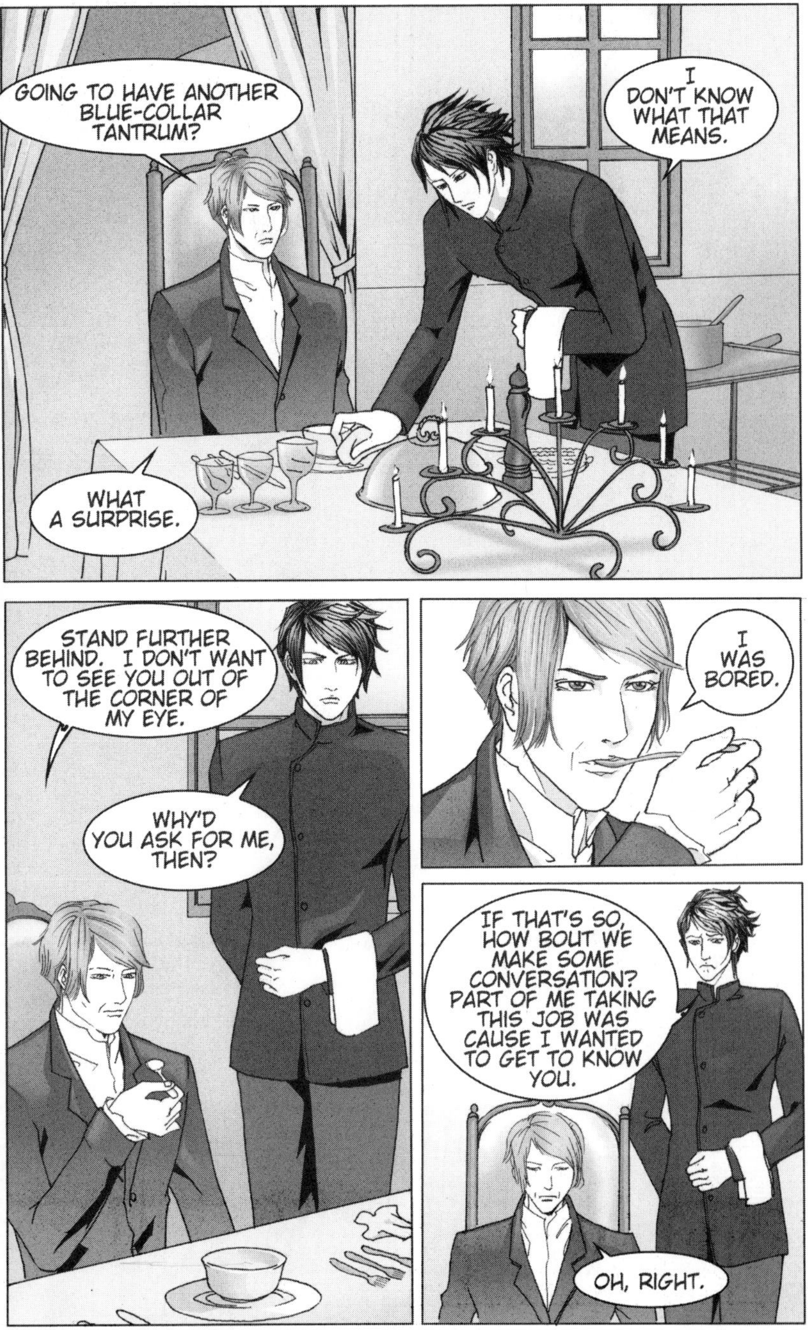
GOING TO HAVE ANOTHER BLUE-COLLAR TANTRUM?
I DON'T KNOW WHAT THAT MEANS.
WHAT A SURPRISE.
STAND FURTHER BEHIND. I DON'T WANT TO SEE YOU OUT OF THE CORNER OF MY EYE.
WHY'D YOU ASK FOR ME, THEN?
I WAS BORED.
IF THAT'S SO, HOW BOUT WE MAKE SOME CONVERSATION? PART OF ME TAKING THIS JOB WAS CAUSE I WANTED TO GET TO KNOW YOU.
OH, RIGHT.

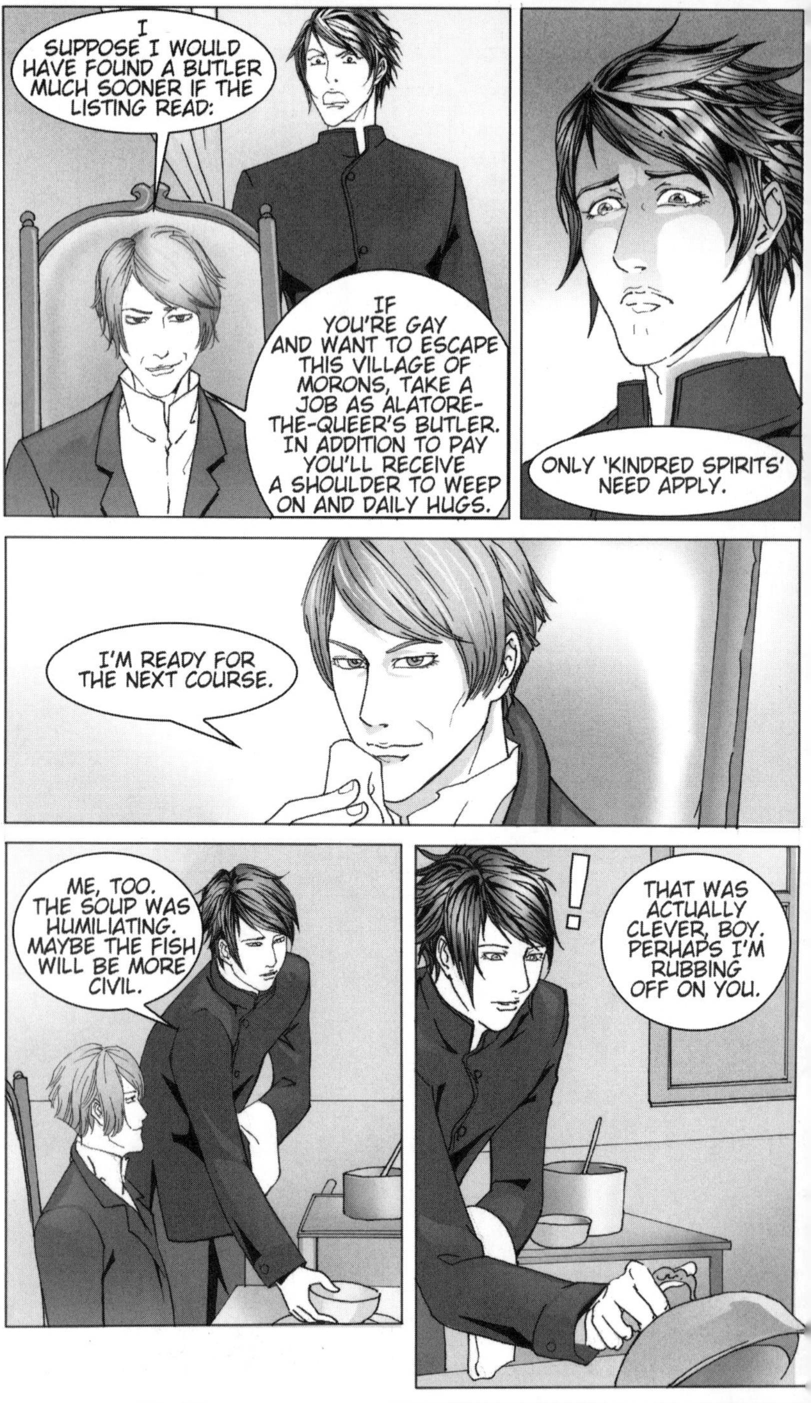
I SUPPOSE I WOULD HAVE FOUND A BUTLER MUCH SOONER IF THE LISTING READ:
IF YOU'RE GAY AND WANT TO ESCAPE THIS VILLAGE OF MORONS, TAKE A JOB AS ALATORE-THE-QUEER'S BUTLER. IN ADDITION TO PAY YOU'LL RECEIVE A SHOULDER TO WEEP ON AND DAILY HUGS.
ONLY 'KINDRED SPIRITS' NEED APPLY.
I'M READY FOR THE NEXT COURSE.
ME, TOO. THE SOUP WAS HUMILIATING. MAYBE THE FISH WILL BE MORE CIVIL.
!
THAT WAS ACTUALLY CLEVER, BOY. PERHAPS I'M RUBBING OFF ON YOU.

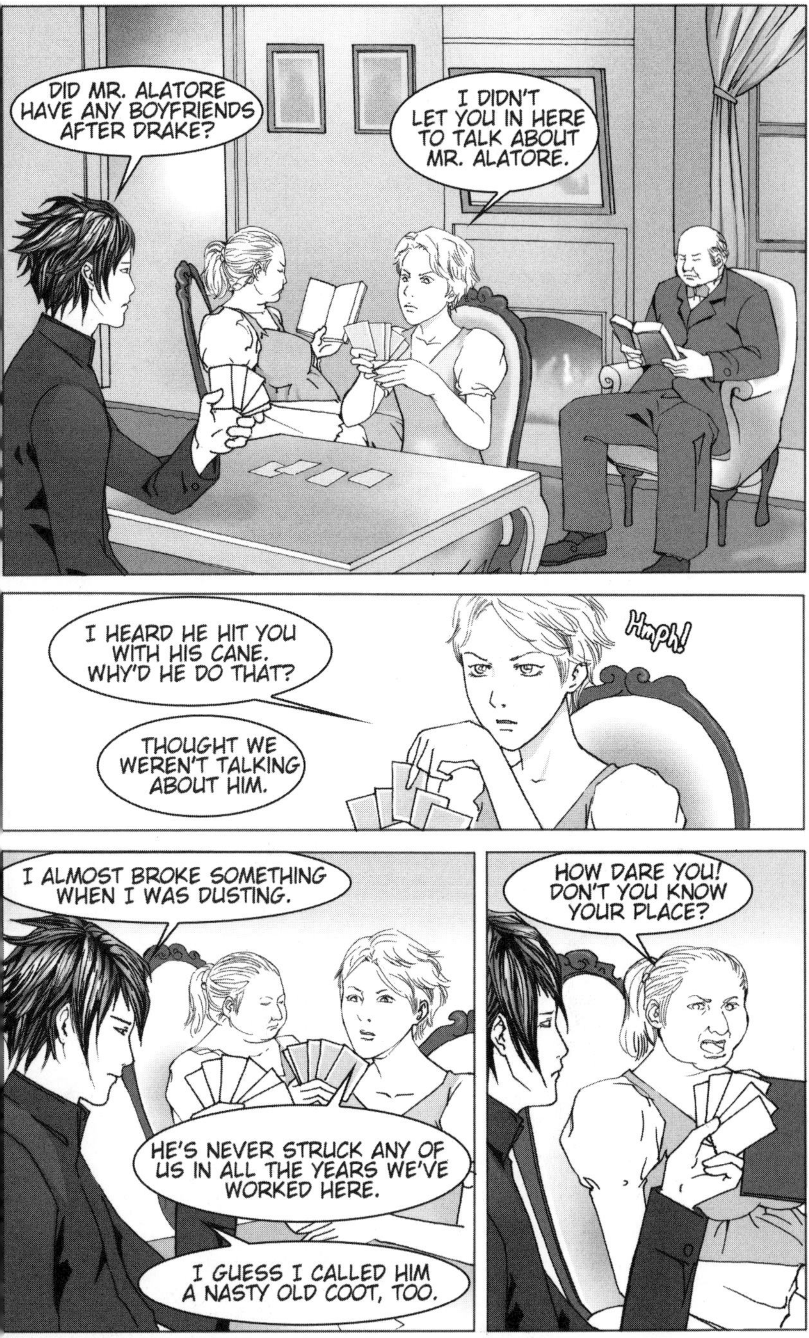
DID MR. ALATORE HAVE ANY BOYFRIENDS AFTER DRAKE?
I DIDN'T LET YOU IN HERE TO TALK ABOUT MR. ALATORE.
I HEARD HE HIT YOU WITH HIS CANE. WHY'D HE DO THAT?
Hmph!
THOUGHT WE WEREN'T TALKING ABOUT HIM.
I ALMOST BROKE SOMETHING WHEN I WAS DUSTING.
HE'S NEVER STRUCK ANY OF US IN ALL THE YEARS WE'VE WORKED HERE.
I GUESS I CALLED HIM A NASTY OLD COOT, TOO.
HOW DARE YOU! DON'T YOU KNOW YOUR PLACE?

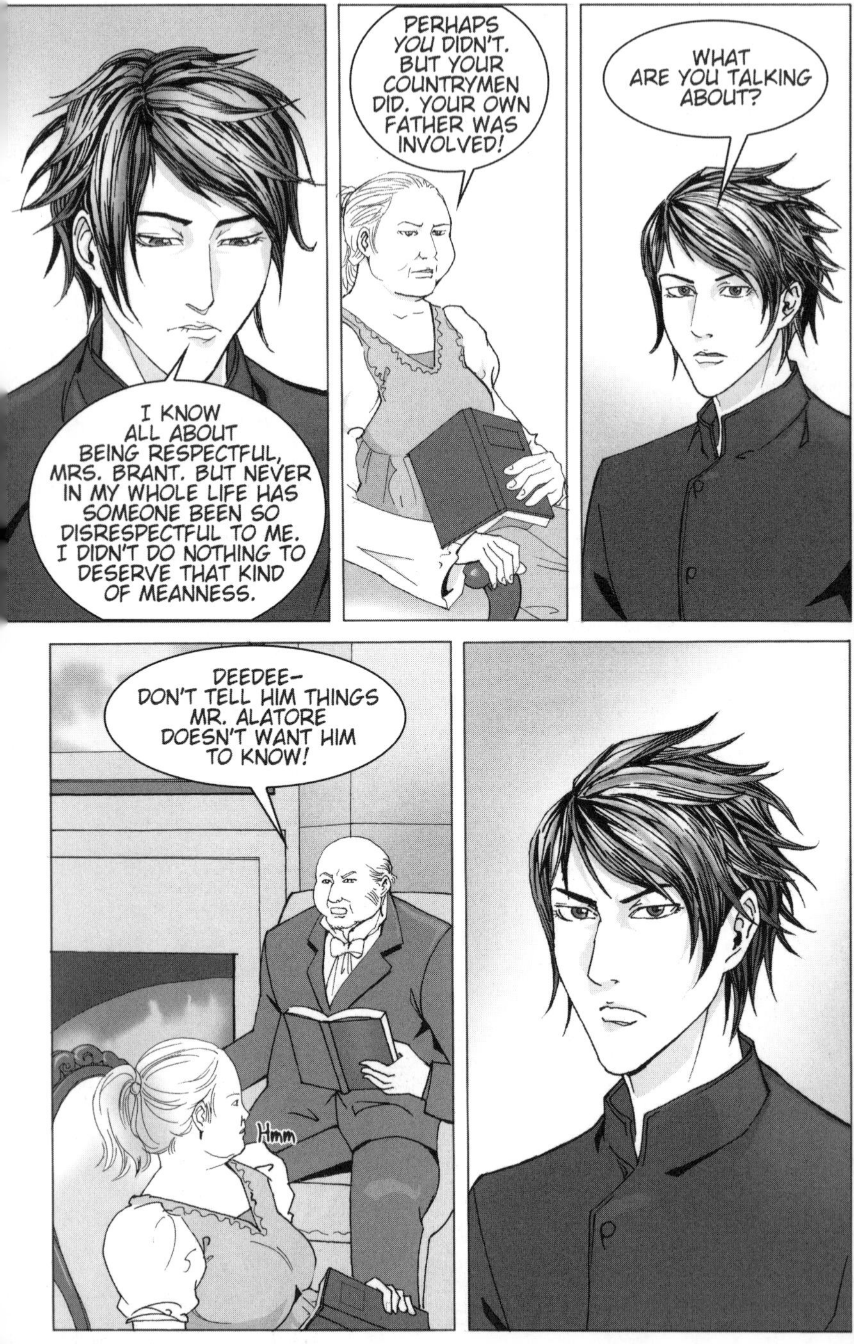
I KNOW ALL ABOUT BEING RESPECTFUL, MRS. BRANT. BUT NEVER IN MY WHOLE LIFE HAS SOMEONE BEEN SO DISRESPECTFUL TO ME. I DIDN'T DO NOTHING TO DESERVE THAT KIND OF MEANNESS.
PERHAPS YOU DIDN'T. BUT YOUR COUNTRYMEN DID. YOUR OWN FATHER WAS INVOLVED!
WHAT ARE YOU TALKING ABOUT?
DEEDEE- DON'T TELL HIM THINGS MR. ALATORE DOESN'T WANT HIM TO KNOW!
Hmm

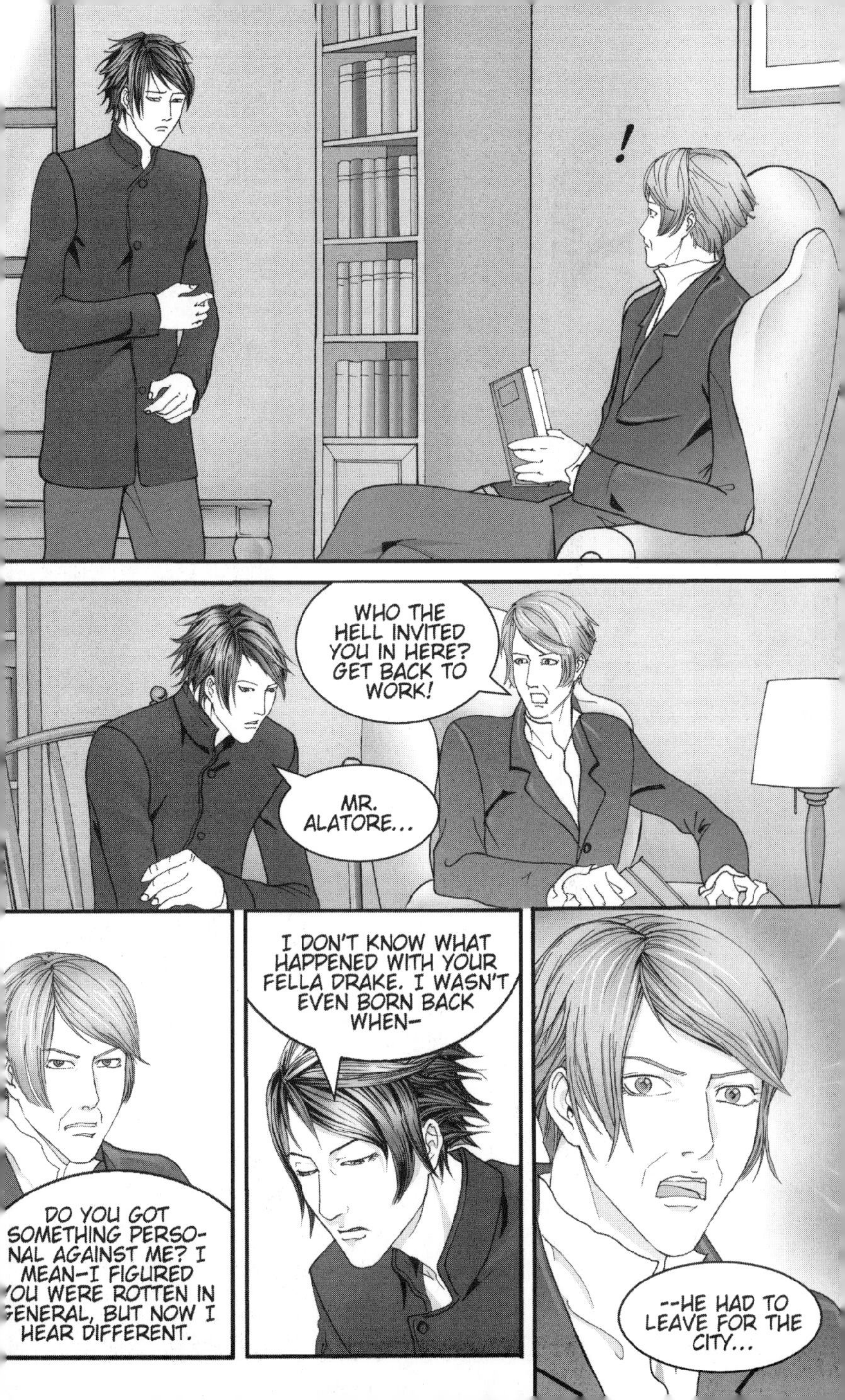
!
WHO THE HELL INVITED YOU IN HERE? GET BACK TO WORK!
MR. ALATORE...
DO YOU GOT SOMETHING PERSO-NAL AGAINST ME? I MEAN–I FIGURED YOU WERE ROTTEN IN GENERAL, BUT NOW I HEAR DIFFERENT.
I DON'T KNOW WHAT HAPPENED WITH YOUR FELLA DRAKE. I WASN'T EVEN BORN BACK WHEN–
--HE HAD TO LEAVE FOR THE CITY...

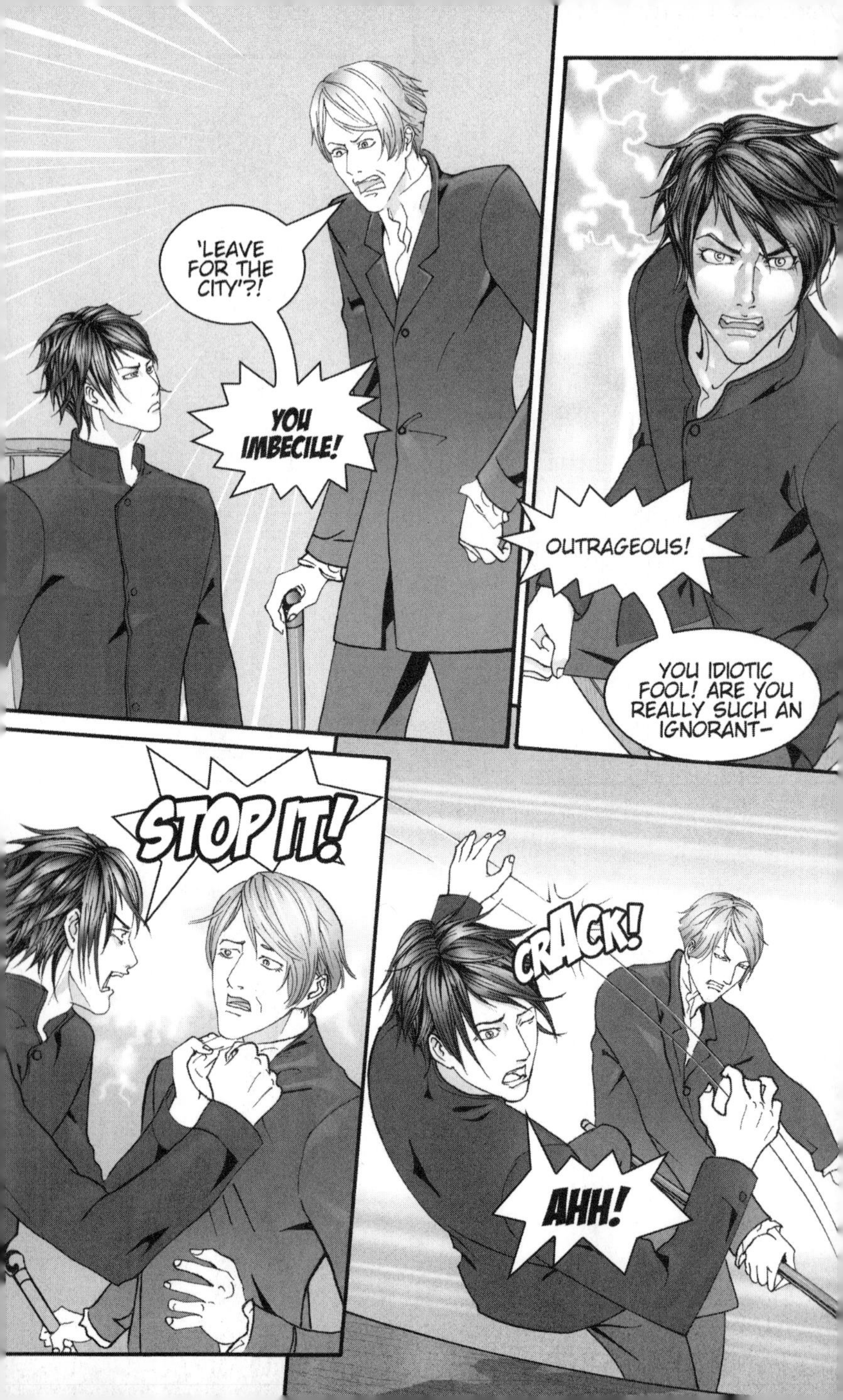
'LEAVE FOR THE CITY'?!
YOU IMBECILE!
OUTRAGEOUS!
YOU IDIOTIC FOOL! ARE YOU REALLY SUCH AN IGNORANT-
STOP IT!
CRACK!
AHH!

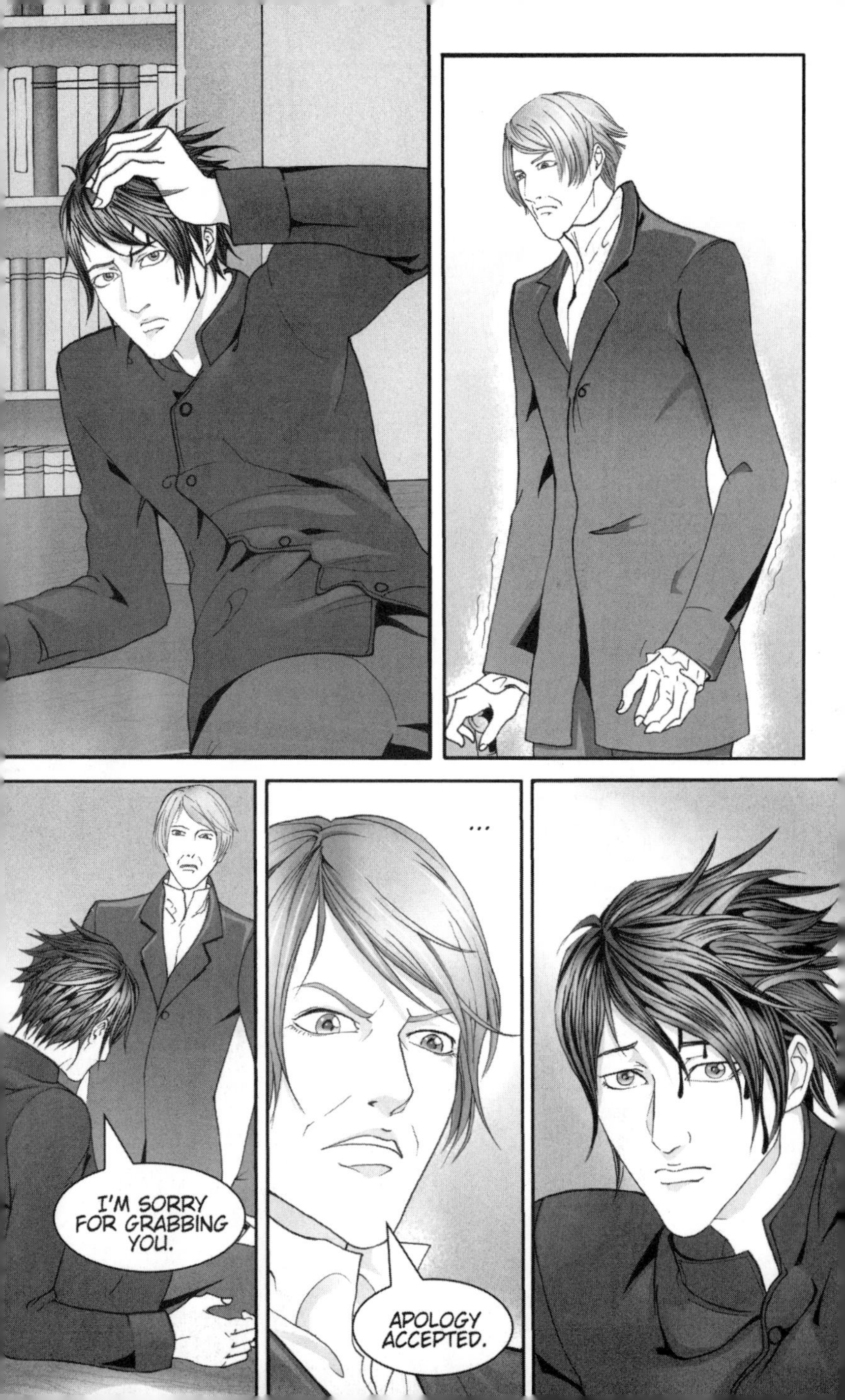
I'M SORRY FOR GRABBING YOU.
APOLOGY ACCEPTED.
...

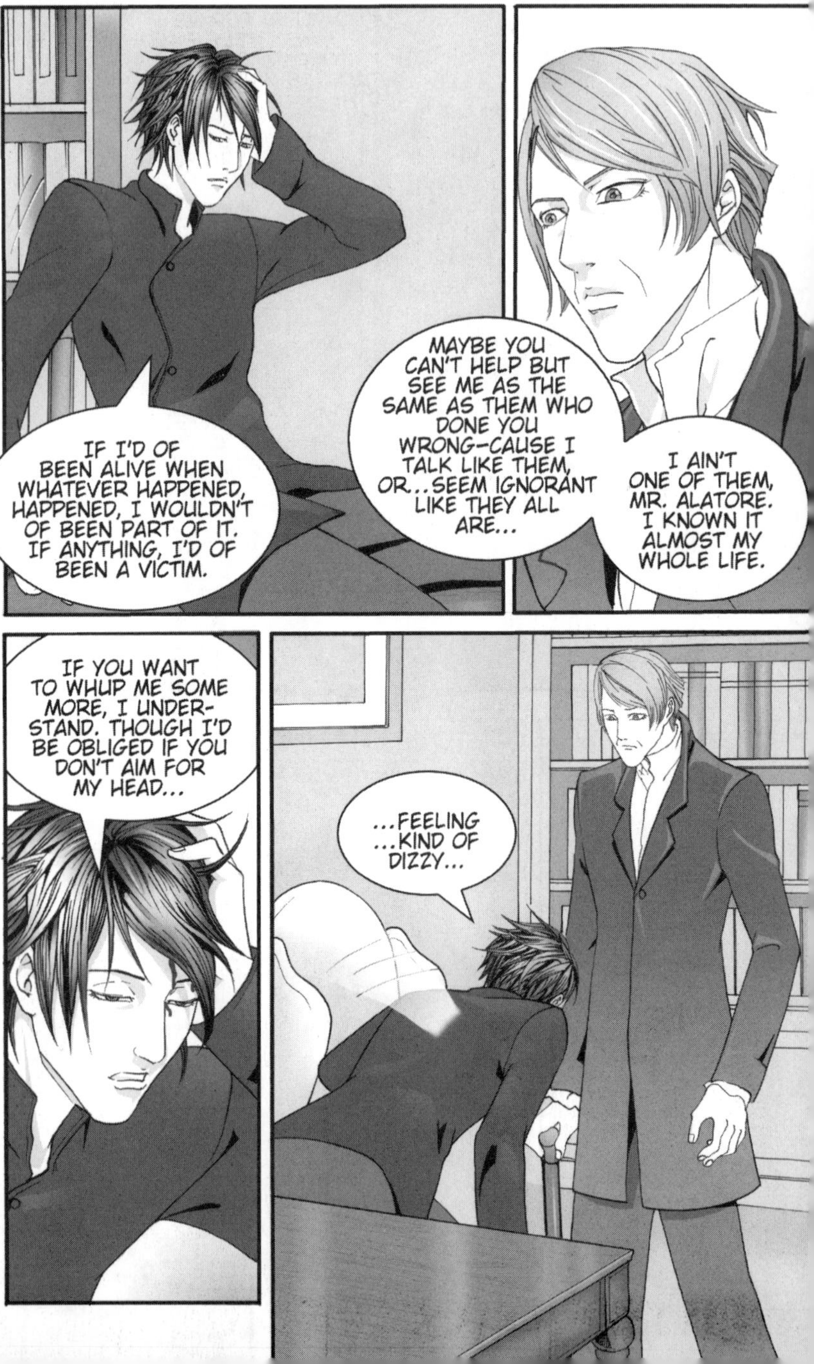
IF I'D OF BEEN ALIVE WHEN WHATEVER HAPPENED, HAPPENED, I WOULDN'T OF BEEN PART OF IT. IF ANYTHING, I'D OF BEEN A VICTIM.
MAYBE YOU CAN'T HELP BUT SEE ME AS THE SAME AS THEM WHO DONE YOU WRONG--CAUSE I TALK LIKE THEM, OR...SEEM IGNORANT LIKE THEY ALL ARE...
I AIN'T ONE OF THEM, MR. ALATORE. I KNOWN IT ALMOST MY WHOLE LIFE.
IF YOU WANT TO WHUP ME SOME MORE, I UNDERSTAND. THOUGH I'D BE OBLIGED IF YOU DON'T AIM FOR MY HEAD...
...FEELING ...KIND OF DIZZY...

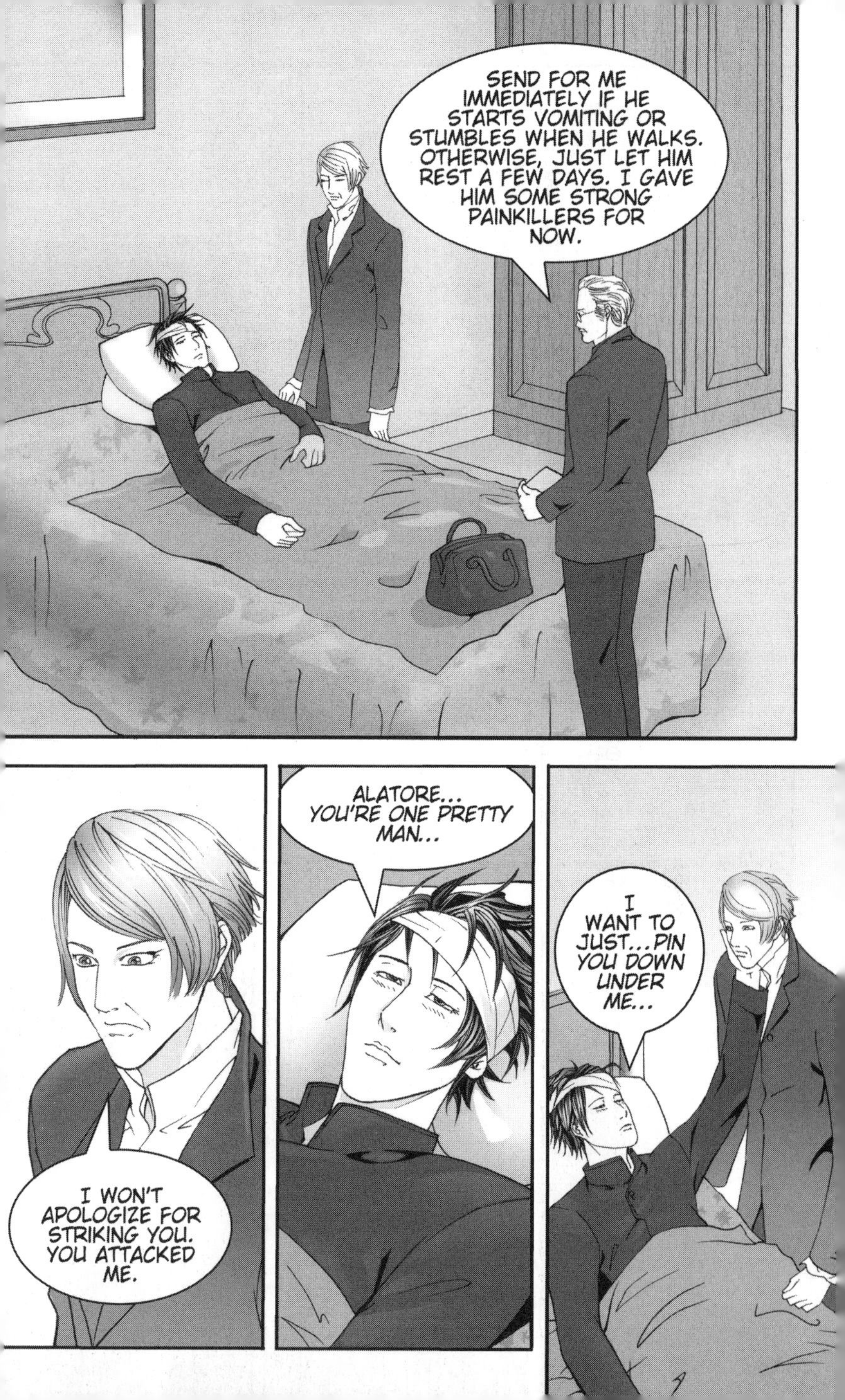
SEND FOR ME IMMEDIATELY IF HE STARTS VOMITING OR STUMBLES WHEN HE WALKS. OTHERWISE, JUST LET HIM REST A FEW DAYS. I GAVE HIM SOME STRONG PAINKILLERS FOR NOW.
I WON'T APOLOGIZE FOR STRIKING YOU. YOU ATTACKED ME.
ALATORE... YOU'RE ONE PRETTY MAN...
I WANT TO JUST...PIN YOU DOWN UNDER ME...

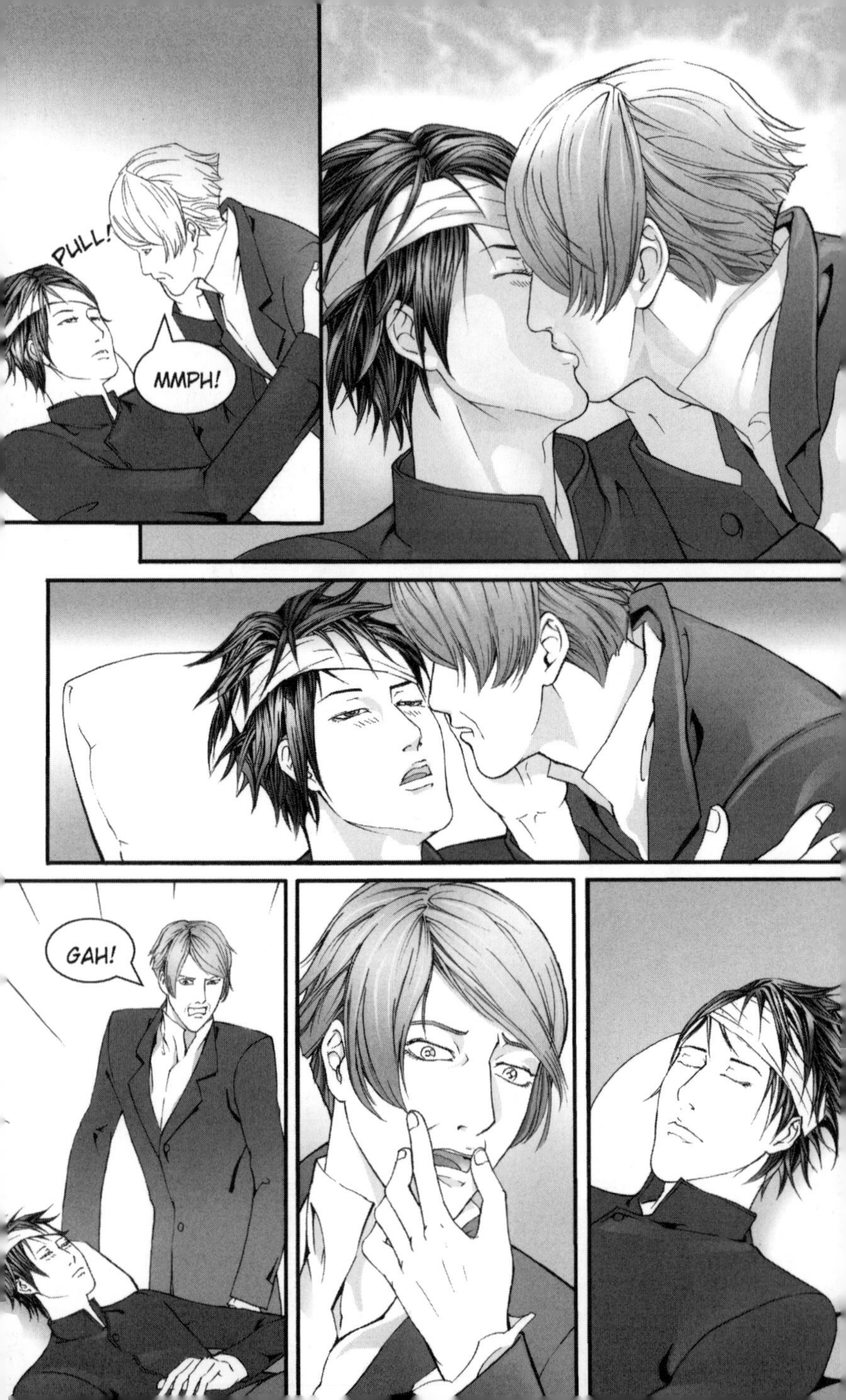
PULL!
MMPH!
GAH!

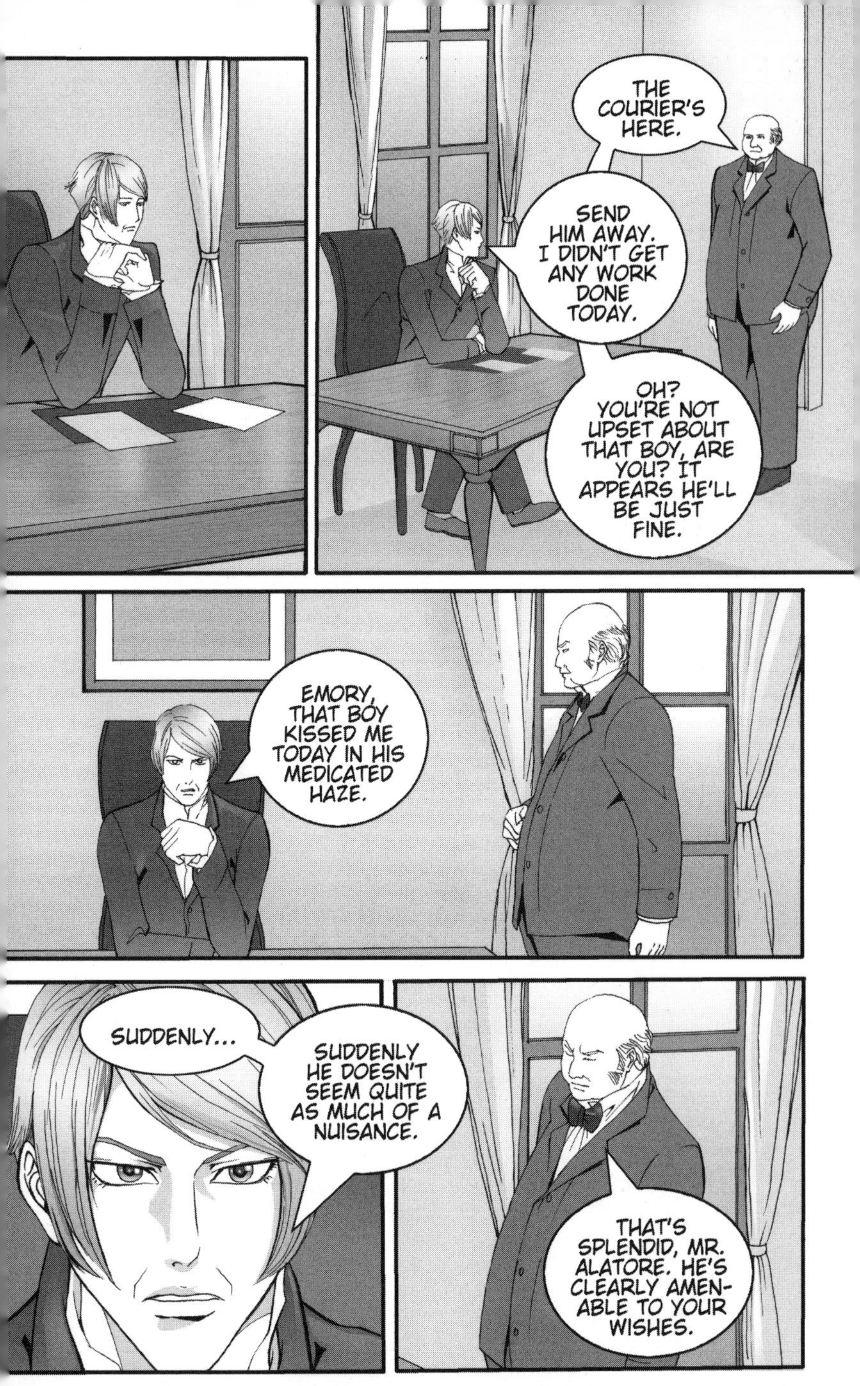
THE COURIER'S HERE.
SEND HIM AWAY. I DIDN'T GET ANY WORK DONE TODAY.
OH? YOU'RE NOT UPSET ABOUT THAT BOY, ARE YOU? IT APPEARS HE'LL BE JUST FINE.
EMORY, THAT BOY KISSED ME TODAY IN HIS MEDICATED HAZE.
SUDDENLY...
SUDDENLY HE DOESN'T SEEM QUITE AS MUCH OF A NUISANCE.
THAT'S SPLENDID, MR. ALATORE. HE'S CLEARLY AMEN-ABLE TO YOUR WISHES.

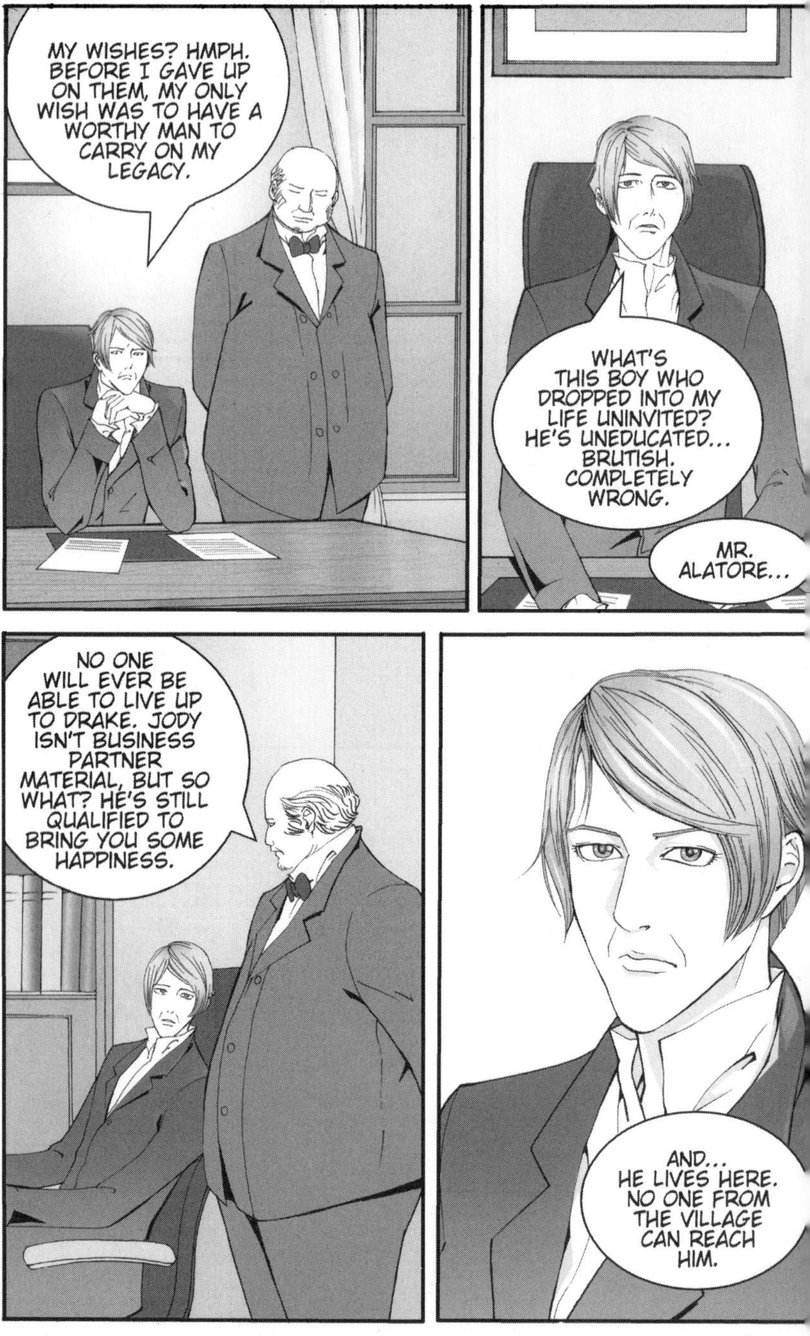
MY WISHES? HMPH. BEFORE I GAVE UP ON THEM, MY ONLY WISH WAS TO HAVE A WORTHY MAN TO CARRY ON MY LEGACY.
WHAT'S THIS BOY WHO DROPPED INTO MY LIFE UNINVITED? HE'S UNEDUCATED... BRUTISH. COMPLETELY WRONG.
MR. ALATORE...
NO ONE WILL EVER BE ABLE TO LIVE UP TO DRAKE. JODY ISN'T BUSINESS PARTNER MATERIAL, BUT SO WHAT? HE'S STILL QUALIFIED TO BRING YOU SOME HAPPINESS.
AND... HE LIVES HERE. NO ONE FROM THE VILLAGE CAN REACH HIM.

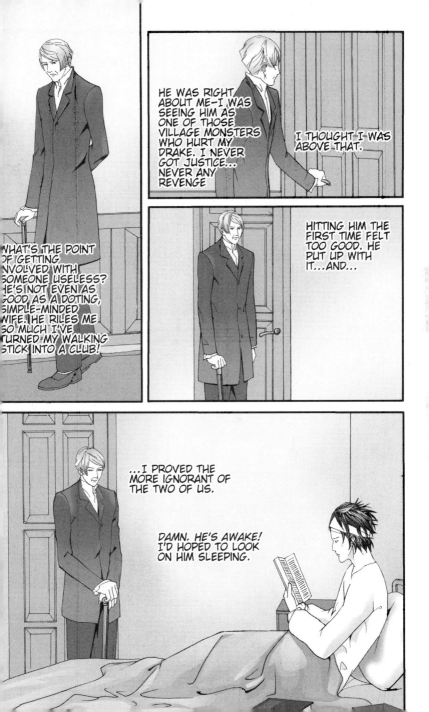

HE WAS RIGHT ABOUT ME—I WAS SEEING HIM AS ONE OF THOSE VILLAGE MONSTERS WHO HURT MY DRAKE. I NEVER GOT JUSTICE... NEVER ANY REVENGE

I THOUGHT I WAS ABOVE THAT.

HITTING HIM THE FIRST TIME FELT TOO GOOD. HE PUT UP WITH IT...AND...

WHAT'S THE POINT OF GETTING INVOLVED WITH SOMEONE USELESS? HE'S NOT EVEN AS GOOD AS A DOTING, SIMPLE-MINDED WIFE. HE RILES ME SO MUCH I'VE TURNED MY WALKING STICK INTO A CLUB!

...I PROVED THE MORE IGNORANT OF THE TWO OF US.

DAMN. HE'S AWAKE! I'D HOPED TO LOOK ON HIM SLEEPING.

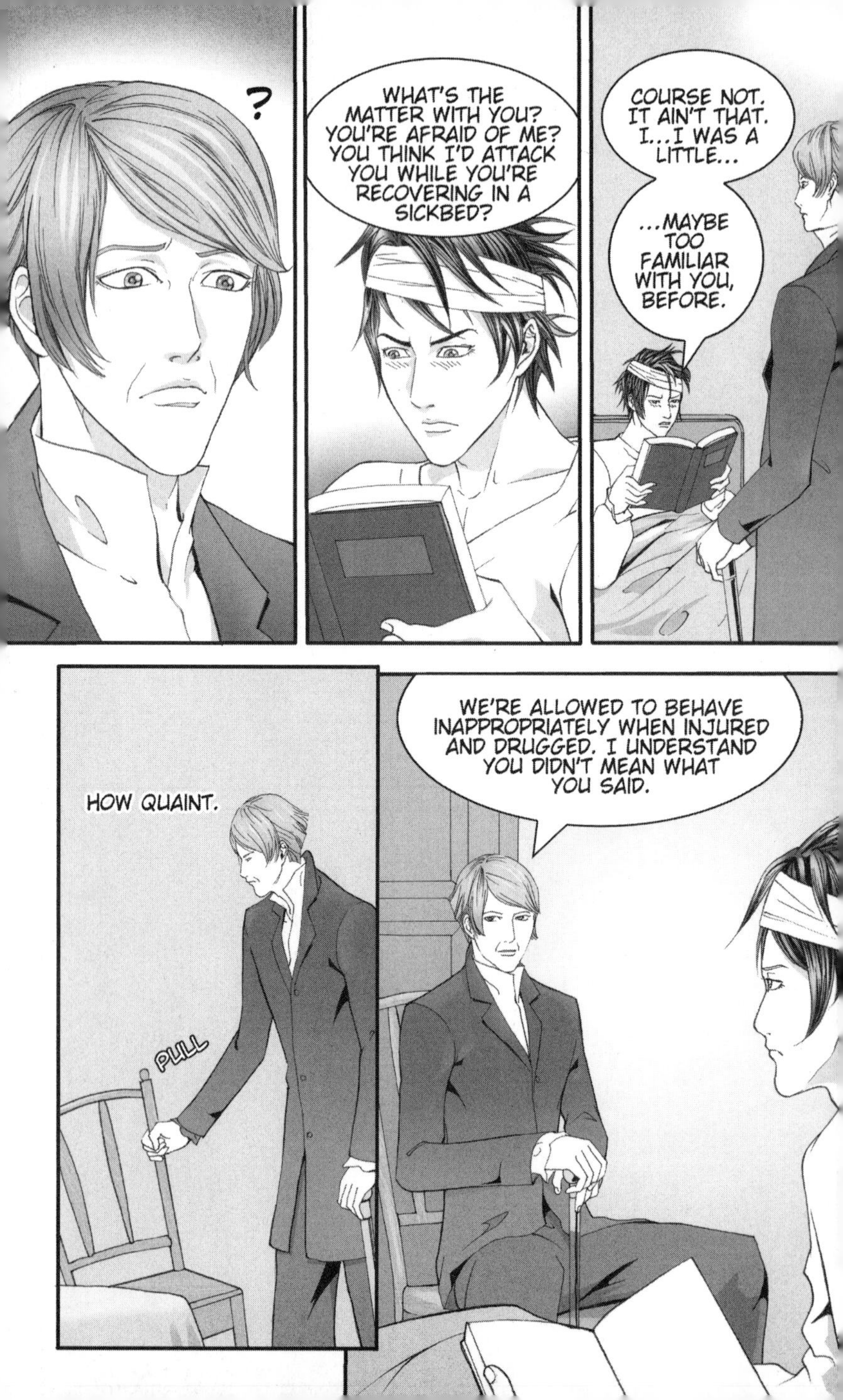
?
WHAT'S THE MATTER WITH YOU? YOU'RE AFRAID OF ME? YOU THINK I'D ATTACK YOU WHILE YOU'RE RECOVERING IN A SICKBED?
COURSE NOT. IT AIN'T THAT. I...I WAS A LITTLE...
...MAYBE TOO FAMILIAR WITH YOU, BEFORE.
HOW QUAINT.
PULL
WE'RE ALLOWED TO BEHAVE INAPPROPRIATELY WHEN INJURED AND DRUGGED. I UNDERSTAND YOU DIDN'T MEAN WHAT YOU SAID.

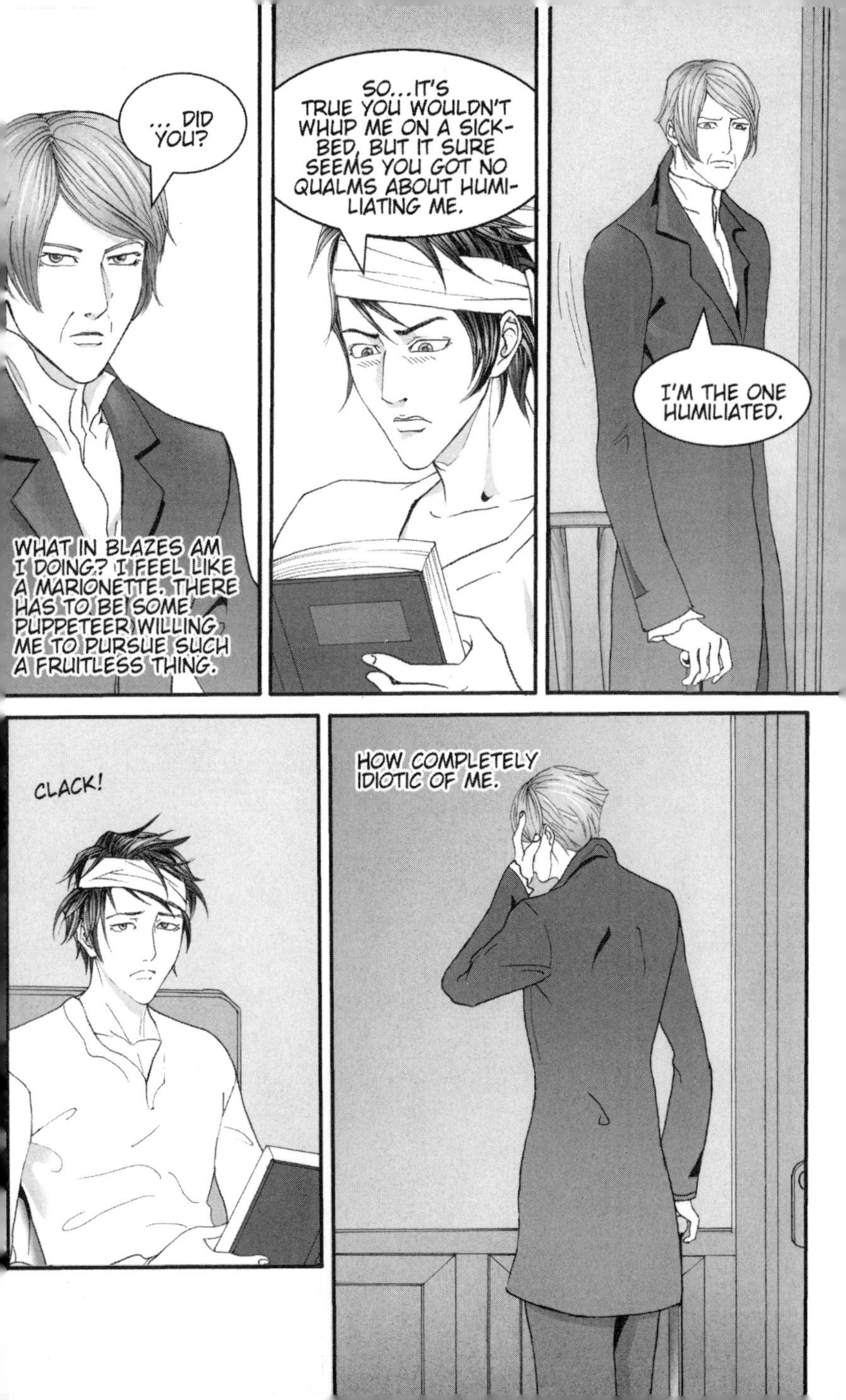
... DID YOU?
WHAT IN BLAZES AM I DOING? I FEEL LIKE A MARIONETTE. THERE HAS TO BE SOME PUPPETEER WILLING ME TO PURSUE SUCH A FRUITLESS THING.
SO...IT'S TRUE YOU WOULDN'T WHUP ME ON A SICK-BED, BUT IT SURE SEEMS YOU GOT NO QUALMS ABOUT HUMI-LIATING ME.
I'M THE ONE HUMILIATED.
CLACK!
HOW COMPLETELY IDIOTIC OF ME.

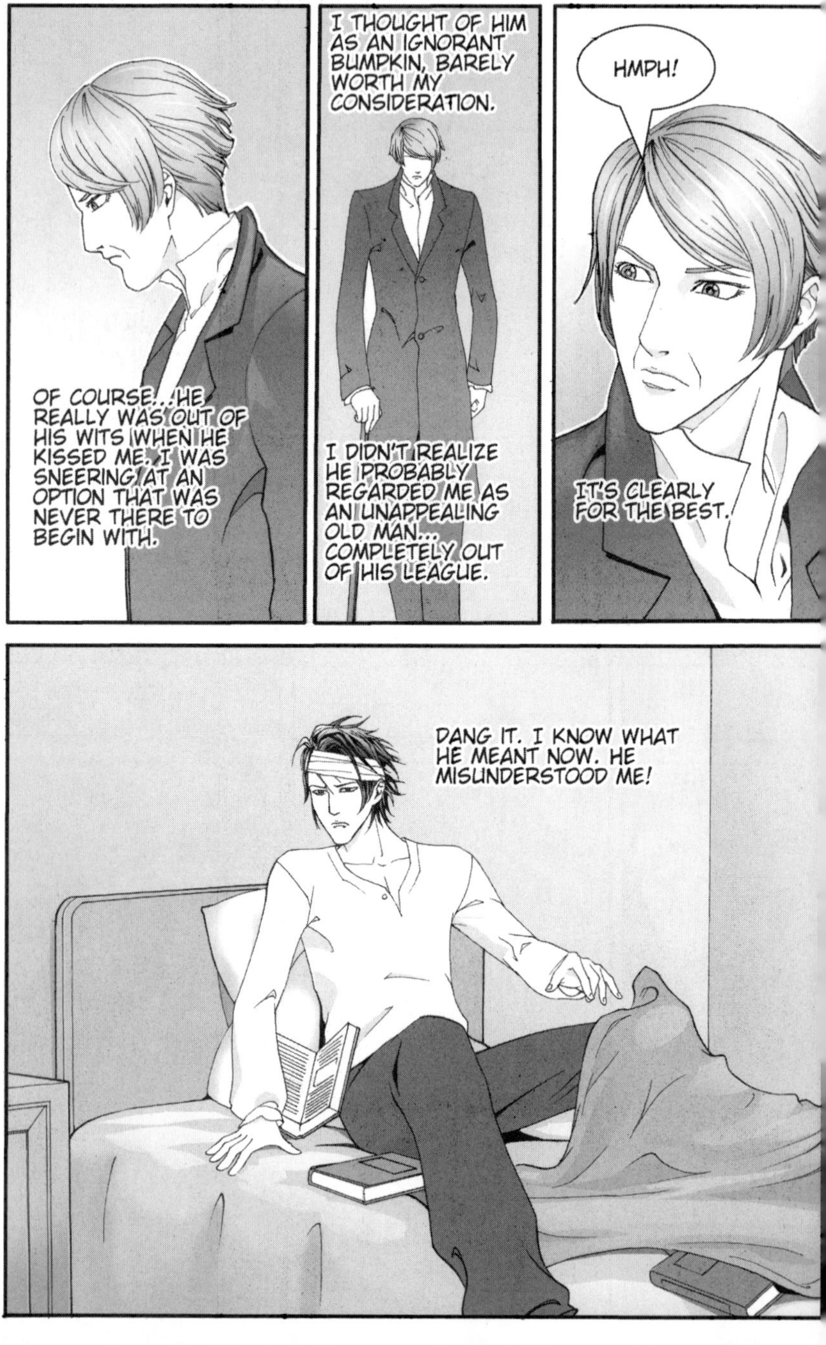
OF COURSE...HE REALLY WAS OUT OF HIS WITS WHEN HE KISSED ME. I WAS SNEERING AT AN OPTION THAT WAS NEVER THERE TO BEGIN WITH.
I THOUGHT OF HIM AS AN IGNORANT BUMPKIN, BARELY WORTH MY CONSIDERATION.
I DIDN'T REALIZE HE PROBABLY REGARDED ME AS AN UNAPPEALING OLD MAN... COMPLETELY OUT OF HIS LEAGUE.
HMPH!
IT'S CLEARLY FOR THE BEST.
DANG IT. I KNOW WHAT HE MEANT NOW. HE MISUNDERSTOOD ME!

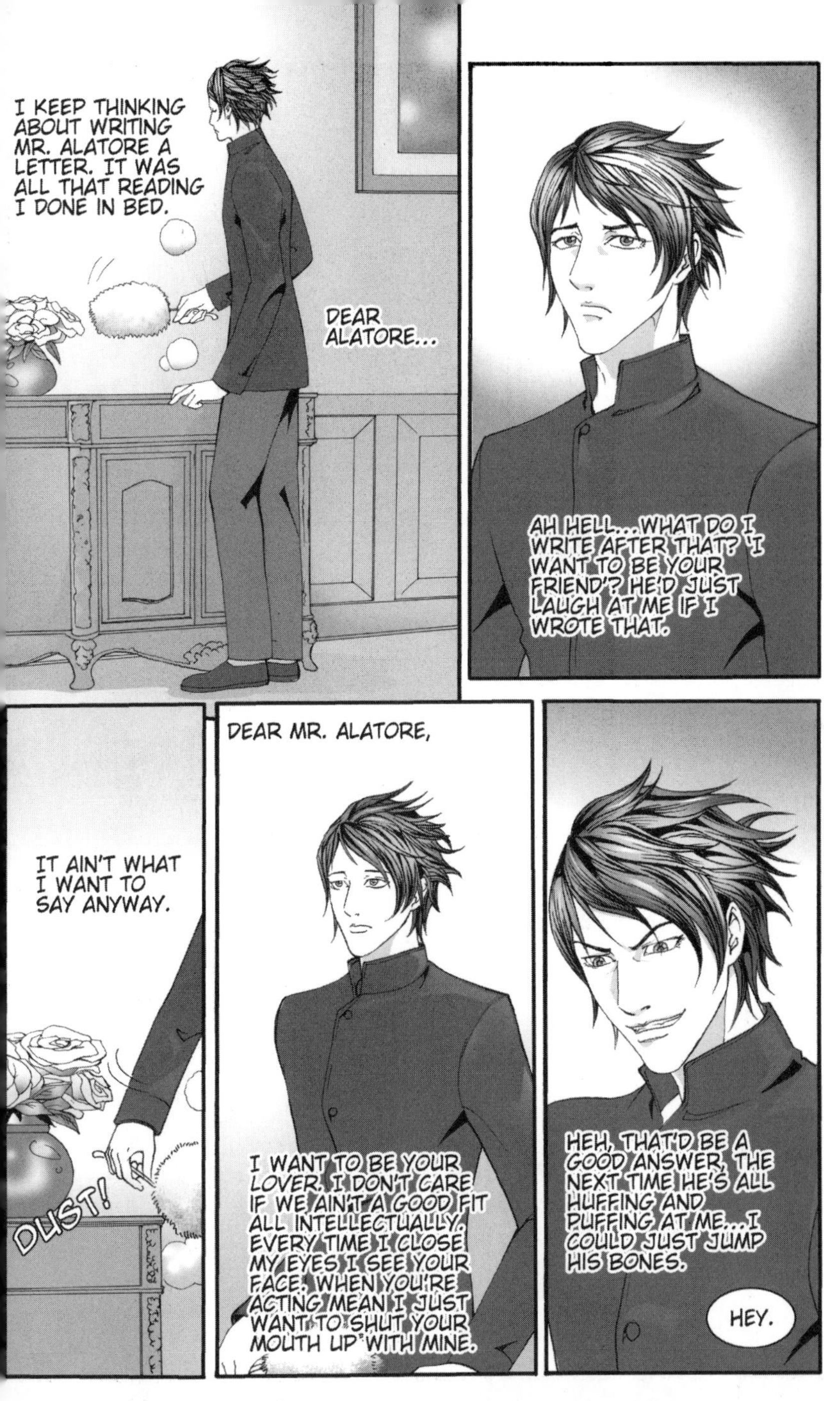

I KEEP THINKING ABOUT WRITING MR. ALATORE A LETTER. IT WAS ALL THAT READING I DONE IN BED.
DEAR ALATORE...
AH HELL... WHAT DO I WRITE AFTER THAT? 'I WANT TO BE YOUR FRIEND'? HE'D JUST LAUGH AT ME IF I WROTE THAT.
IT AIN'T WHAT I WANT TO SAY ANYWAY.
DUST!
DEAR MR. ALATORE,
I WANT TO BE YOUR LOVER. I DON'T CARE IF WE AIN'T A GOOD FIT ALL INTELLECTUALLY. EVERY TIME I CLOSE MY EYES I SEE YOUR FACE. WHEN YOU'RE ACTING MEAN I JUST WANT TO SHUT YOUR MOUTH UP WITH MINE.
HEH, THAT'D BE A GOOD ANSWER, THE NEXT TIME HE'S ALL HUFFING AND PUFFING AT ME... I COULD JUST JUMP HIS BONES.
HEY.

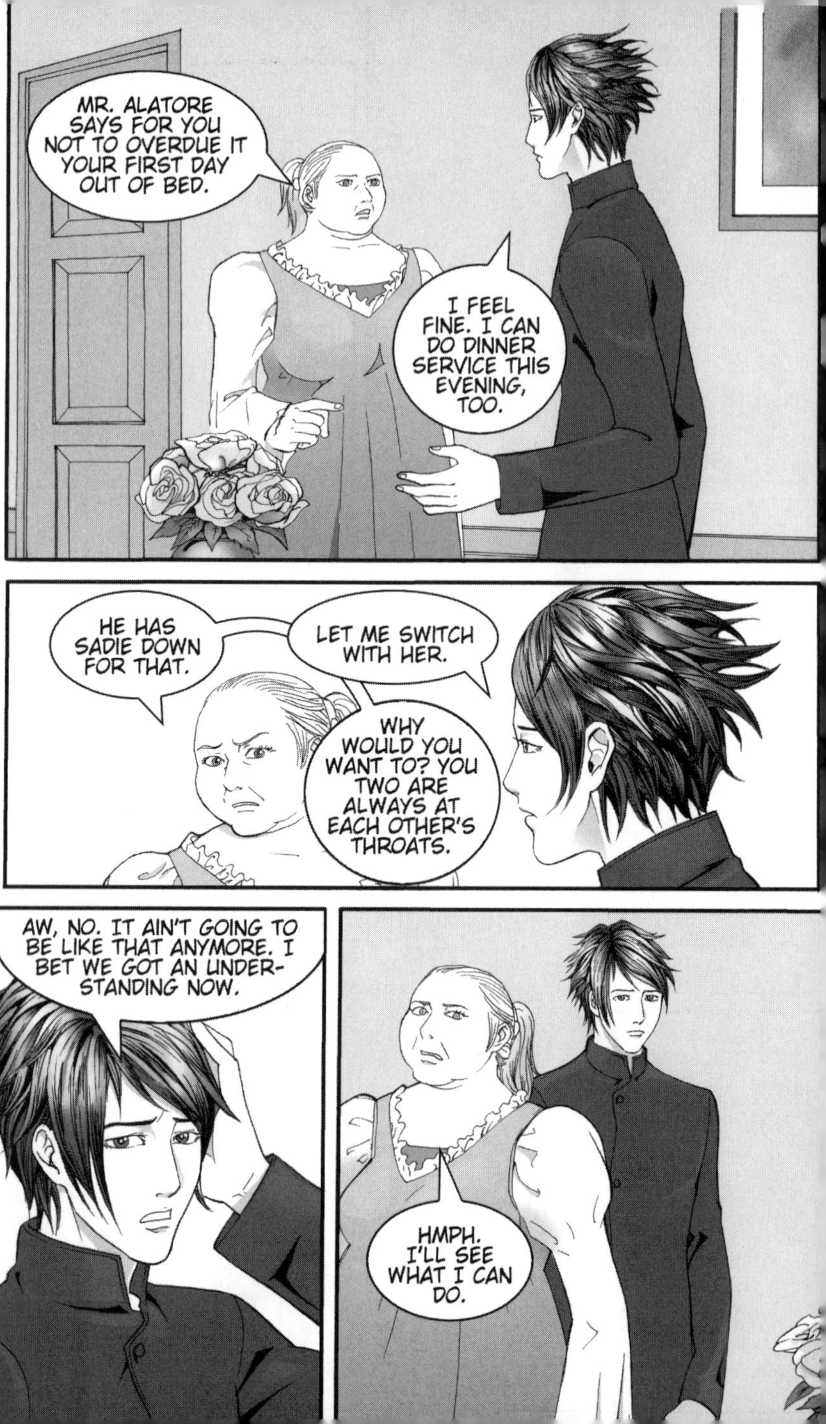
MR. ALATORE SAYS FOR YOU NOT TO OVERDUE IT YOUR FIRST DAY OUT OF BED.
I FEEL FINE. I CAN DO DINNER SERVICE THIS EVENING, TOO.
HE HAS SADIE DOWN FOR THAT.
LET ME SWITCH WITH HER.
WHY WOULD YOU WANT TO? YOU TWO ARE ALWAYS AT EACH OTHER'S THROATS.
AW, NO. IT AIN'T GOING TO BE LIKE THAT ANYMORE. I BET WE GOT AN UNDER-STANDING NOW.
HMPH. I'LL SEE WHAT I CAN DO.

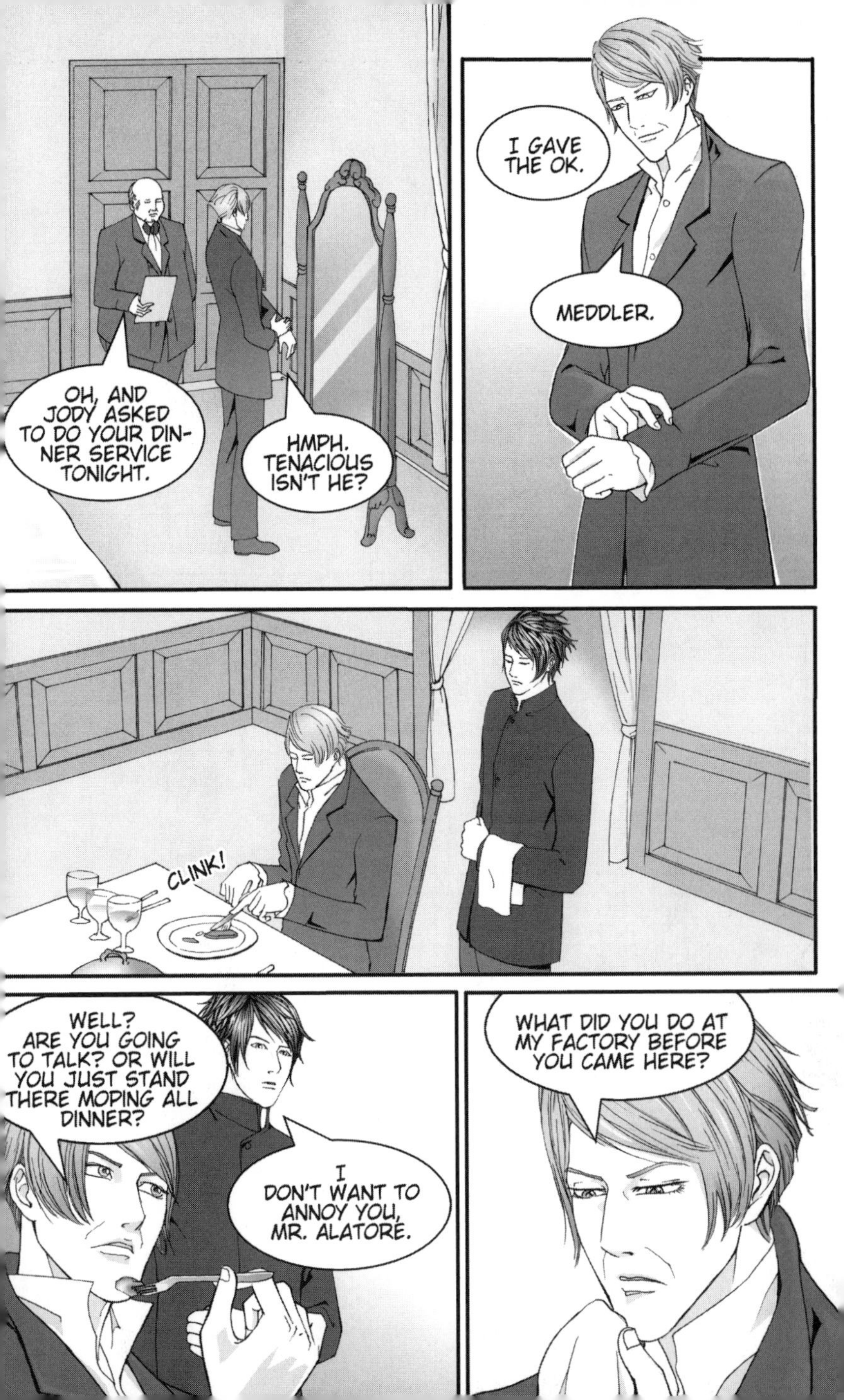
OH, AND JODY ASKED TO DO YOUR DIN-NER SERVICE TONIGHT.
HMPH. TENACIOUS ISN'T HE?
I GAVE THE OK.
MEDDLER.
CLINK!
WELL? ARE YOU GOING TO TALK? OR WILL YOU JUST STAND THERE MOPING ALL DINNER?
I DON'T WANT TO ANNOY YOU, MR. ALATORE.
WHAT DID YOU DO AT MY FACTORY BEFORE YOU CAME HERE?

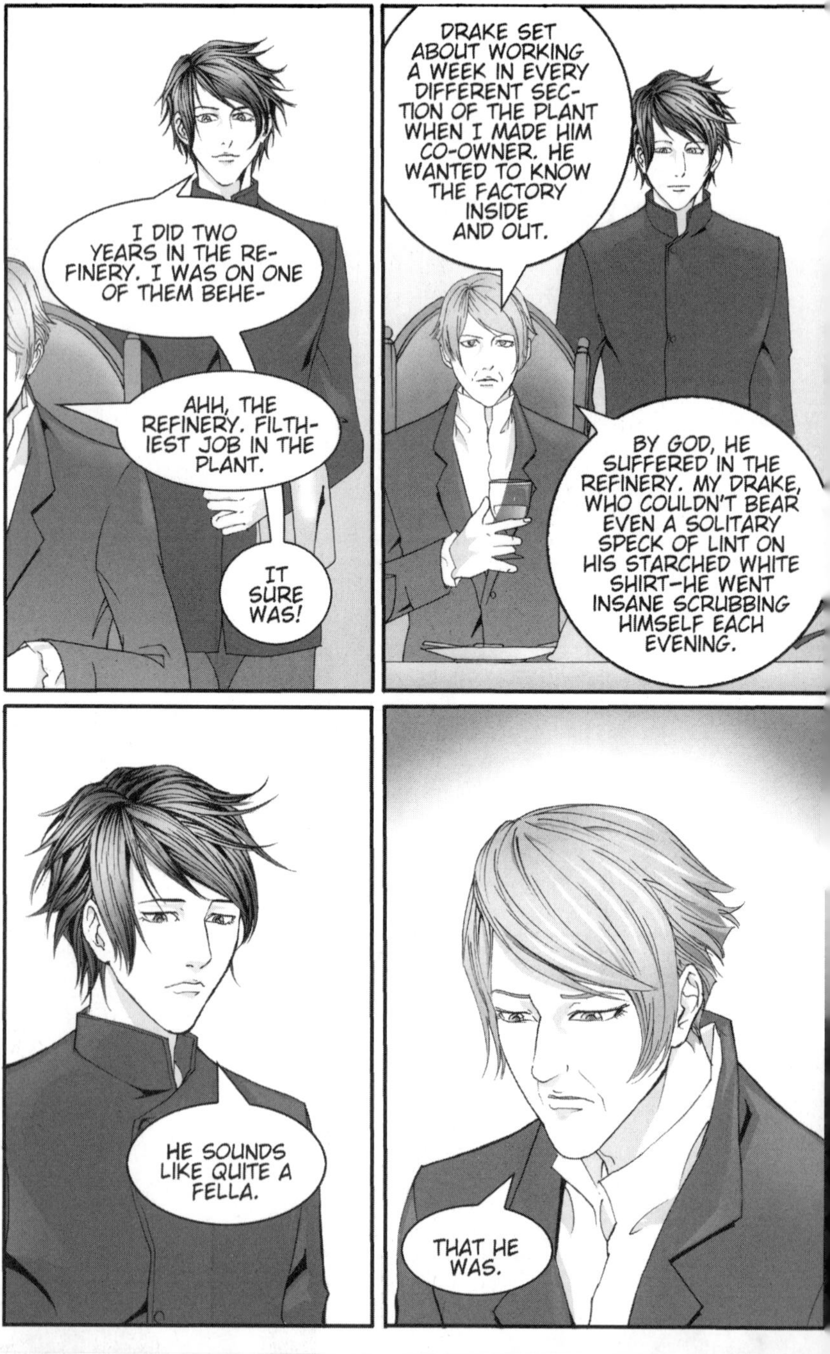
I DID TWO YEARS IN THE RE-FINERY. I WAS ON ONE OF THEM BEHE-
AHH, THE REFINERY. FILTH-IEST JOB IN THE PLANT.
IT SURE WAS!
DRAKE SET ABOUT WORKING A WEEK IN EVERY DIFFERENT SEC-TION OF THE PLANT WHEN I MADE HIM CO-OWNER. HE WANTED TO KNOW THE FACTORY INSIDE AND OUT.
BY GOD, HE SUFFERED IN THE REFINERY. MY DRAKE, WHO COULDN'T BEAR EVEN A SOLITARY SPECK OF LINT ON HIS STARCHED WHITE SHIRT–HE WENT INSANE SCRUBBING HIMSELF EACH EVENING.
HE SOUNDS LIKE QUITE A FELLA.
THAT HE WAS.

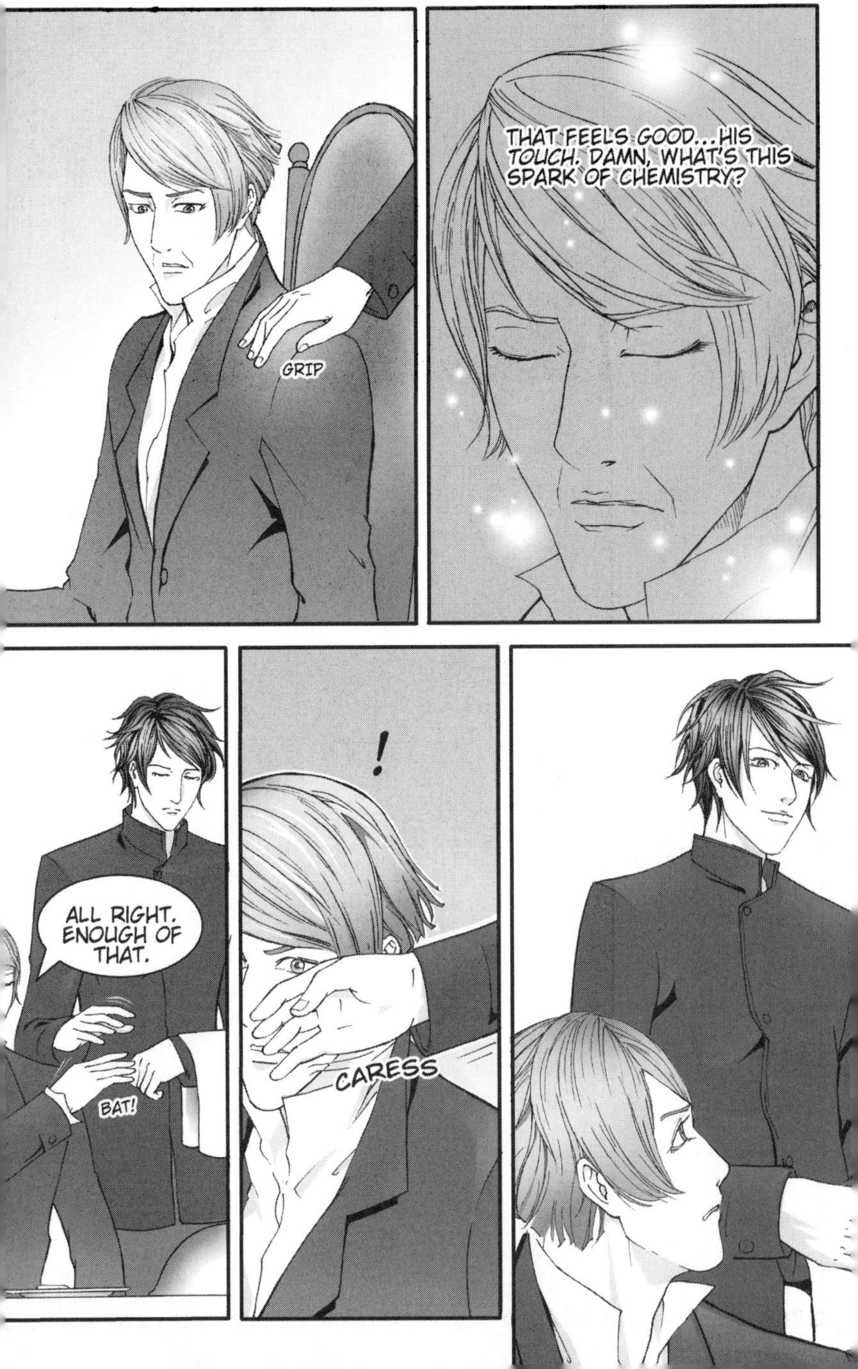
GRIP
THAT FEELS GOOD...HIS TOUCH. DAMN, WHAT'S THIS SPARK OF CHEMISTRY?
ALL RIGHT. ENOUGH OF THAT.
BAT!
!
CARESS

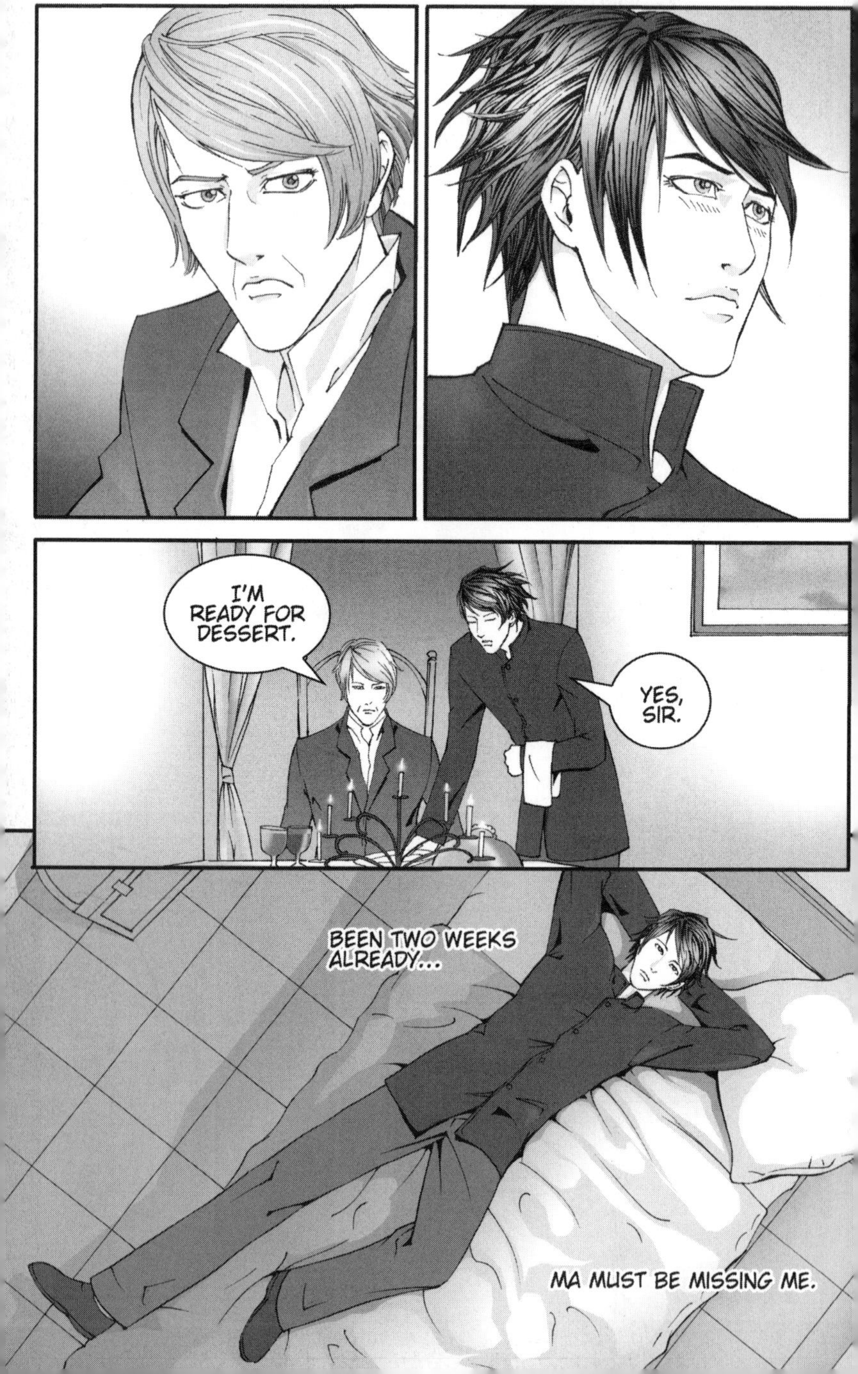
I'M READY FOR DESSERT.
YES, SIR.
BEEN TWO WEEKS ALREADY...
MA MUST BE MISSING ME.

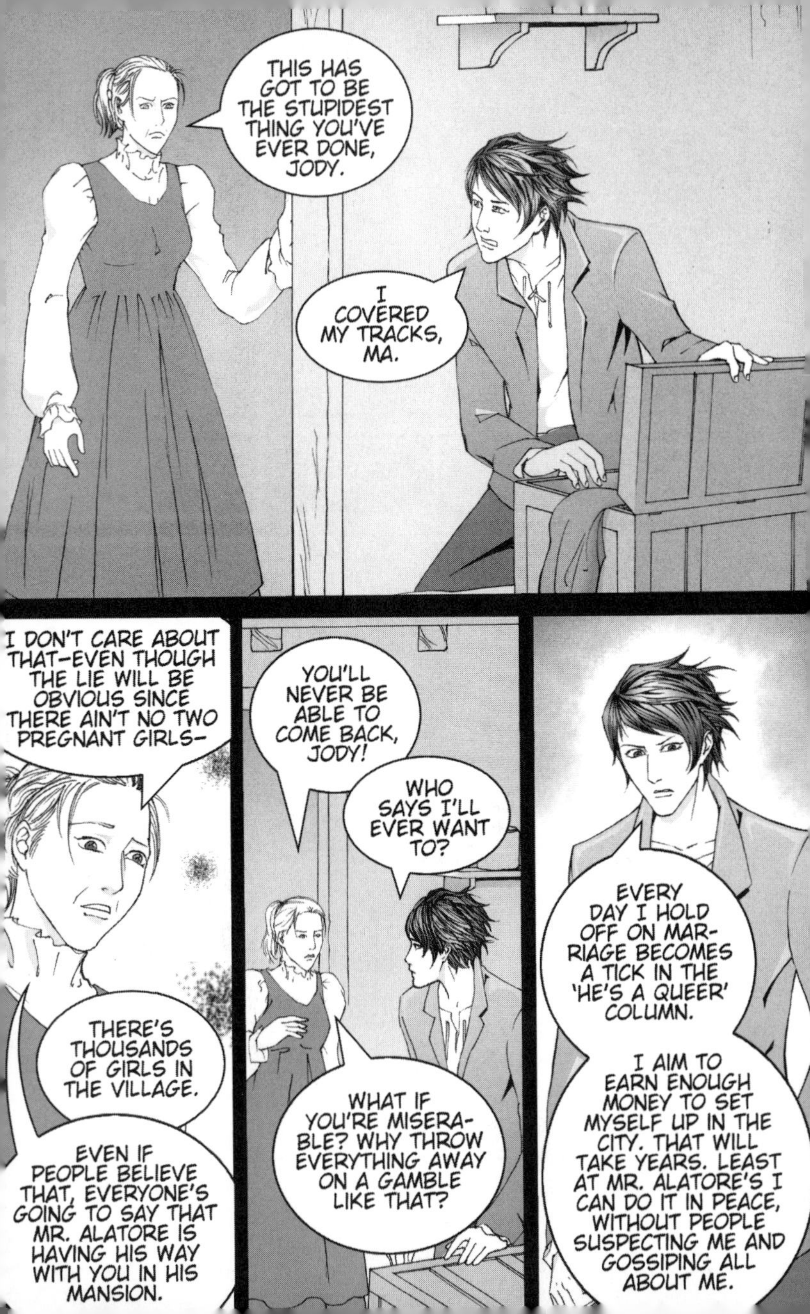
THIS HAS GOT TO BE THE STUPIDEST THING YOU'VE EVER DONE, JODY.
I COVERED MY TRACKS, MA.
I DON'T CARE ABOUT THAT—EVEN THOUGH THE LIE WILL BE OBVIOUS SINCE THERE AIN'T NO TWO PREGNANT GIRLS—
THERE'S THOUSANDS OF GIRLS IN THE VILLAGE.
EVEN IF PEOPLE BELIEVE THAT, EVERYONE'S GOING TO SAY THAT MR. ALATORE IS HAVING HIS WAY WITH YOU IN HIS MANSION.
YOU'LL NEVER BE ABLE TO COME BACK, JODY!
WHO SAYS I'LL EVER WANT TO?
WHAT IF YOU'RE MISERA-BLE? WHY THROW EVERYTHING AWAY ON A GAMBLE LIKE THAT?
EVERY DAY I HOLD OFF ON MAR-RIAGE BECOMES A TICK IN THE 'HE'S A QUEER' COLUMN.
I AIM TO EARN ENOUGH MONEY TO SET MYSELF UP IN THE CITY. THAT WILL TAKE YEARS. LEAST AT MR. ALATORE'S I CAN DO IT IN PEACE, WITHOUT PEOPLE SUSPECTING ME AND GOSSIPING ALL ABOUT ME.

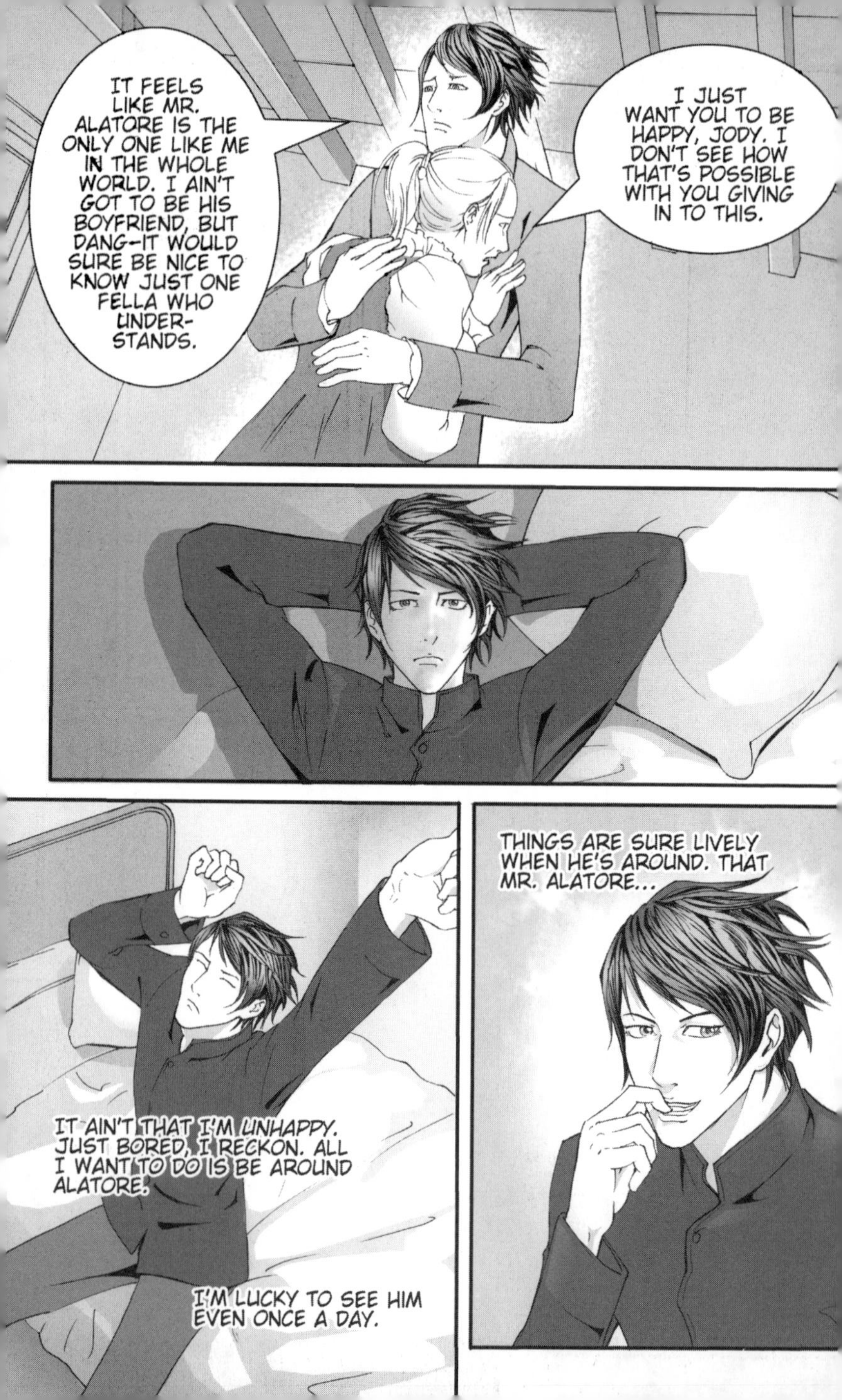
IT FEELS LIKE MR. ALATORE IS THE ONLY ONE LIKE ME IN THE WHOLE WORLD. I AIN'T GOT TO BE HIS BOYFRIEND, BUT DANG--IT WOULD SURE BE NICE TO KNOW JUST ONE FELLA WHO UNDER-STANDS.
I JUST WANT YOU TO BE HAPPY, JODY. I DON'T SEE HOW THAT'S POSSIBLE WITH YOU GIVING IN TO THIS.
IT AIN'T THAT I'M *UNHAPPY*. JUST BORED, I RECKON. ALL I WANT TO DO IS BE AROUND ALATORE.
I'M LUCKY TO SEE HIM EVEN ONCE A DAY.
THINGS ARE SURE LIVELY WHEN HE'S AROUND. THAT MR. ALATORE...

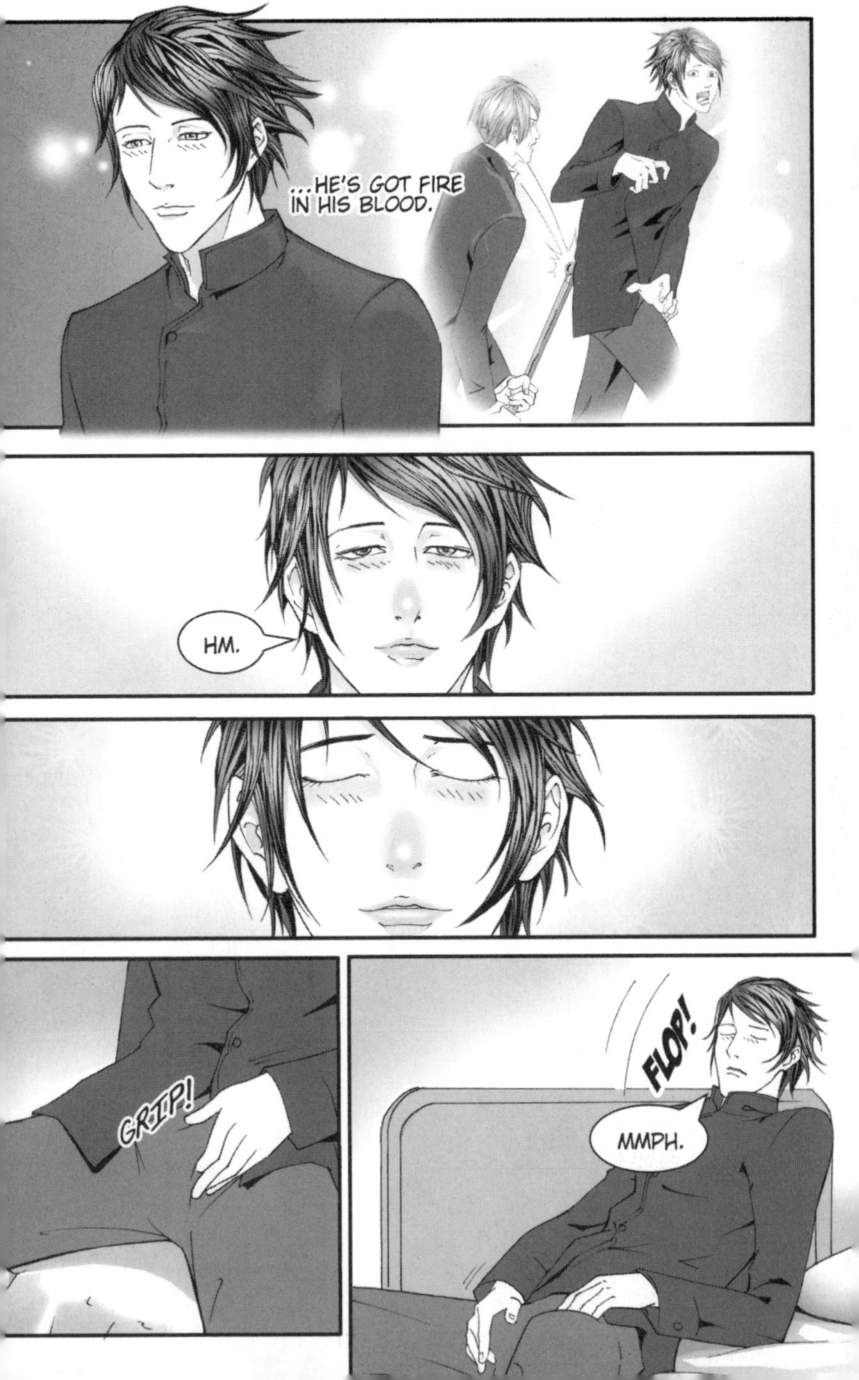
...HE'S GOT FIRE IN HIS BLOOD.
HM.
FLOP!
MMPH.
GRIP!

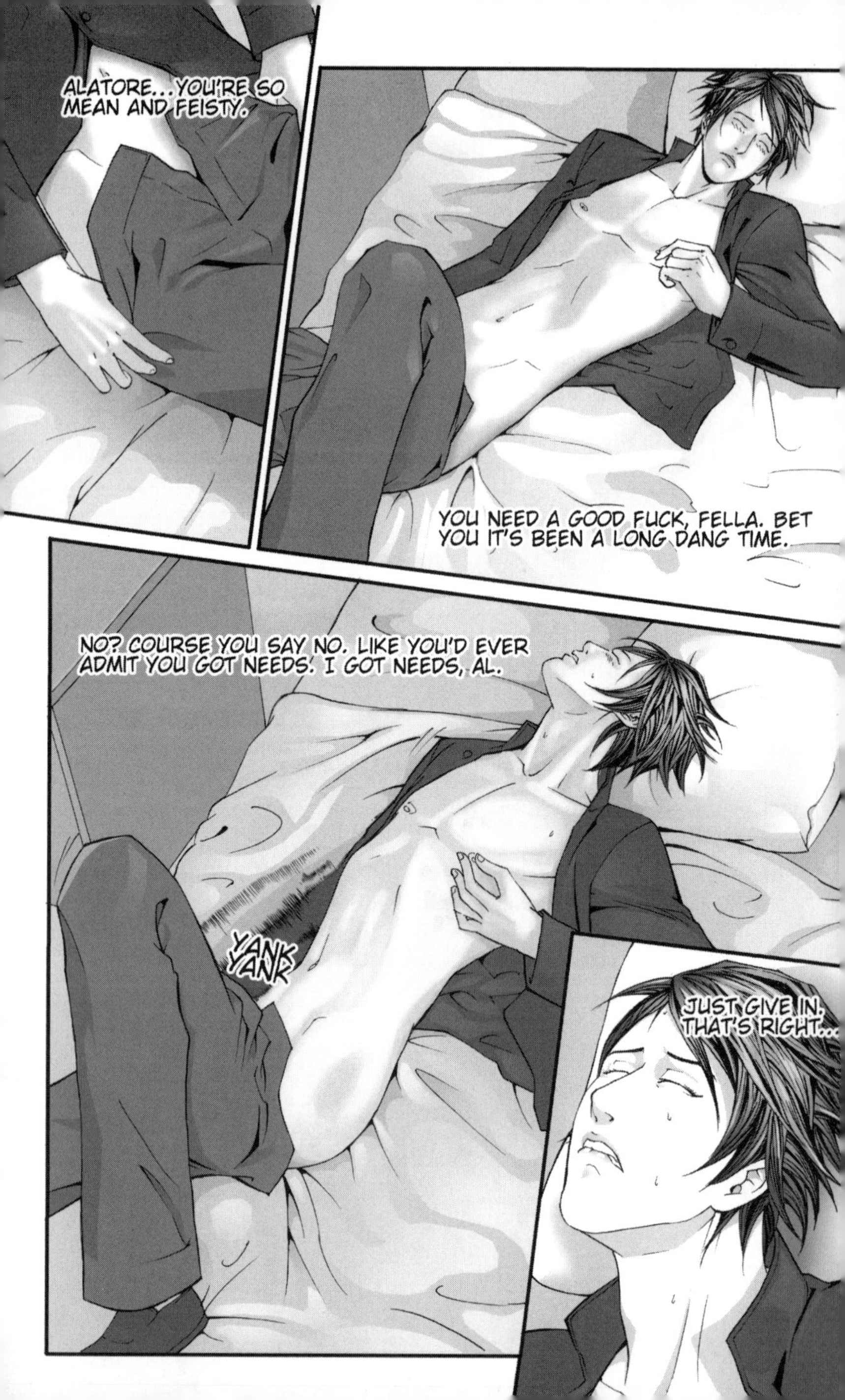
ALATORE...YOU'RE SO MEAN AND FEISTY.
YOU NEED A GOOD FUCK, FELLA. BET YOU IT'S BEEN A LONG DANG TIME.
NO? COURSE YOU SAY NO. LIKE YOU'D EVER ADMIT YOU GOT NEEDS. I GOT NEEDS, AL.
YANK YANK
JUST GIVE IN. THAT'S RIGHT...

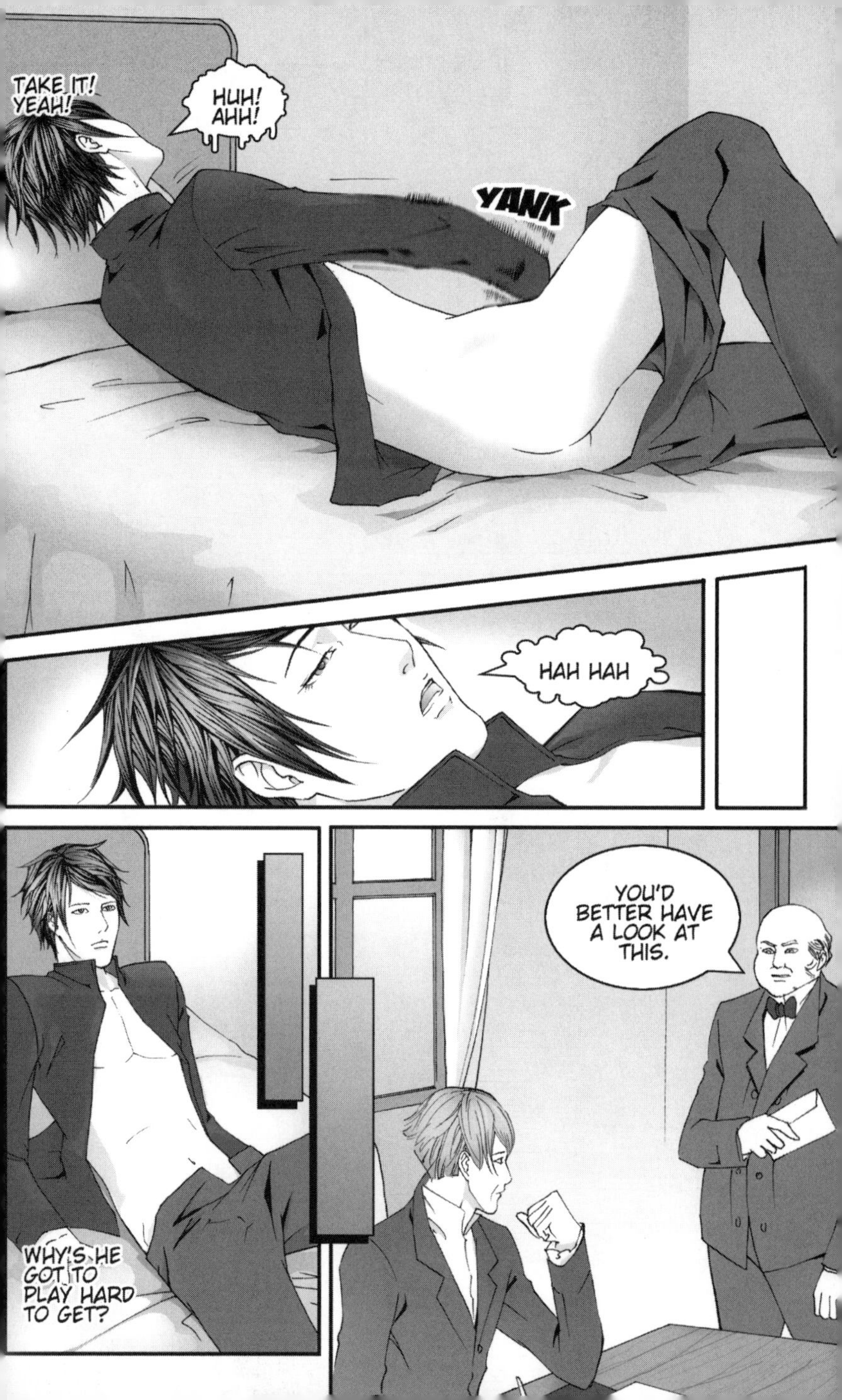
TAKE IT! YEAH!
HUH! AHH!
YANK
HAH HAH
YOU'D BETTER HAVE A LOOK AT THIS.
WHY'S HE GOT TO PLAY HARD TO GET?

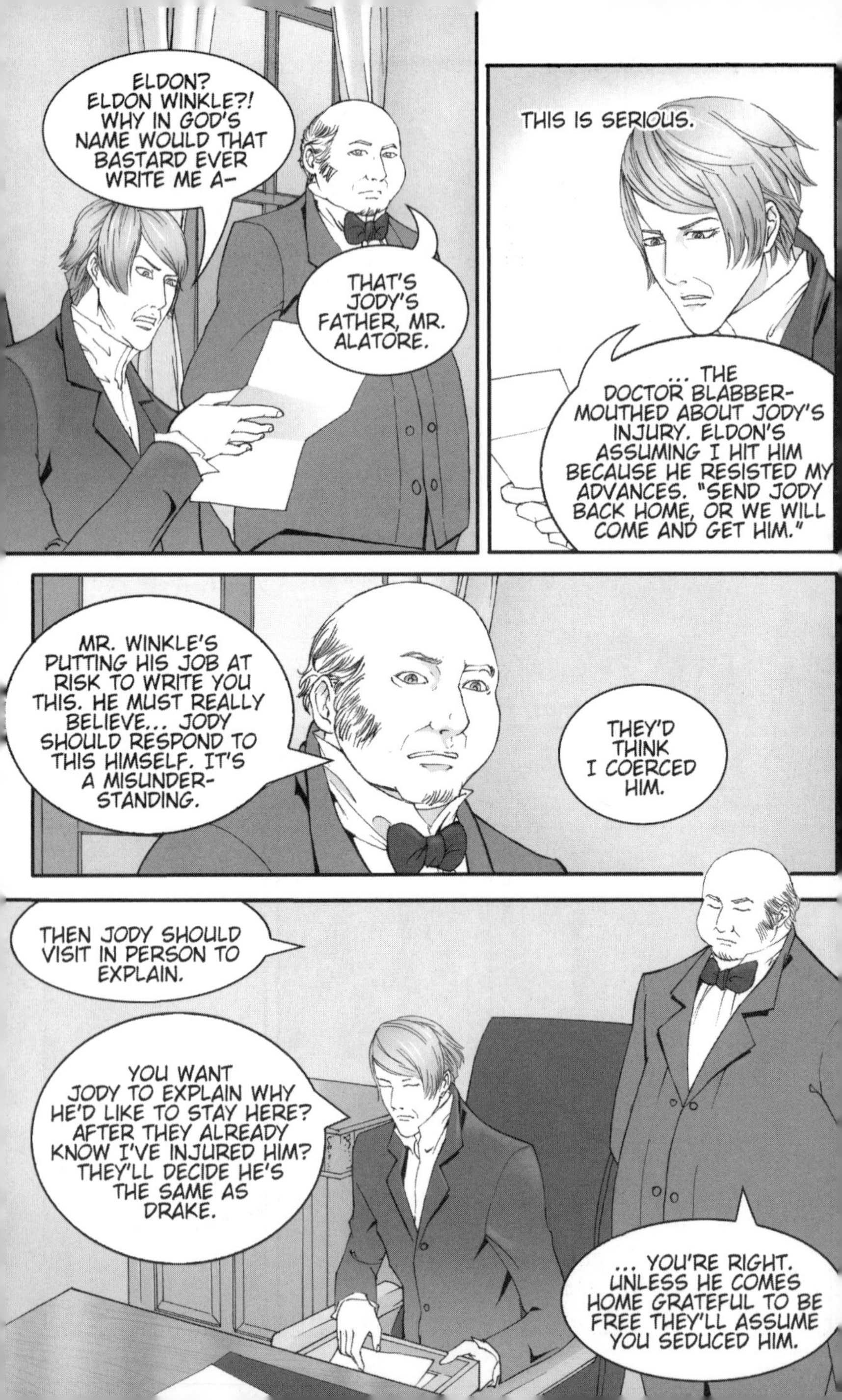
ELDON? ELDON WINKLE?! WHY IN GOD'S NAME WOULD THAT BASTARD EVER WRITE ME A-
THAT'S JODY'S FATHER, MR. ALATORE.
THIS IS SERIOUS.
... THE DOCTOR BLABBER-MOUTHED ABOUT JODY'S INJURY. ELDON'S ASSUMING I HIT HIM BECAUSE HE RESISTED MY ADVANCES. "SEND JODY BACK HOME, OR WE WILL COME AND GET HIM."
MR. WINKLE'S PUTTING HIS JOB AT RISK TO WRITE YOU THIS. HE MUST REALLY BELIEVE... JODY SHOULD RESPOND TO THIS HIMSELF. IT'S A MISUNDER-STANDING.
THEY'D THINK I COERCED HIM.
THEN JODY SHOULD VISIT IN PERSON TO EXPLAIN.
YOU WANT JODY TO EXPLAIN WHY HE'D LIKE TO STAY HERE? AFTER THEY ALREADY KNOW I'VE INJURED HIM? THEY'LL DECIDE HE'S THE SAME AS DRAKE.
... YOU'RE RIGHT. UNLESS HE COMES HOME GRATEFUL TO BE FREE THEY'LL ASSUME YOU SEDUCED HIM.

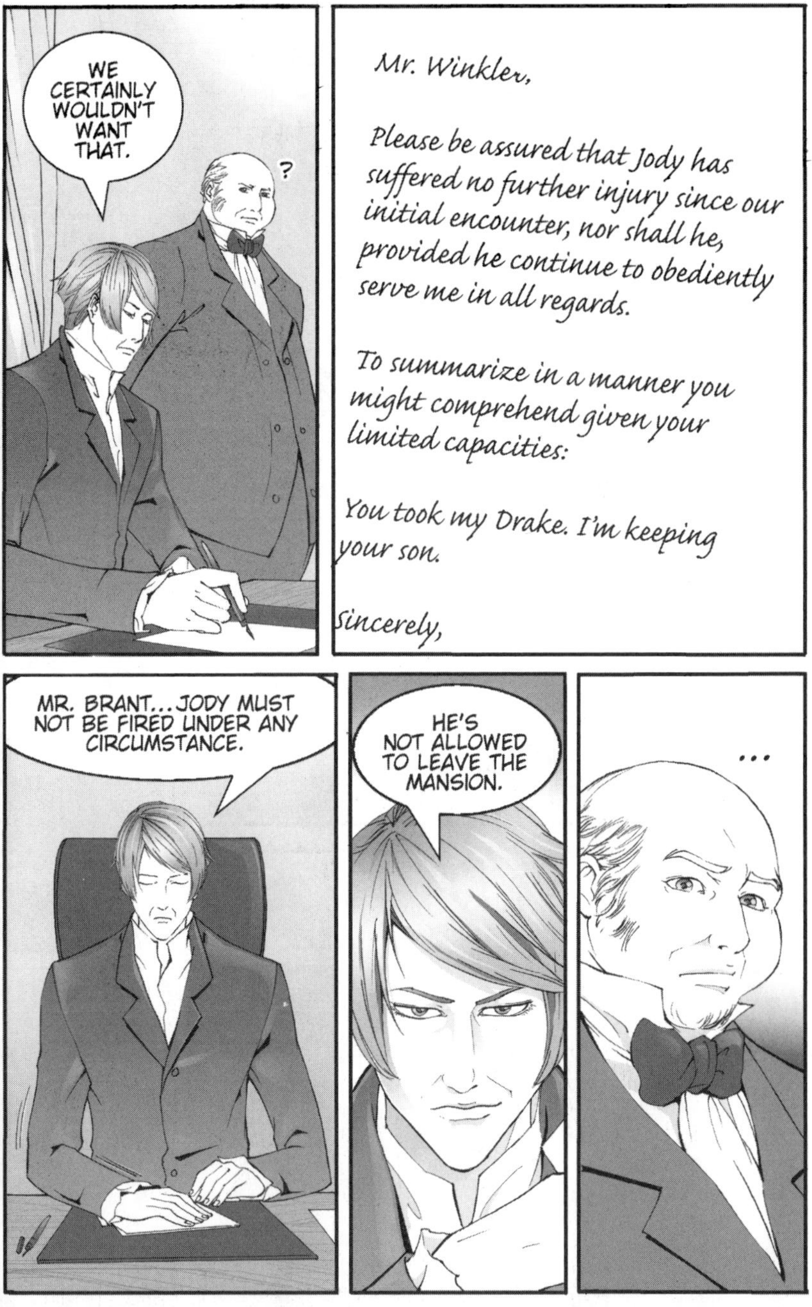
WE CERTAINLY WOULDN'T WANT THAT.
?
Mr. Winkler,
Please be assured that Jody has suffered no further injury since our initial encounter, nor shall he, provided he continue to obediently serve me in all regards.
To summarize in a manner you might comprehend given your limited capacities:
You took my Drake. I'm keeping your son.
Sincerely,
MR. BRANT... JODY MUST NOT BE FIRED UNDER ANY CIRCUMSTANCE.
HE'S NOT ALLOWED TO LEAVE THE MANSION.
...

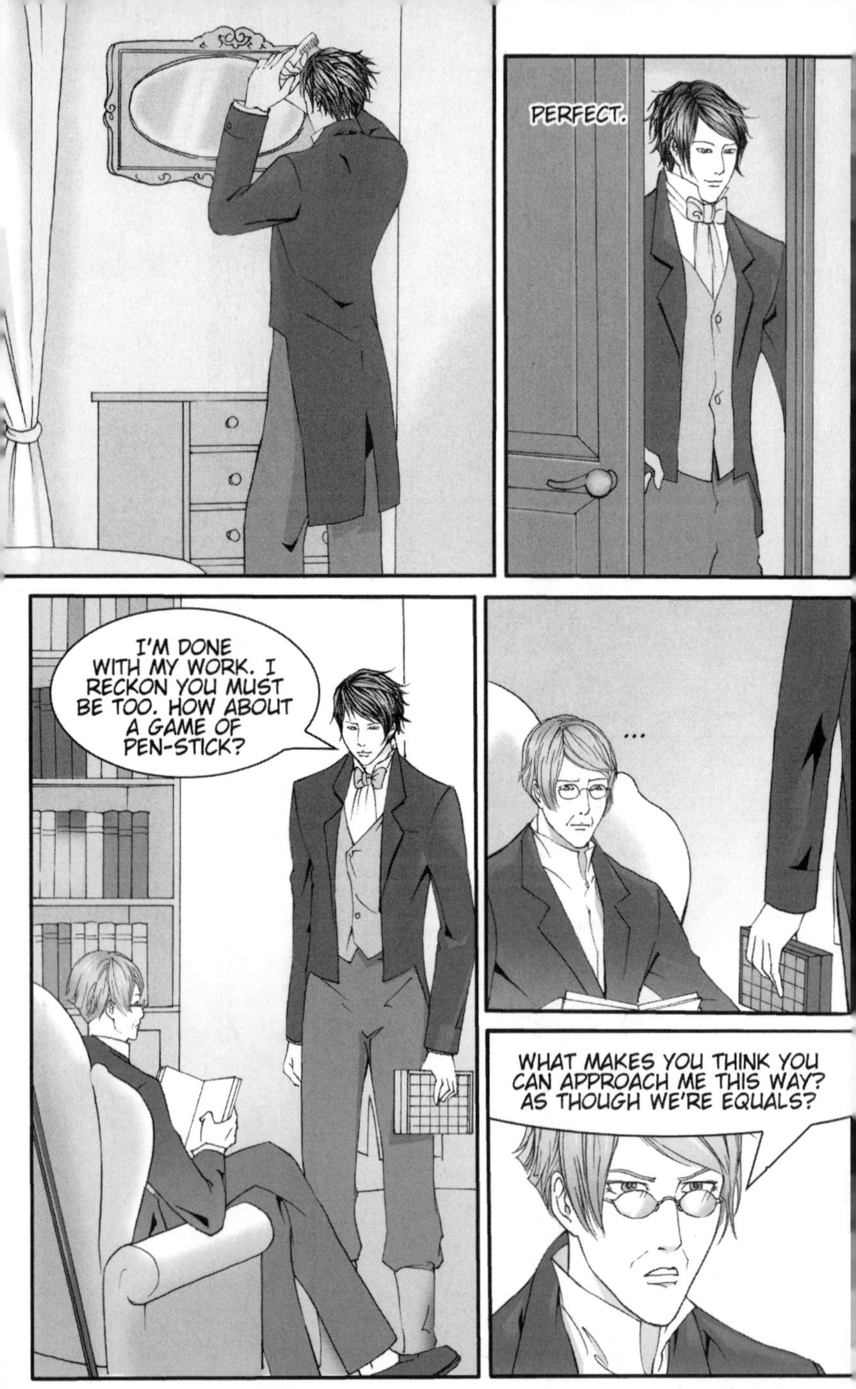

PERFECT.
I'M DONE WITH MY WORK. I RECKON YOU MUST BE TOO. HOW ABOUT A GAME OF PEN-STICK?
...
WHAT MAKES YOU THINK YOU CAN APPROACH ME THIS WAY? AS THOUGH WE'RE EQUALS?

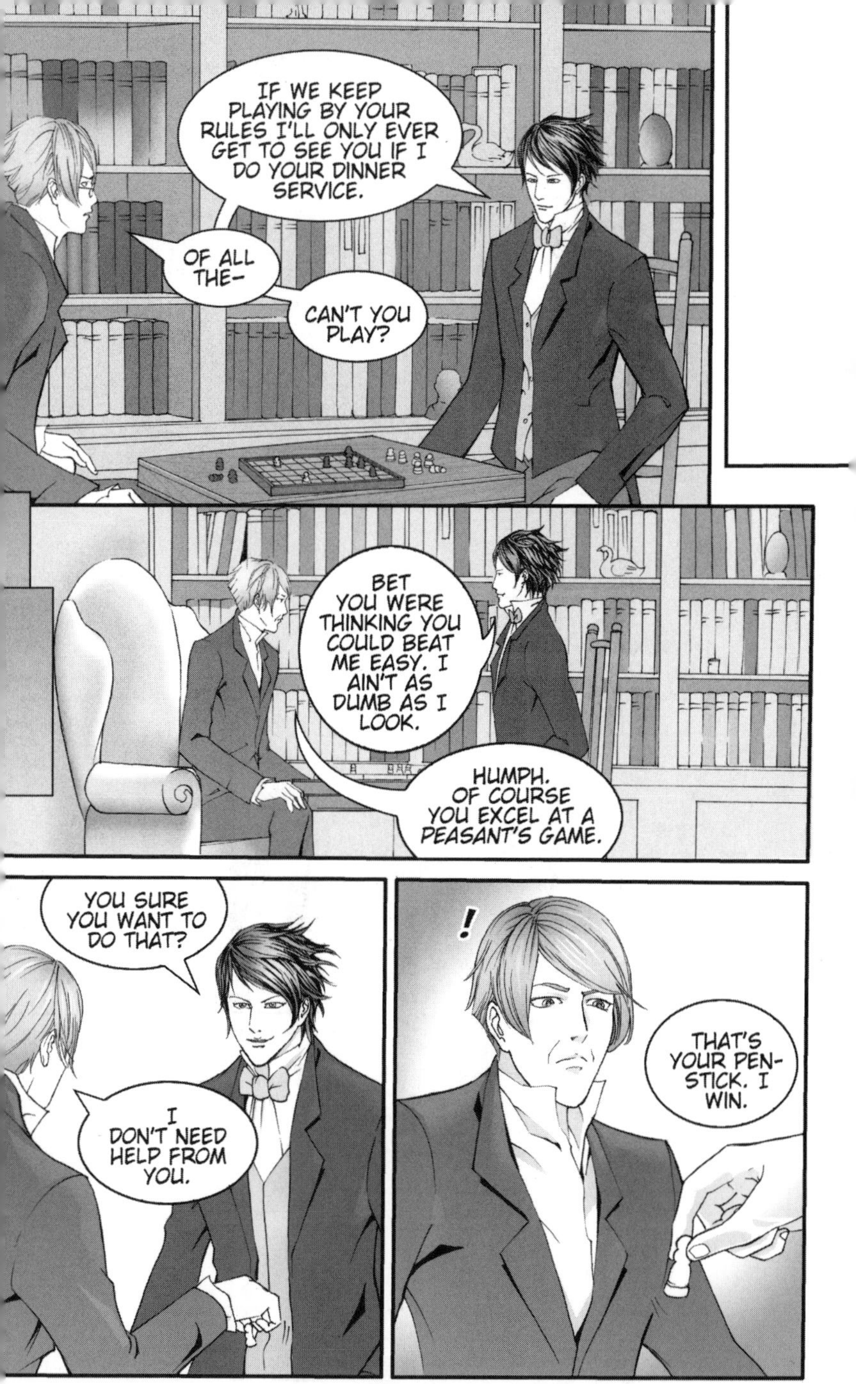
IF WE KEEP PLAYING BY YOUR RULES I'LL ONLY EVER GET TO SEE YOU IF I DO YOUR DINNER SERVICE.
OF ALL THE-
CAN'T YOU PLAY?
BET YOU WERE THINKING YOU COULD BEAT ME EASY. I AIN'T AS DUMB AS I LOOK.
HUMPH. OF COURSE YOU EXCEL AT A PEASANT'S GAME.
YOU SURE YOU WANT TO DO THAT?
I DON'T NEED HELP FROM YOU.
!
THAT'S YOUR PEN-STICK. I WIN.

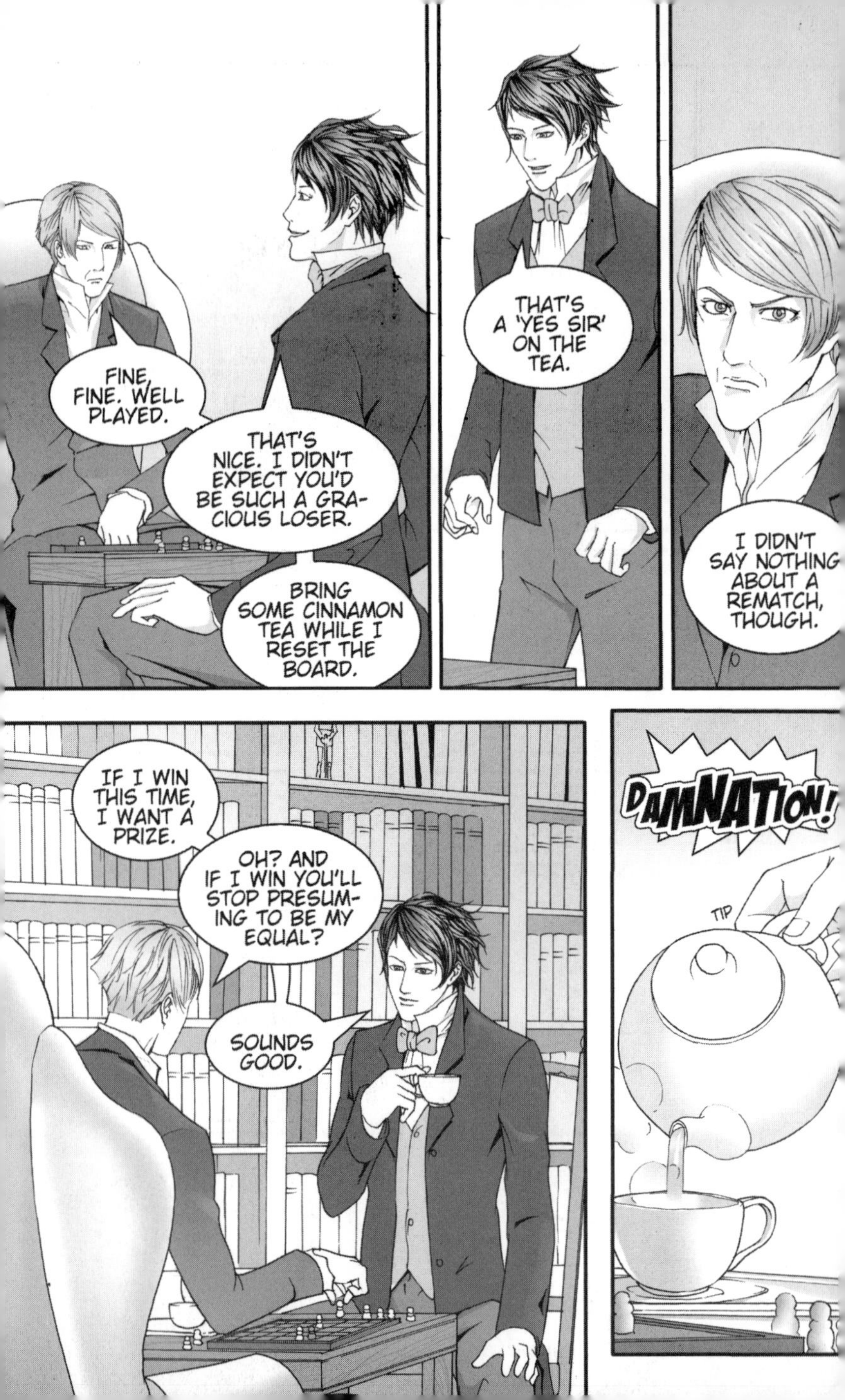
FINE, FINE. WELL PLAYED.
THAT'S NICE. I DIDN'T EXPECT YOU'D BE SUCH A GRA-CIOUS LOSER.
BRING SOME CINNAMON TEA WHILE I RESET THE BOARD.
THAT'S A 'YES SIR' ON THE TEA.
I DIDN'T SAY NOTHING ABOUT A REMATCH, THOUGH.
IF I WIN THIS TIME, I WANT A PRIZE.
OH? AND IF I WIN YOU'LL STOP PRESUM-ING TO BE MY EQUAL?
SOUNDS GOOD.
DAMNATION!
TIP

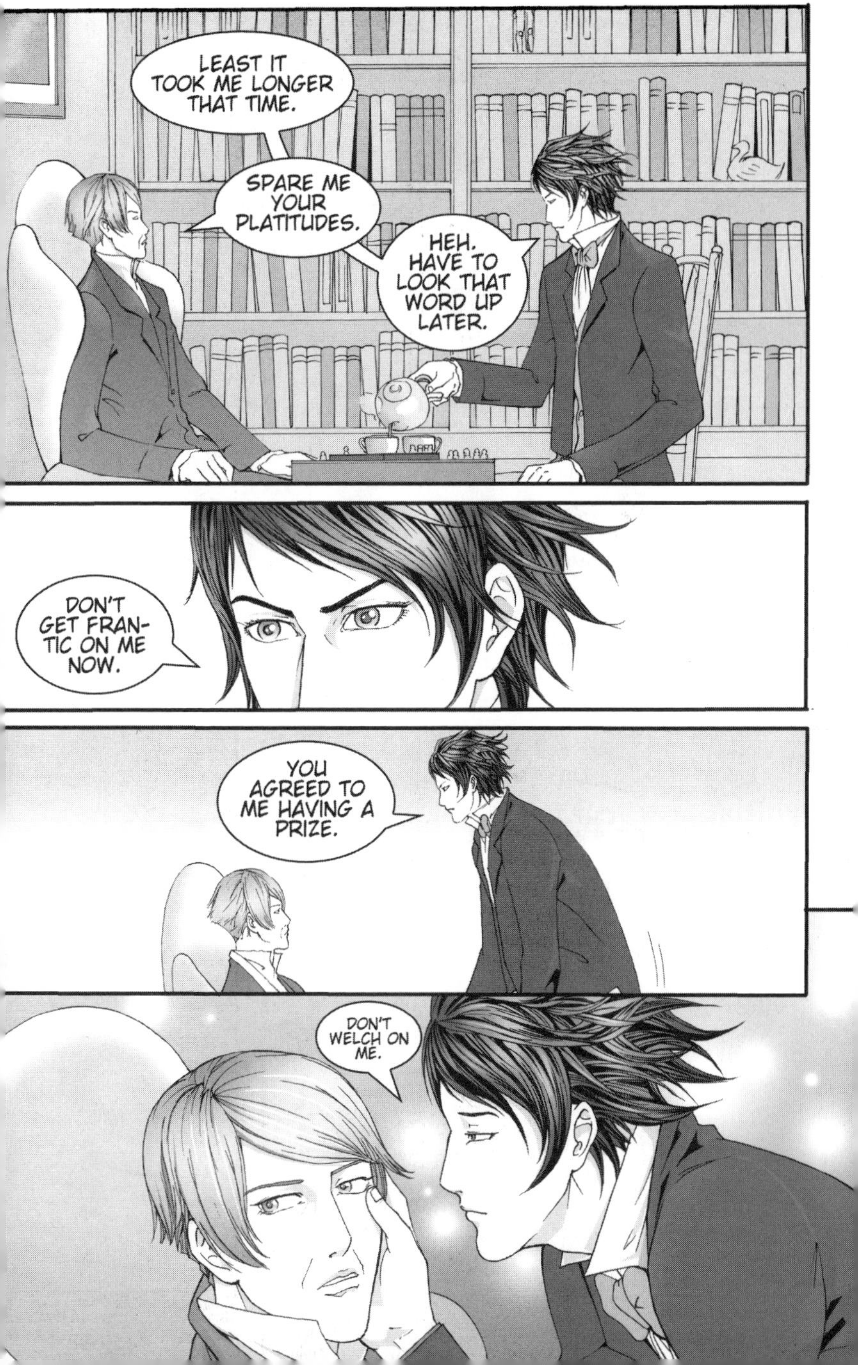
LEAST IT TOOK ME LONGER THAT TIME.
SPARE ME YOUR PLATITUDES.
HEH. HAVE TO LOOK THAT WORD UP LATER.
DON'T GET FRAN-TIC ON ME NOW.
YOU AGREED TO ME HAVING A PRIZE.
DON'T WELCH ON ME.

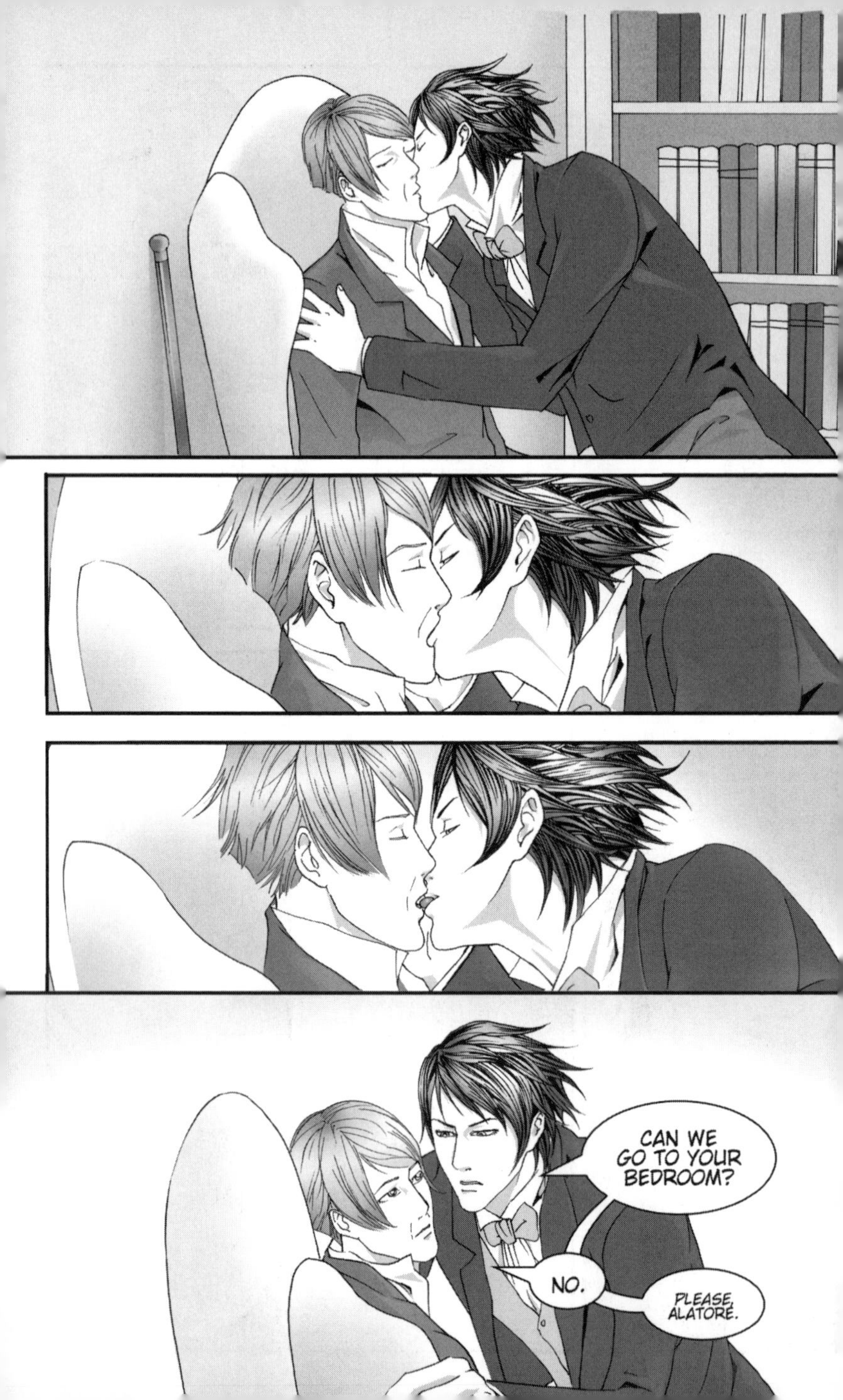
CAN WE GO TO YOUR BEDROOM?
NO.
PLEASE, ALATORE.

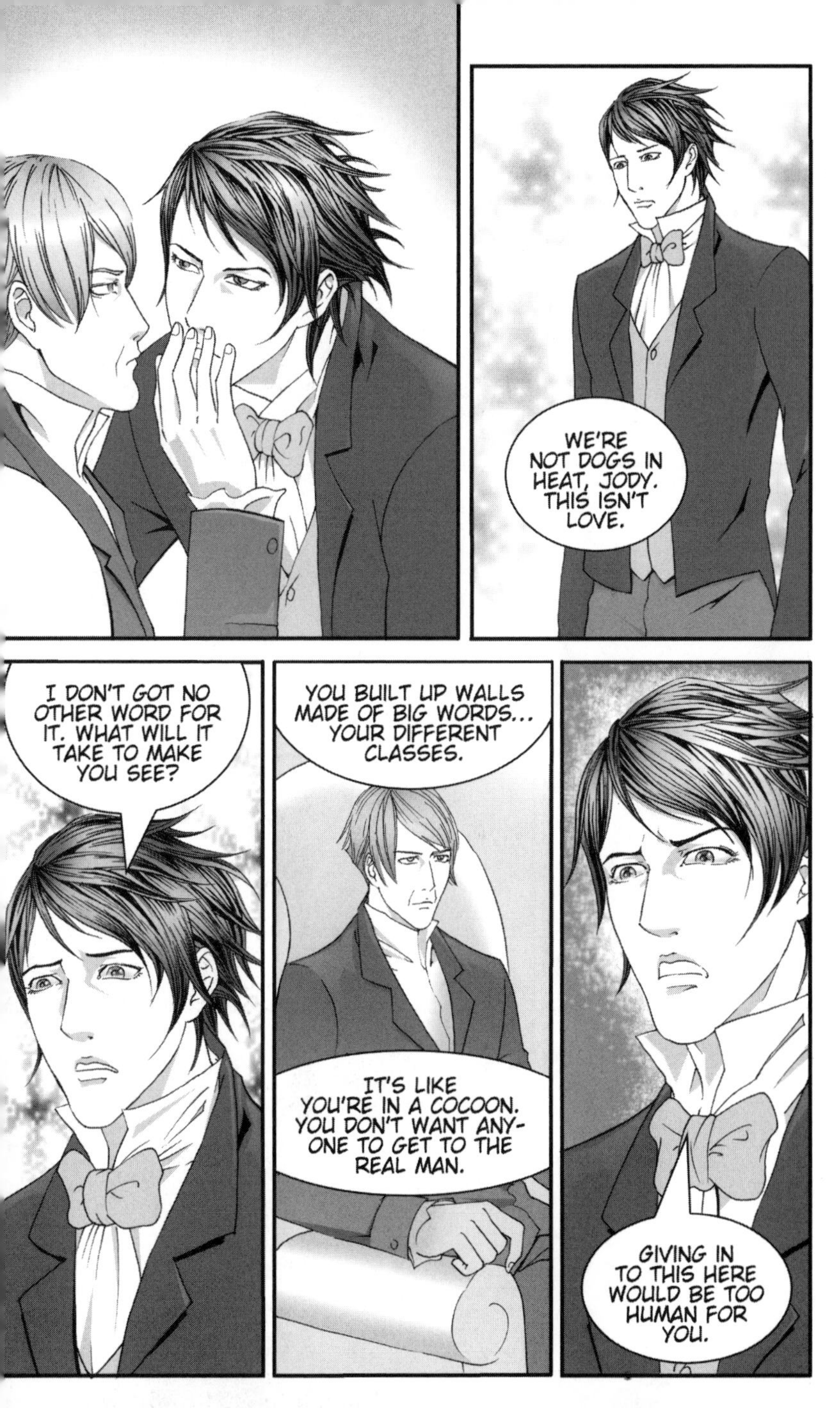
WE'RE NOT DOGS IN HEAT, JODY. THIS ISN'T LOVE.
I DON'T GOT NO OTHER WORD FOR IT. WHAT WILL IT TAKE TO MAKE YOU SEE?
YOU BUILT UP WALLS MADE OF BIG WORDS... YOUR DIFFERENT CLASSES.
IT'S LIKE YOU'RE IN A COCOON. YOU DON'T WANT ANY-ONE TO GET TO THE REAL MAN.
GIVING IN TO THIS HERE WOULD BE TOO HUMAN FOR YOU.

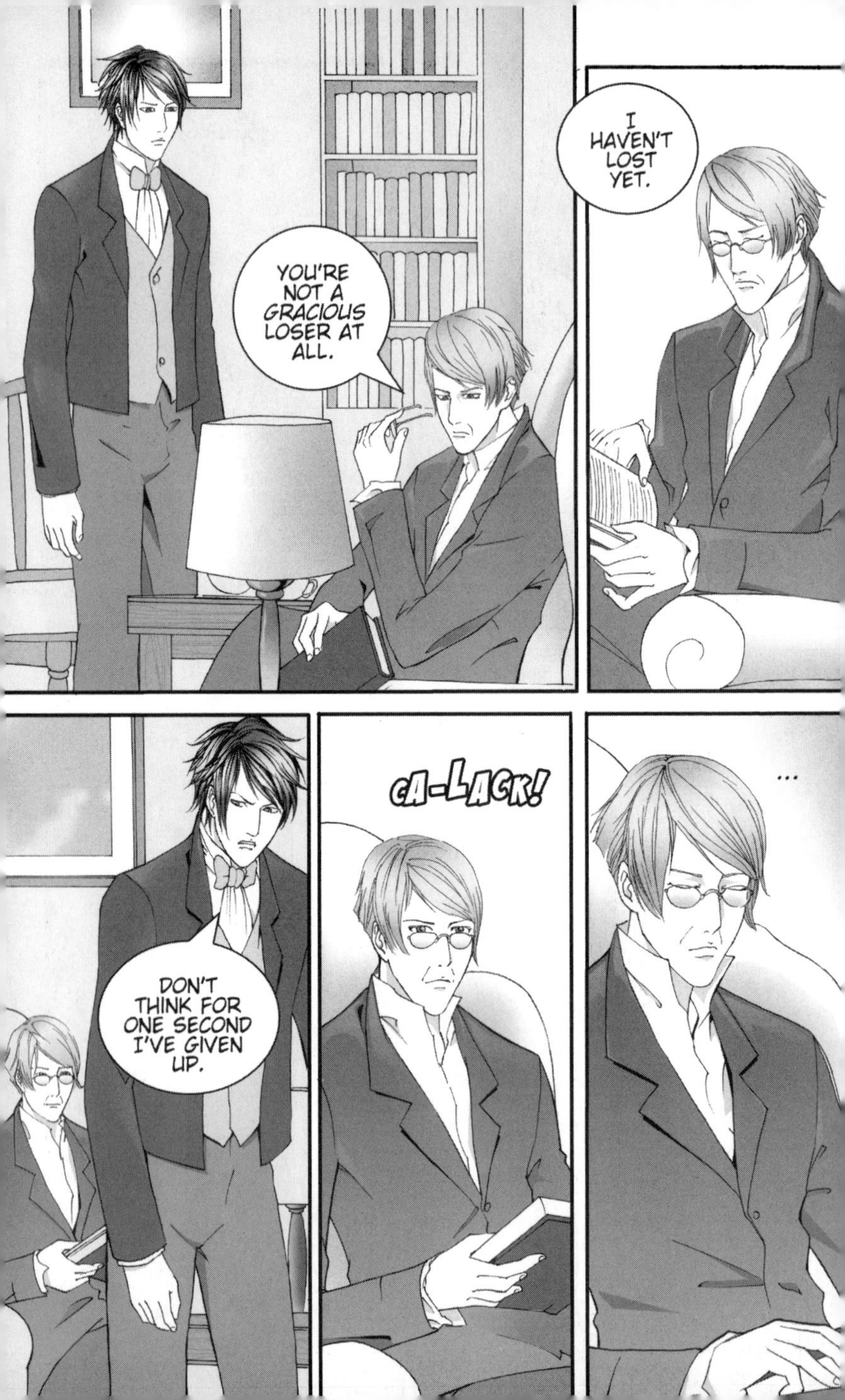
YOU'RE NOT A GRACIOUS LOSER AT ALL.
I HAVEN'T LOST YET.
DON'T THINK FOR ONE SECOND I'VE GIVEN UP.
CA-LACK!
...

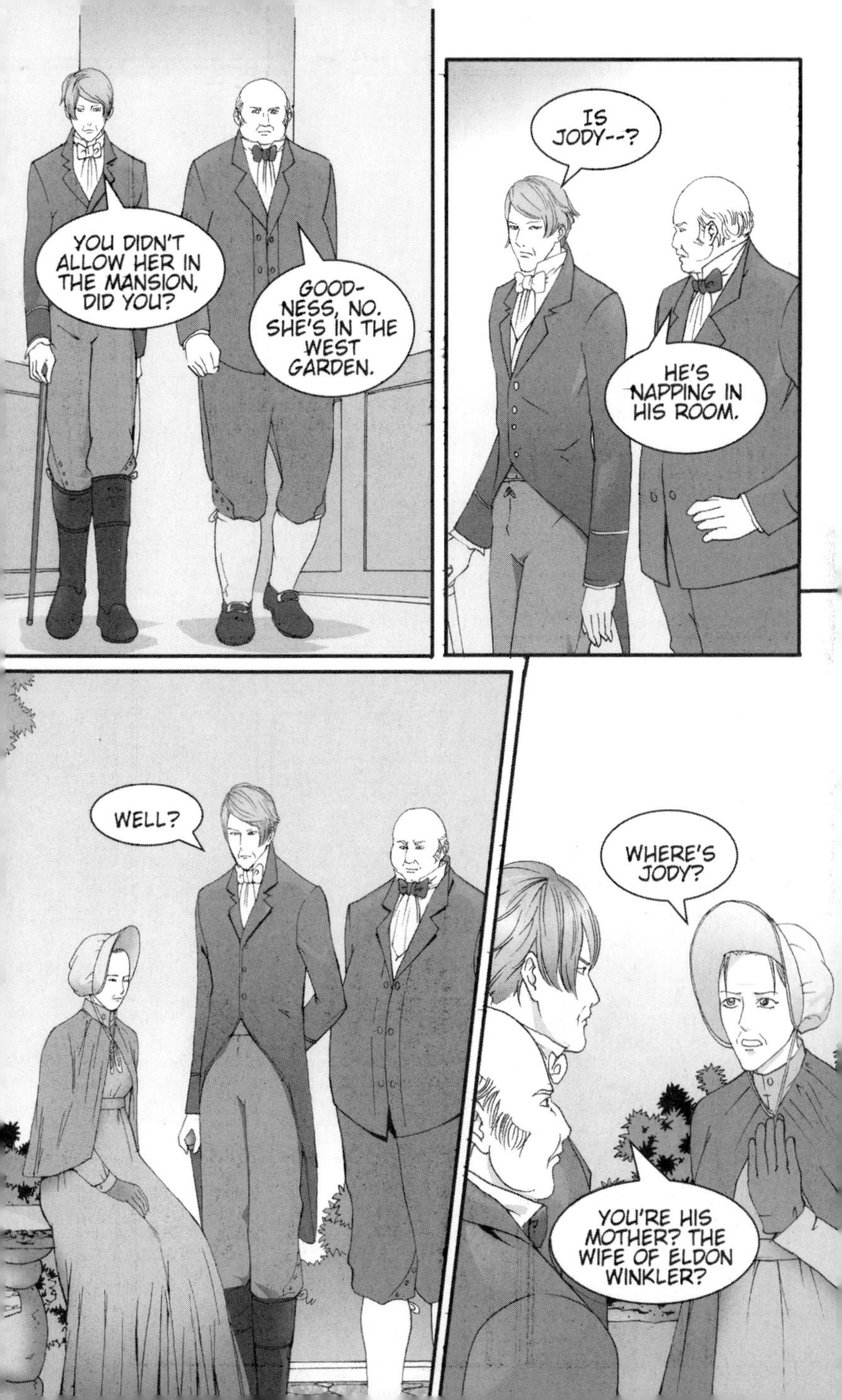
YOU DIDN'T ALLOW HER IN THE MANSION, DID YOU?
GOOD-NESS, NO. SHE'S IN THE WEST GARDEN.
IS JODY--?
HE'S NAPPING IN HIS ROOM.
WELL?
WHERE'S JODY?
YOU'RE HIS MOTHER? THE WIFE OF ELDON WINKLER?

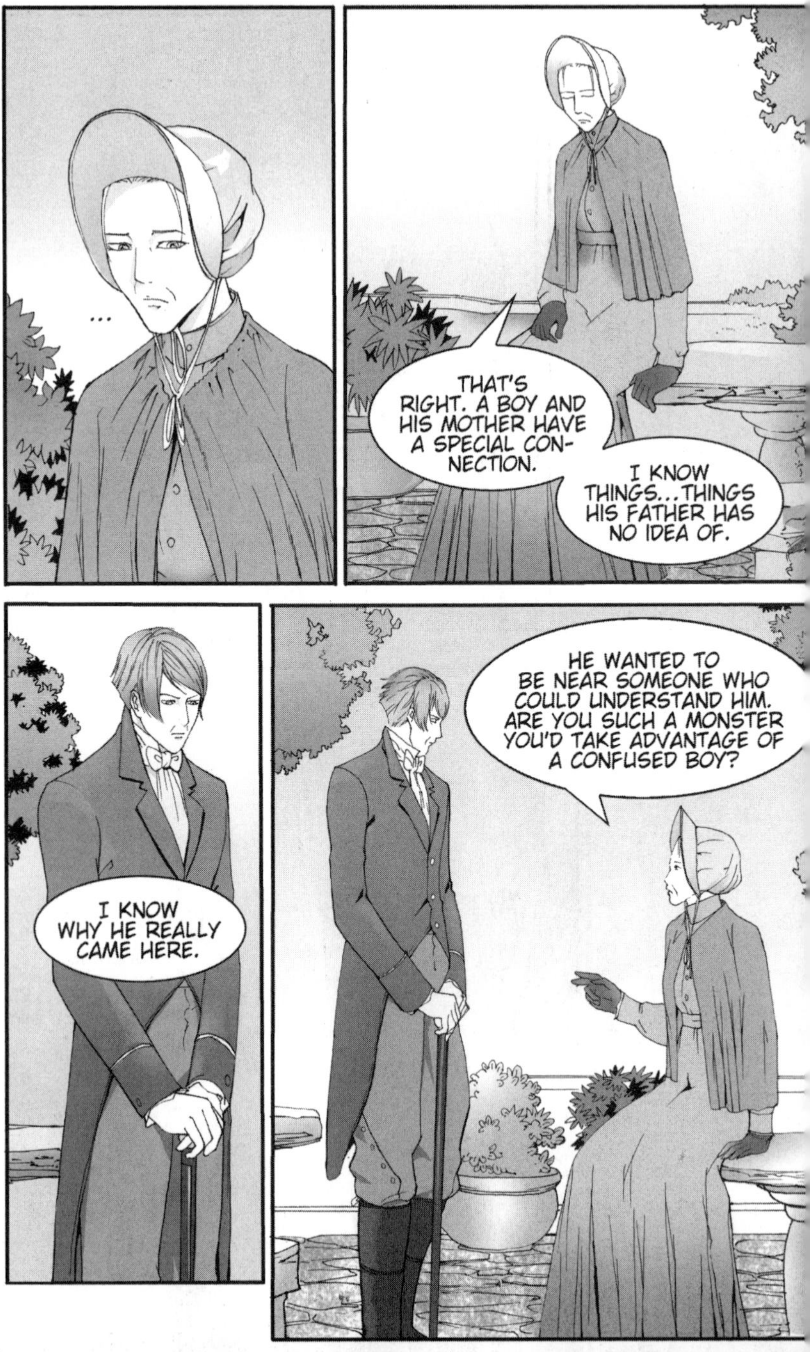
...
THAT'S RIGHT. A BOY AND HIS MOTHER HAVE A SPECIAL CON-NECTION.
I KNOW THINGS...THINGS HIS FATHER HAS NO IDEA OF.
I KNOW WHY HE REALLY CAME HERE.
HE WANTED TO BE NEAR SOMEONE WHO COULD UNDERSTAND HIM. ARE YOU SUCH A MONSTER YOU'D TAKE ADVANTAGE OF A CONFUSED BOY?

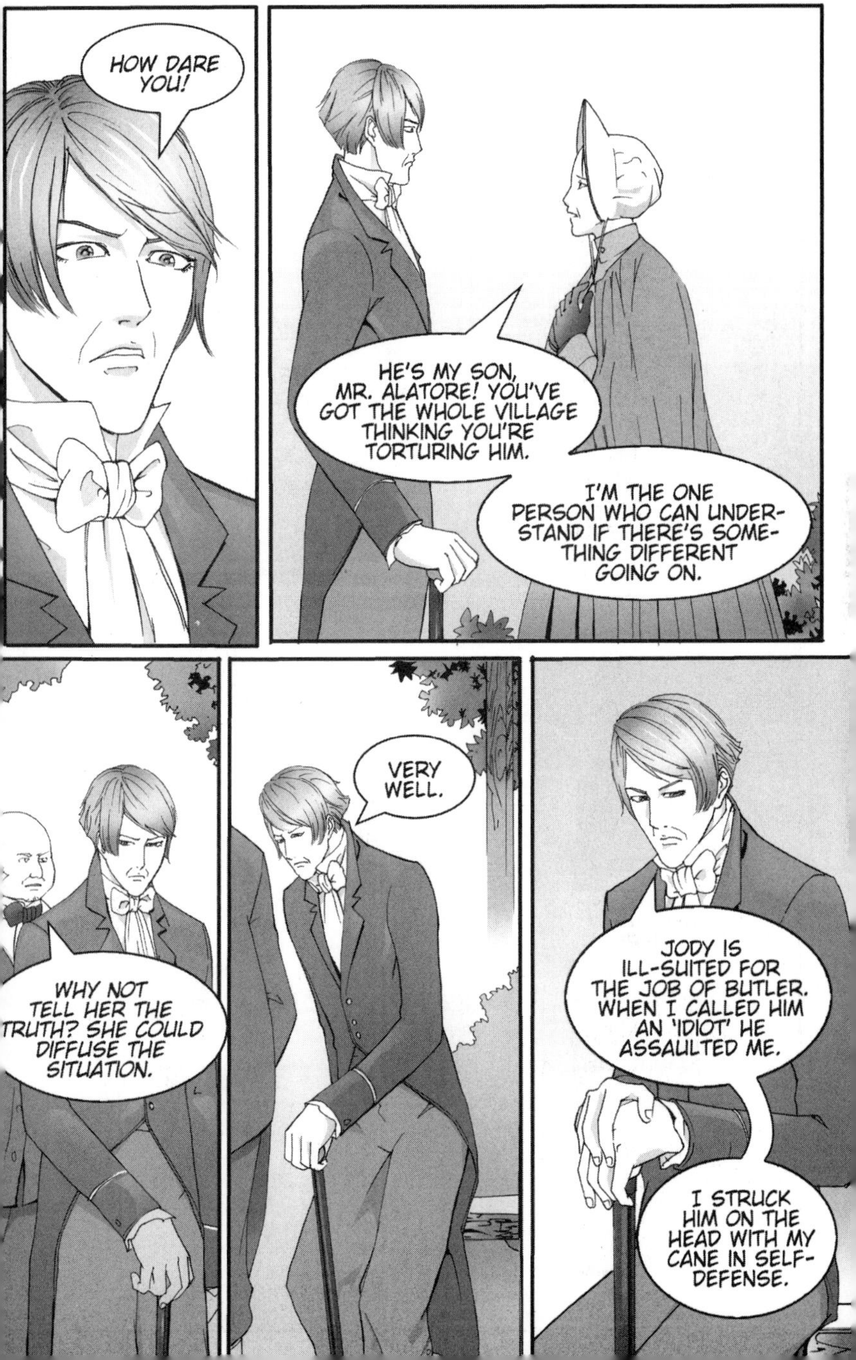
HOW DARE YOU!
HE'S MY SON, MR. ALATORE! YOU'VE GOT THE WHOLE VILLAGE THINKING YOU'RE TORTURING HIM.
I'M THE ONE PERSON WHO CAN UNDER-STAND IF THERE'S SOME-THING DIFFERENT GOING ON.
WHY NOT TELL HER THE TRUTH? SHE COULD DIFFUSE THE SITUATION.
VERY WELL.
JODY IS ILL-SUITED FOR THE JOB OF BUTLER. WHEN I CALLED HIM AN 'IDIOT' HE ASSAULTED ME.
I STRUCK HIM ON THE HEAD WITH MY CANE IN SELF-DEFENSE.

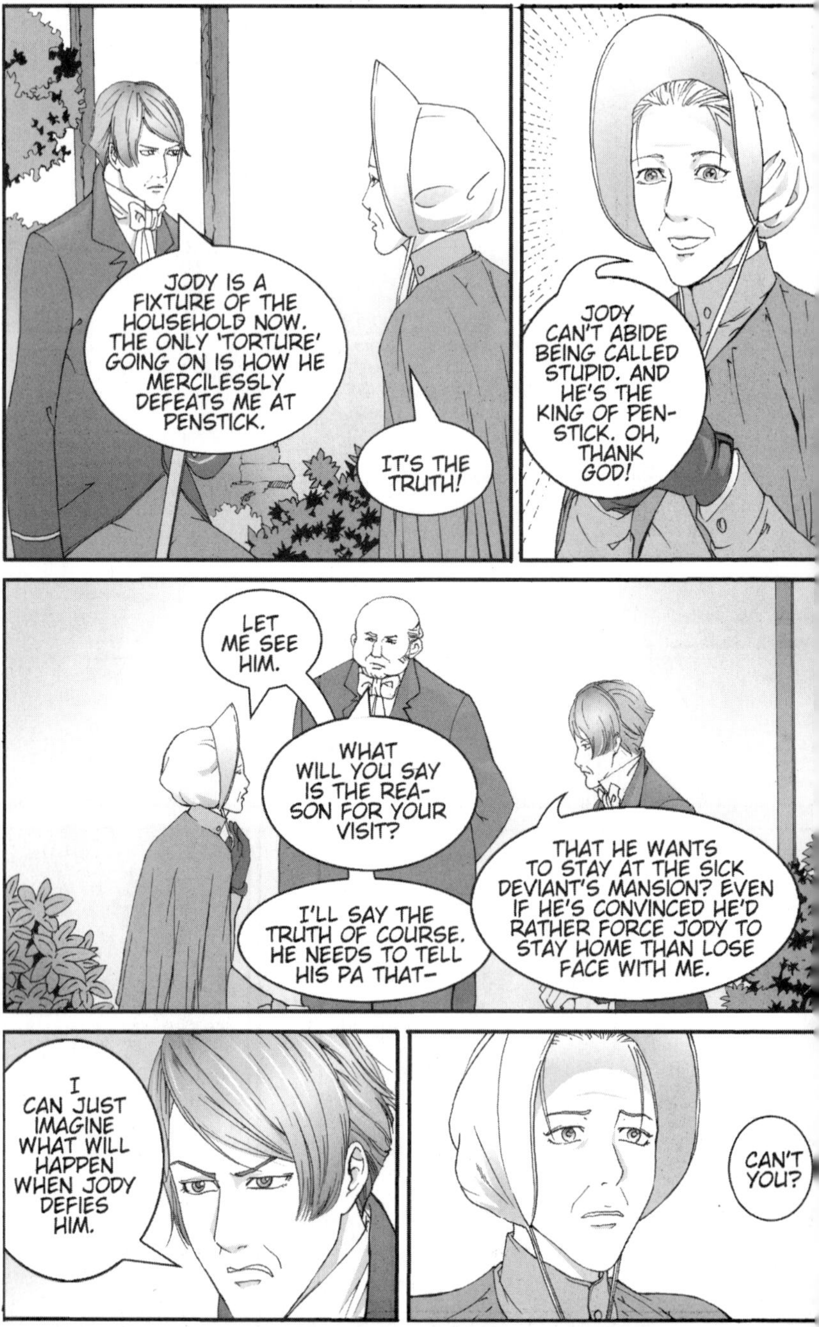
JODY IS A FIXTURE OF THE HOUSEHOLD NOW. THE ONLY 'TORTURE' GOING ON IS HOW HE MERCILESSLY DEFEATS ME AT PENSTICK.
IT'S THE TRUTH!
JODY CAN'T ABIDE BEING CALLED STUPID. AND HE'S THE KING OF PEN-STICK. OH, THANK GOD!
LET ME SEE HIM.
WHAT WILL YOU SAY IS THE REA-SON FOR YOUR VISIT?
I'LL SAY THE TRUTH OF COURSE. HE NEEDS TO TELL HIS PA THAT-
THAT HE WANTS TO STAY AT THE SICK DEVIANT'S MANSION? EVEN IF HE'S CONVINCED HE'D RATHER FORCE JODY TO STAY HOME THAN LOSE FACE WITH ME.
I CAN JUST IMAGINE WHAT WILL HAPPEN WHEN JODY DEFIES HIM.
CAN'T YOU?

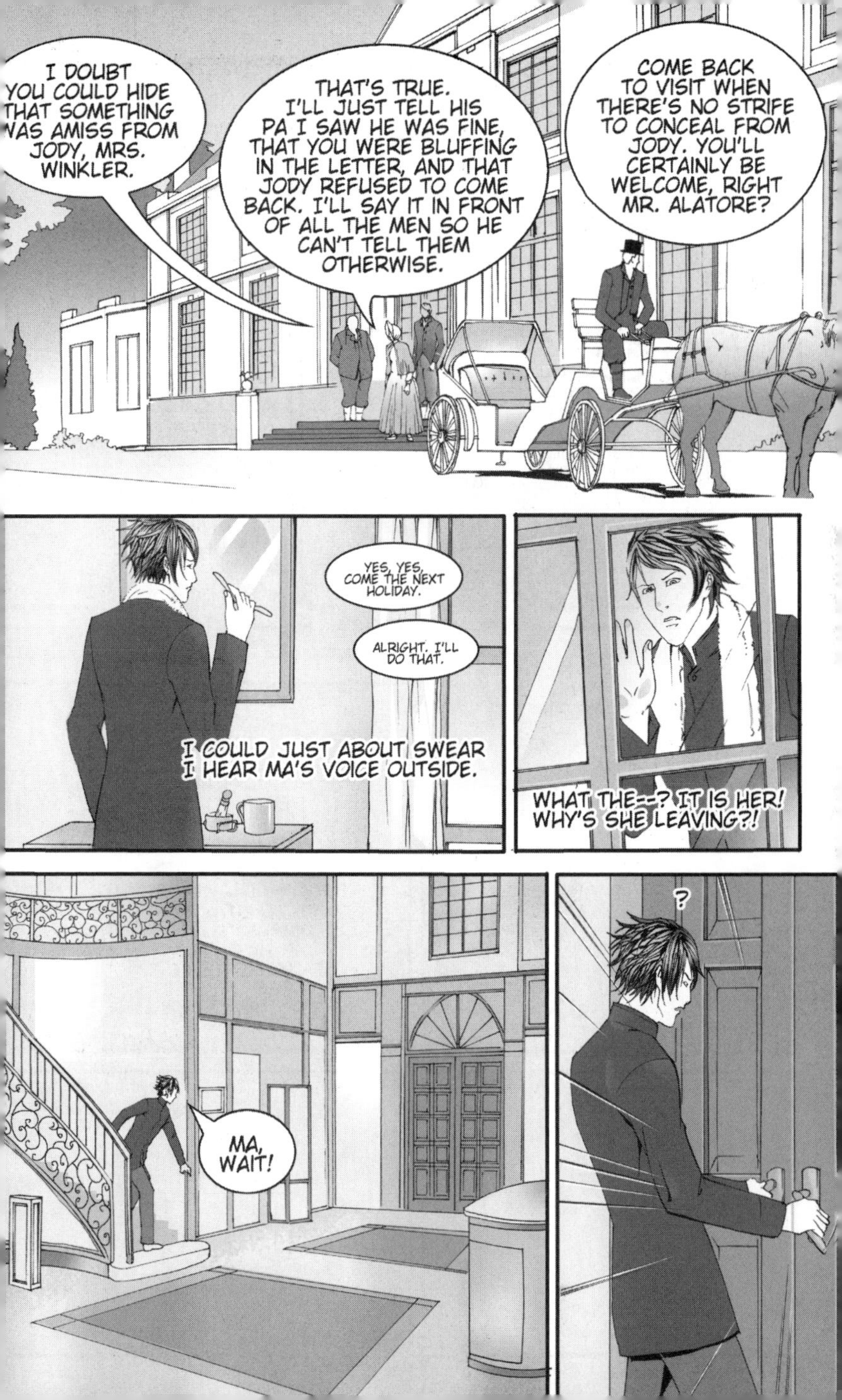
I DOUBT YOU COULD HIDE THAT SOMETHING WAS AMISS FROM JODY, MRS. WINKLER.
THAT'S TRUE. I'LL JUST TELL HIS PA I SAW HE WAS FINE, THAT YOU WERE BLUFFING IN THE LETTER, AND THAT JODY REFUSED TO COME BACK. I'LL SAY IT IN FRONT OF ALL THE MEN SO HE CAN'T TELL THEM OTHERWISE.
COME BACK TO VISIT WHEN THERE'S NO STRIFE TO CONCEAL FROM JODY. YOU'LL CERTAINLY BE WELCOME, RIGHT MR. ALATORE?
YES, YES, COME THE NEXT HOLIDAY.
ALRIGHT. I'LL DO THAT.
I COULD JUST ABOUT SWEAR I HEAR MA'S VOICE OUTSIDE.
WHAT THE--? IT IS HER! WHY'S SHE LEAVING?!
MA, WAIT!
?

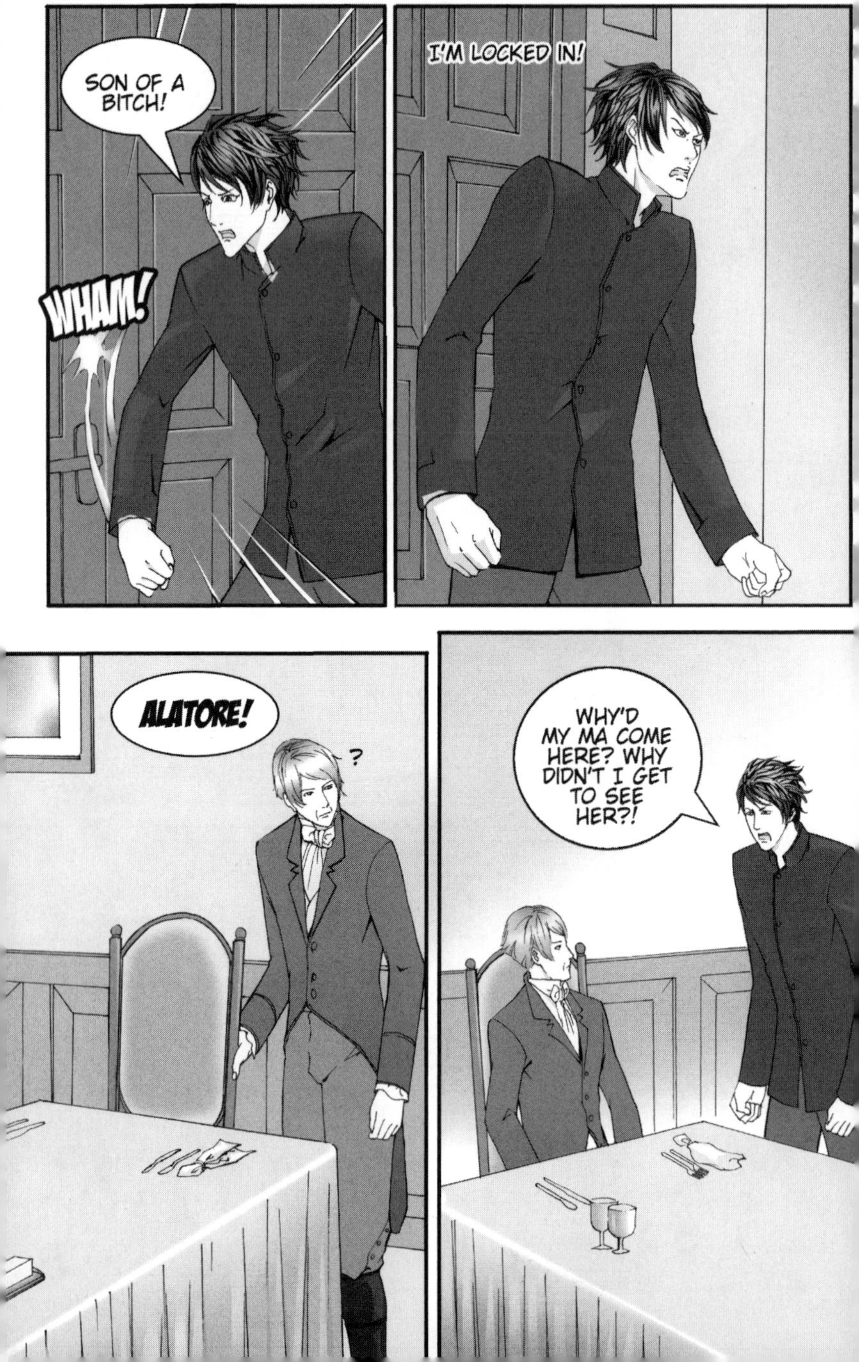
SON OF A BITCH!
WHAM!
I'M LOCKED IN!
ALATORE!
?
WHY'D MY MA COME HERE? WHY DIDN'T I GET TO SEE HER?!

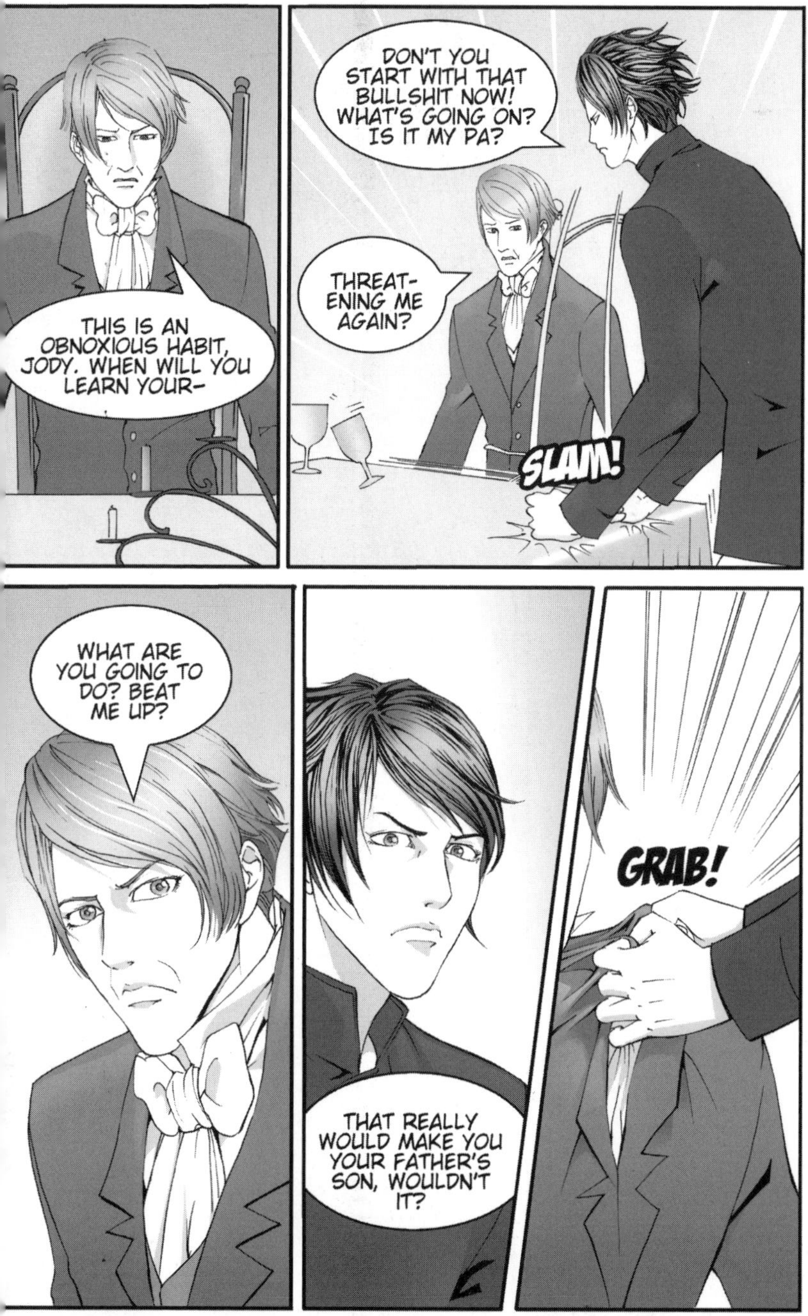
THIS IS AN OBNOXIOUS HABIT, JODY. WHEN WILL YOU LEARN YOUR-
DON'T YOU START WITH THAT BULLSHIT NOW! WHAT'S GOING ON? IS IT MY PA?
THREAT- ENING ME AGAIN?
SLAM!
WHAT ARE YOU GOING TO DO? BEAT ME UP?
THAT REALLY WOULD MAKE YOU YOUR FATHER'S SON, WOULDN'T IT?
GRAB!

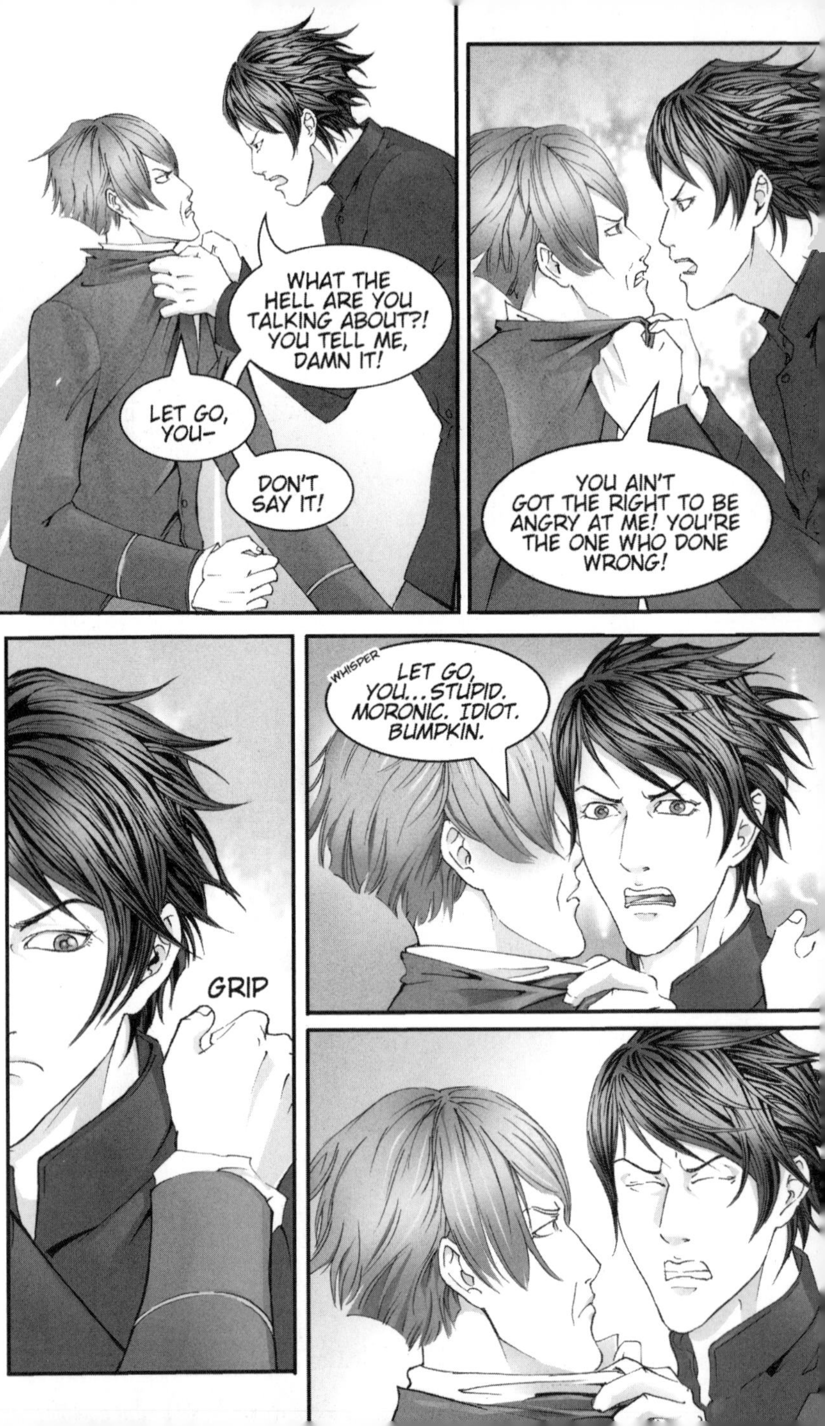
WHAT THE HELL ARE YOU TALKING ABOUT?! YOU TELL ME, DAMN IT!
LET GO, YOU-
DON'T SAY IT!
YOU AIN'T GOT THE RIGHT TO BE ANGRY AT ME! YOU'RE THE ONE WHO DONE WRONG!
GRIP
WHISPER
LET GO, YOU...STUPID. MORONIC. IDIOT. BUMPKIN.

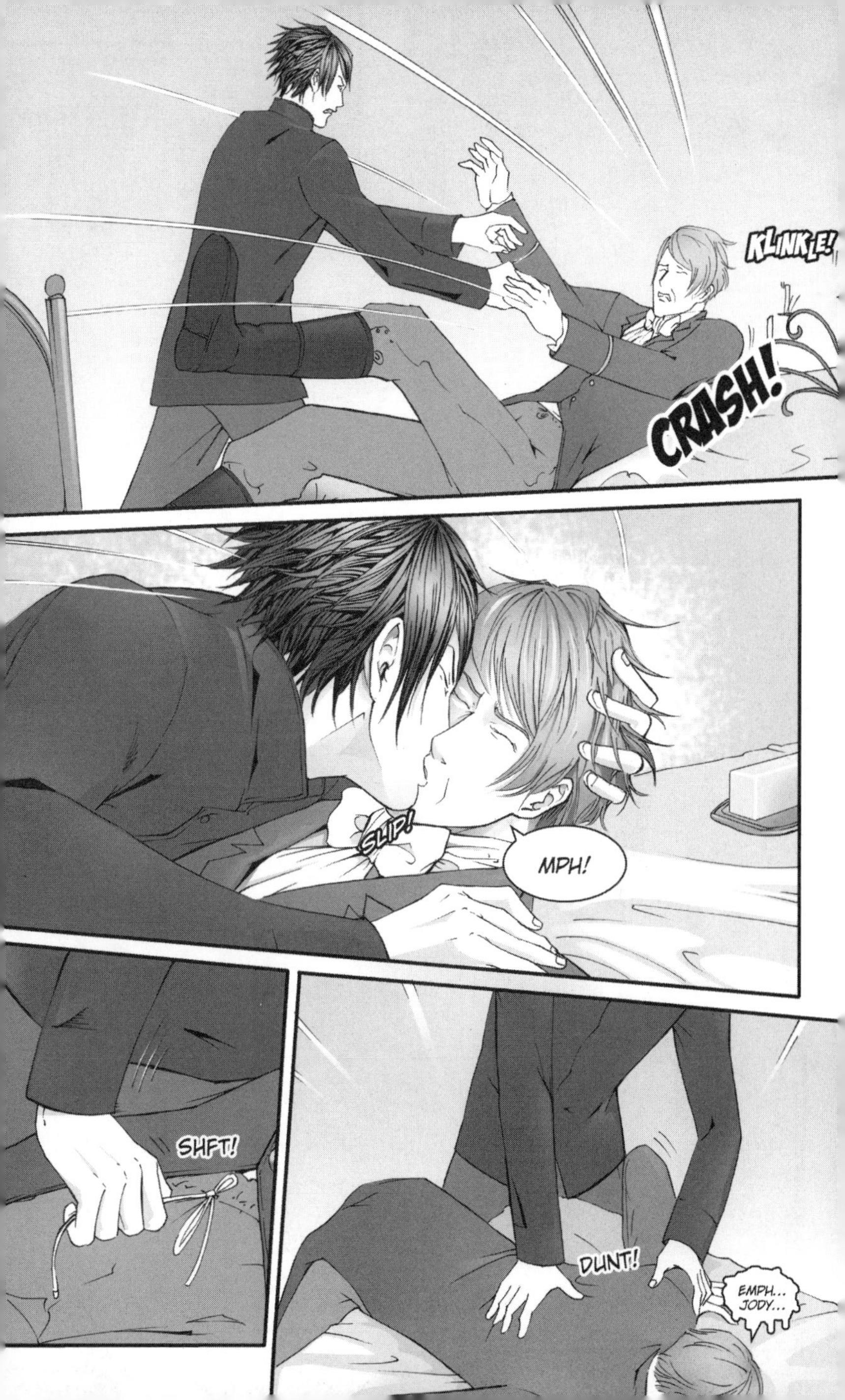
KLINKLE!
CRASH!
SLIP!
MPH!
SHFT!
DUNT!
EMPH... JODY...

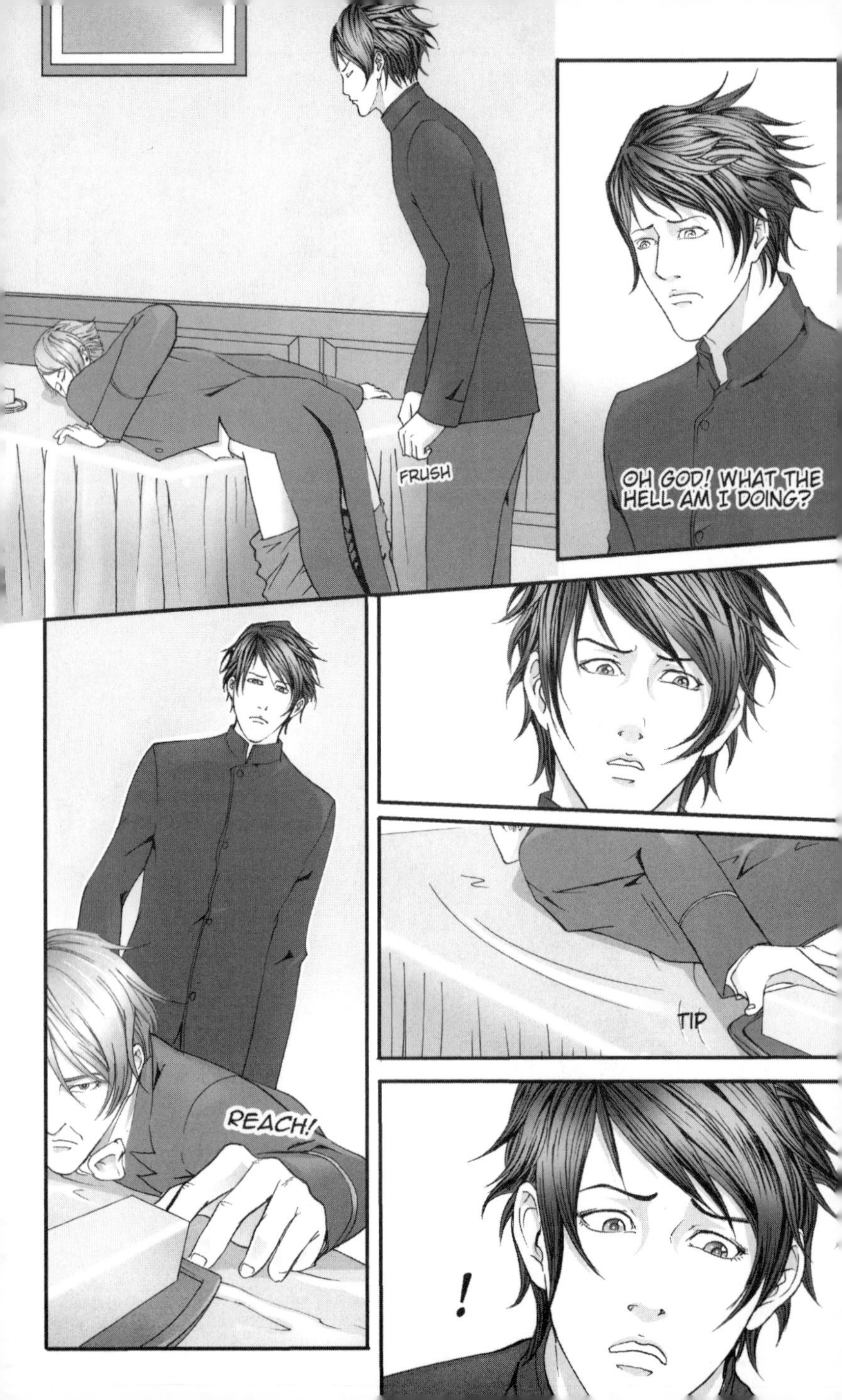
FRUSH
OH GOD! WHAT THE HELL AM I DOING?
REACH!
TIP
!

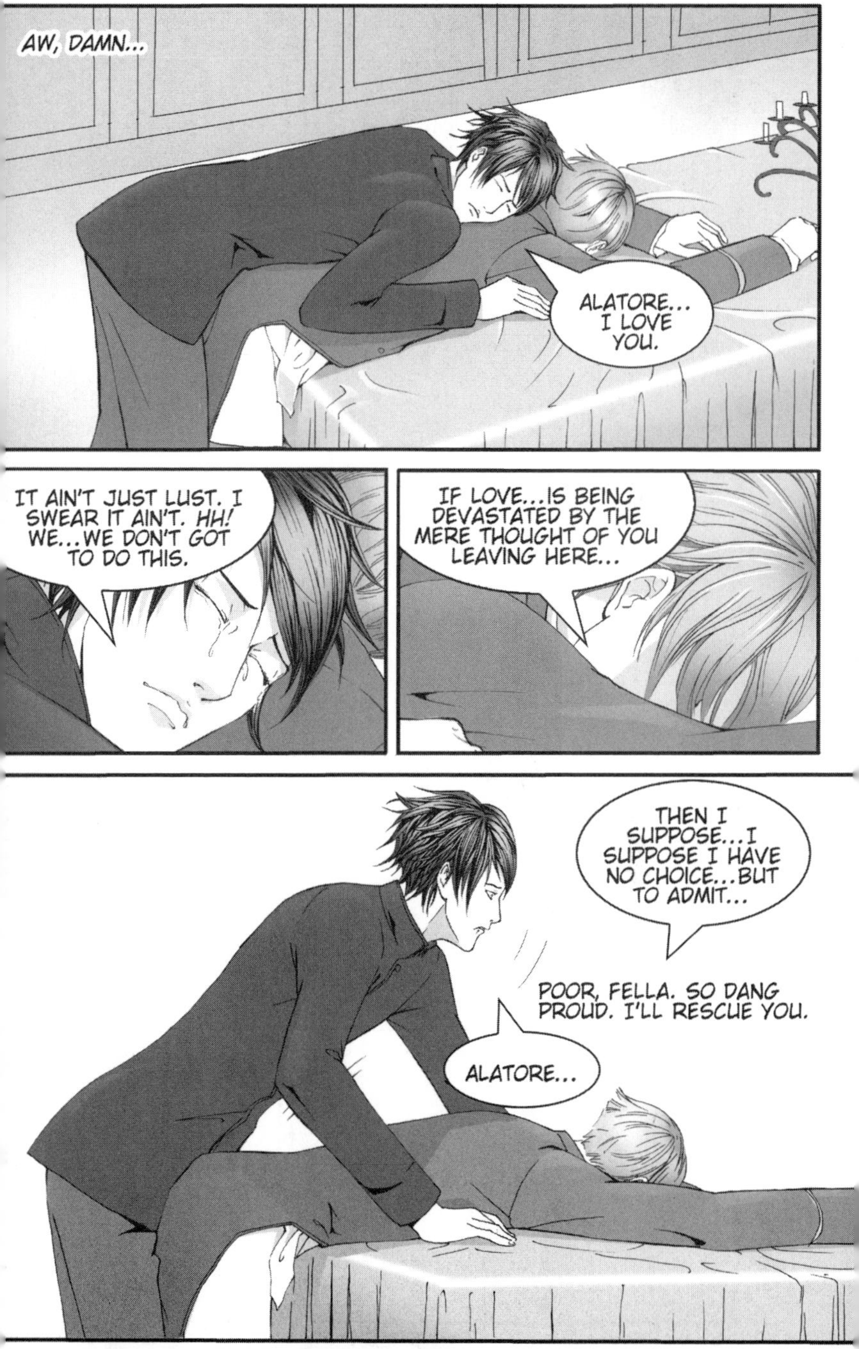
AW, DAMN...
ALATORE... I LOVE YOU.
IT AIN'T JUST LUST. I SWEAR IT AIN'T. HH! WE...WE DON'T GOT TO DO THIS.
IF LOVE...IS BEING DEVASTATED BY THE MERE THOUGHT OF YOU LEAVING HERE...
THEN I SUPPOSE...I SUPPOSE I HAVE NO CHOICE...BUT TO ADMIT...
POOR, FELLA. SO DANG PROUD. I'LL RESCUE YOU.
ALATORE...

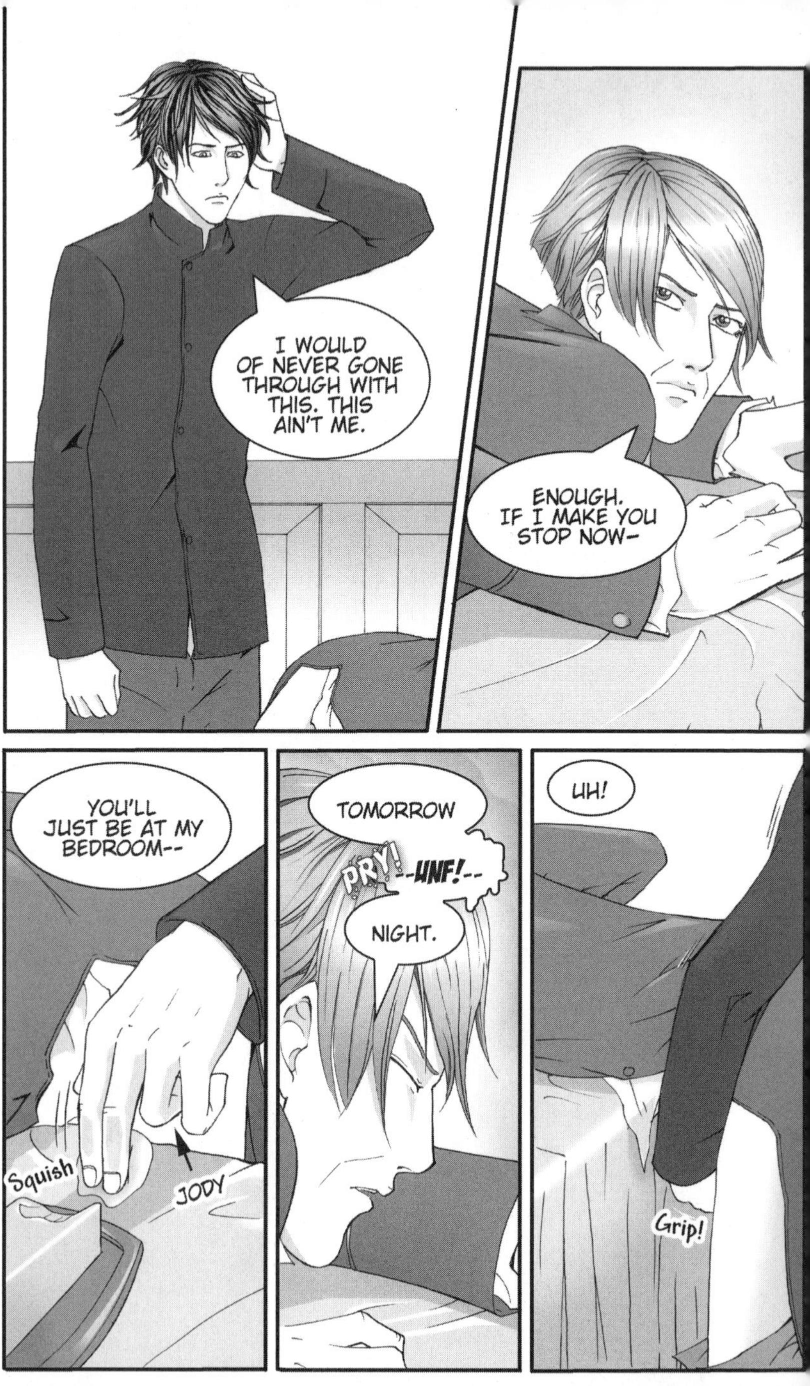
I WOULD OF NEVER GONE THROUGH WITH THIS. THIS AIN'T ME.
ENOUGH. IF I MAKE YOU STOP NOW–
YOU'LL JUST BE AT MY BEDROOM--
Squish
JODY
TOMORROW
PRY!
--UNF!--
NIGHT.
UH!
Grip!

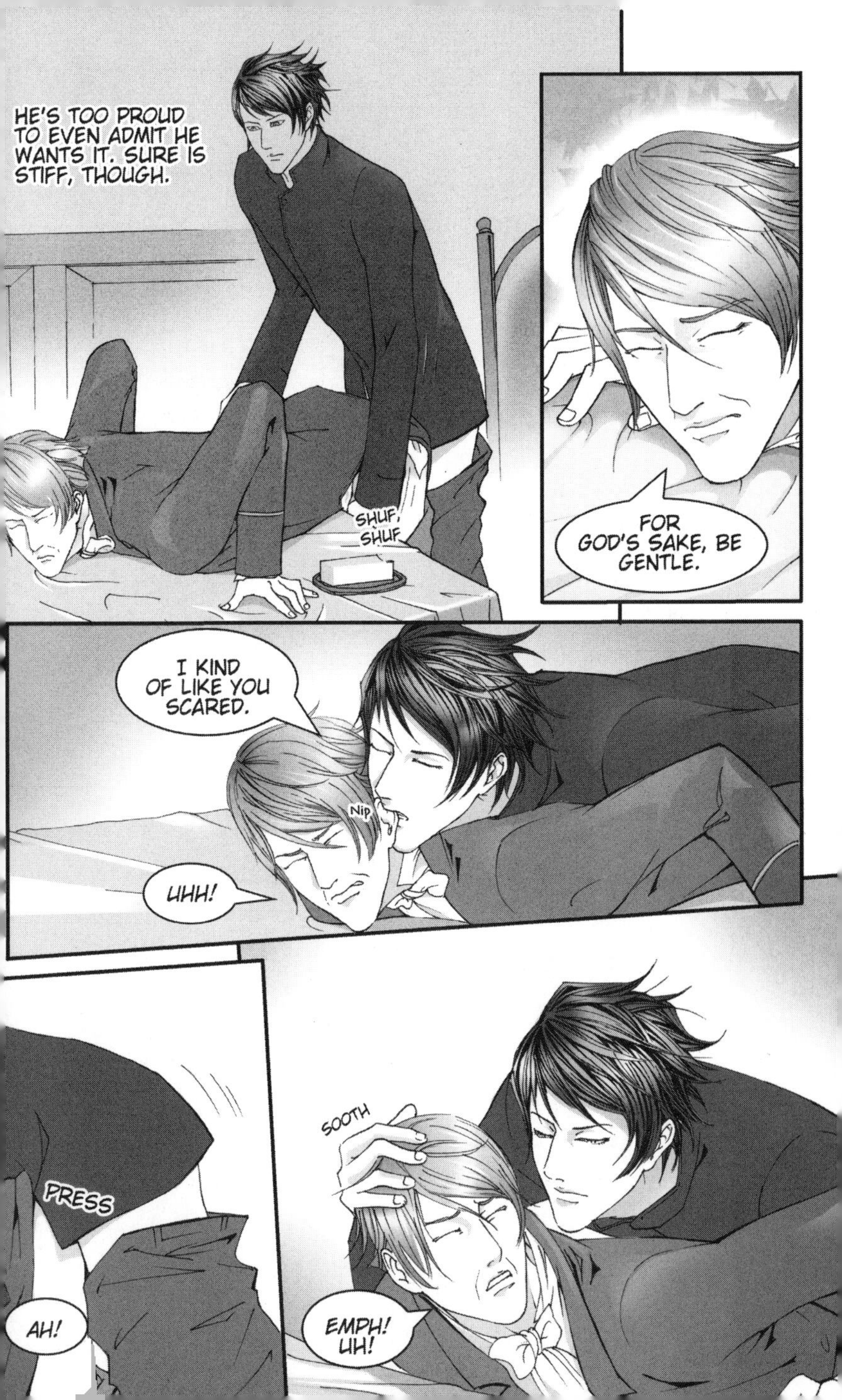
HE'S TOO PROUD TO EVEN ADMIT HE WANTS IT. SURE IS STIFF, THOUGH.
SHUF, SHUF
FOR GOD'S SAKE, BE GENTLE.
I KIND OF LIKE YOU SCARED.
Nip
UHH!
PRESS
AH!
SOOTH
EMPH! UH!

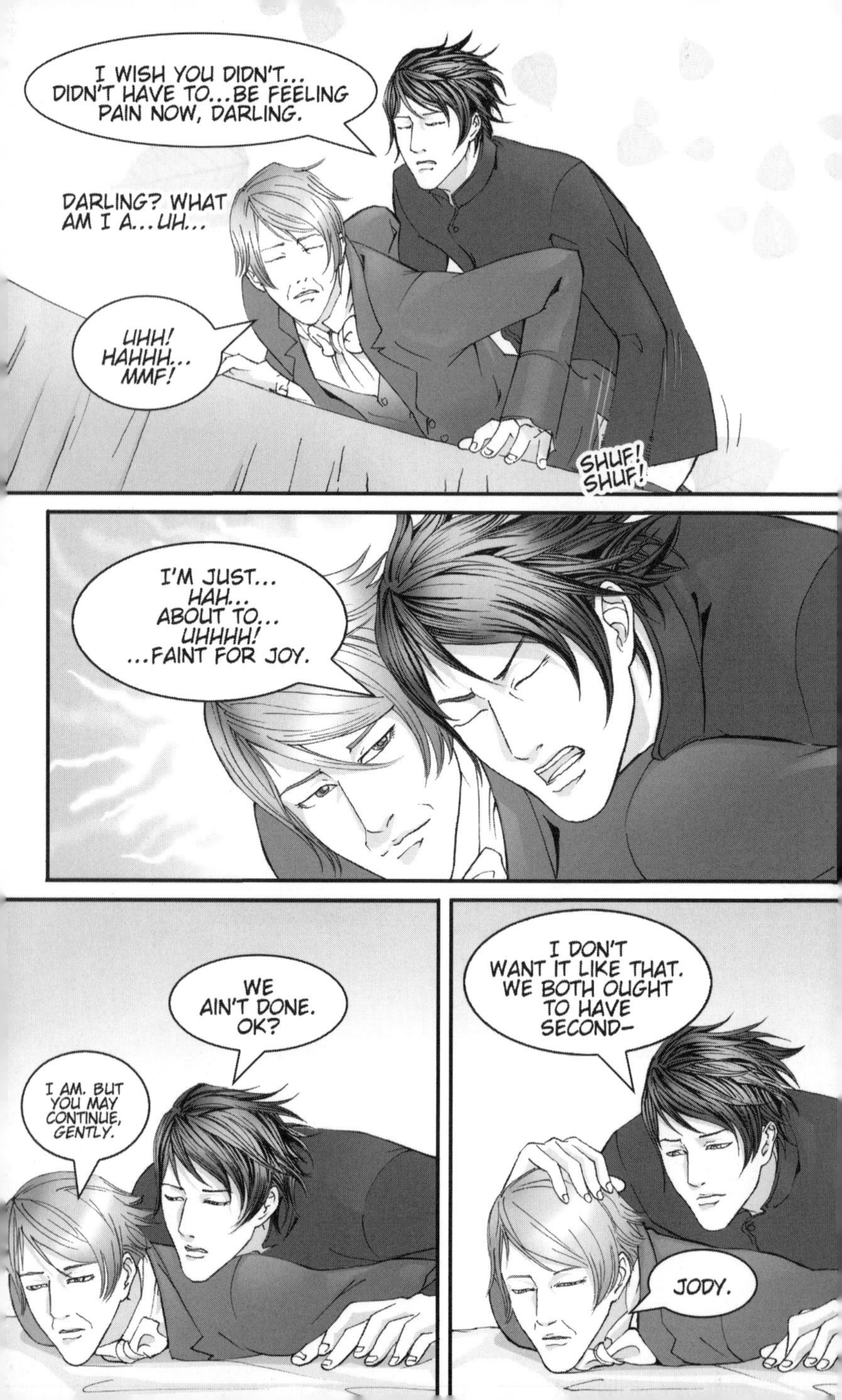
I WISH YOU DIDN'T... DIDN'T HAVE TO...BE FEELING PAIN NOW, DARLING.
DARLING? WHAT AM I A...UH...
UHH! HAHHH... MMF!
SHUF! SHUF!
I'M JUST... HAH... ABOUT TO... UHHHH! ...FAINT FOR JOY.
WE AIN'T DONE. OK?
I AM. BUT YOU MAY CONTINUE, GENTLY.
I DON'T WANT IT LIKE THAT. WE BOTH OUGHT TO HAVE SECOND–
JODY.

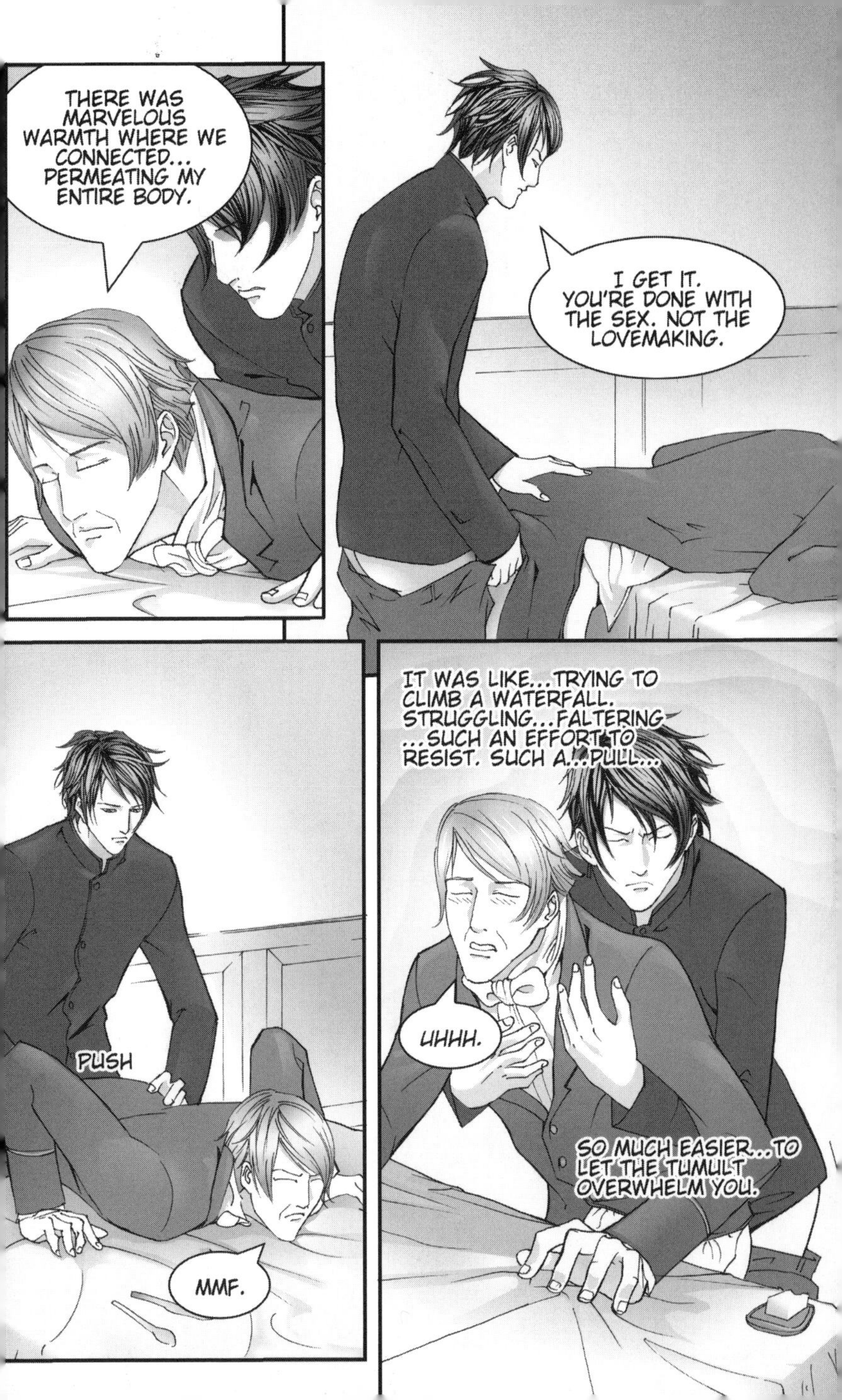
THERE WAS MARVELOUS WARMTH WHERE WE CONNECTED... PERMEATING MY ENTIRE BODY.
I GET IT. YOU'RE DONE WITH THE SEX. NOT THE LOVEMAKING.
PUSH
MMF.
IT WAS LIKE...TRYING TO CLIMB A WATERFALL. STRUGGLING...FALTERING ...SUCH AN EFFORT TO RESIST. SUCH A...PULL...
UHHH.
SO MUCH EASIER...TO LET THE TUMULT OVERWHELM YOU.

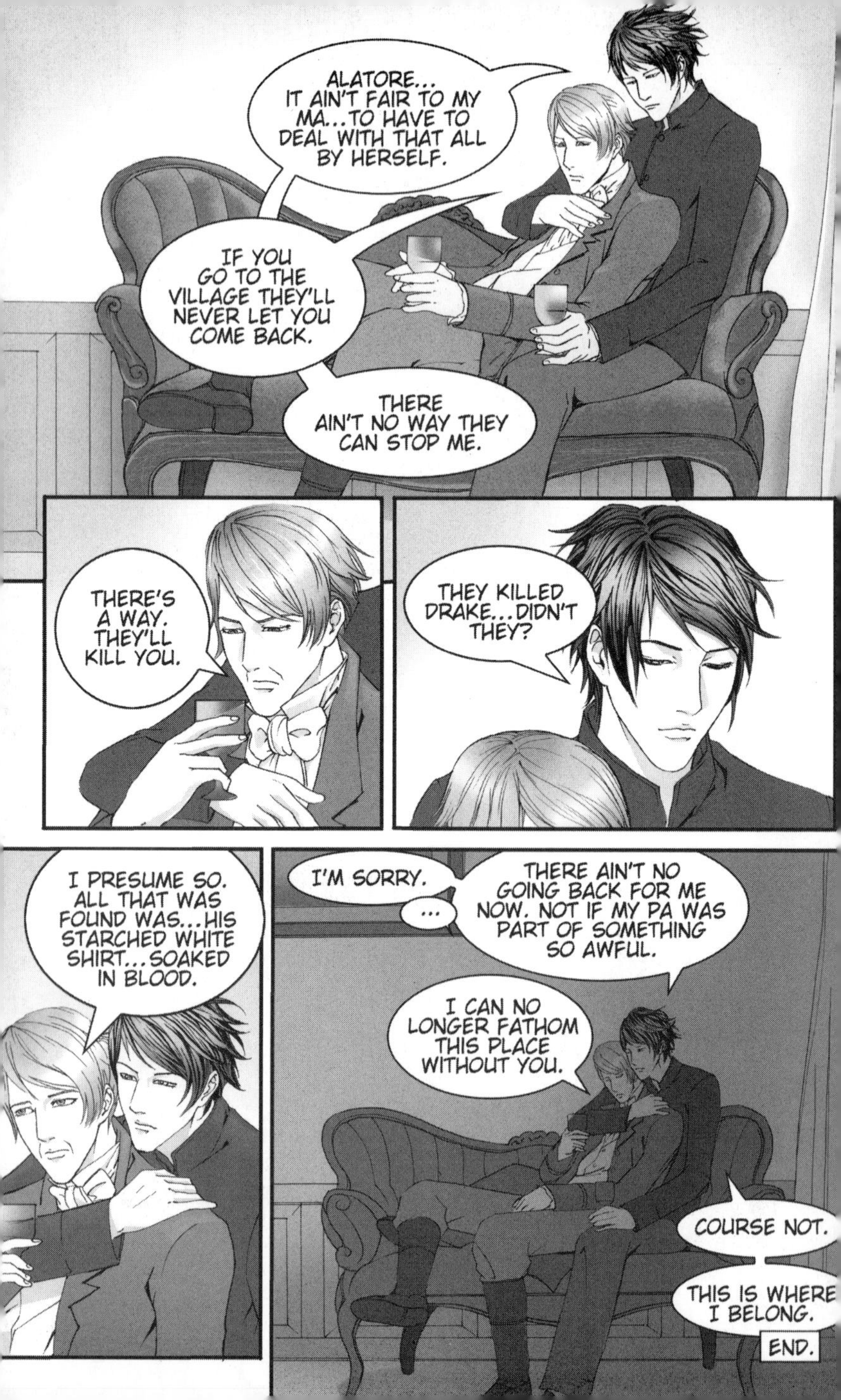
ALATORE... IT AIN'T FAIR TO MY MA...TO HAVE TO DEAL WITH THAT ALL BY HERSELF.
IF YOU GO TO THE VILLAGE THEY'LL NEVER LET YOU COME BACK.
THERE AIN'T NO WAY THEY CAN STOP ME.
THERE'S A WAY. THEY'LL KILL YOU.
THEY KILLED DRAKE...DIDN'T THEY?
I PRESUME SO. ALL THAT WAS FOUND WAS...HIS STARCHED WHITE SHIRT...SOAKED IN BLOOD.
I'M SORRY.
...
THERE AIN'T NO GOING BACK FOR ME NOW. NOT IF MY PA WAS PART OF SOMETHING SO AWFUL.
I CAN NO LONGER FATHOM THIS PLACE WITHOUT YOU.
COURSE NOT.
THIS IS WHERE I BELONG.
END.

The street urchin Vanqisher has been taken in by **Cain the Dark**, medieval Italy's most **infamous** warrior.

Cain made it clear early on that his interest in Vanquisher was far from innocent. What's not clear is what Cain truly is. Vanquisher once saw **black wings** on Cain's back. Why is the church so **obsessed** with destroying Cain?

VOL.2

CAIN

Le Peruggine

Coming in March 2008!

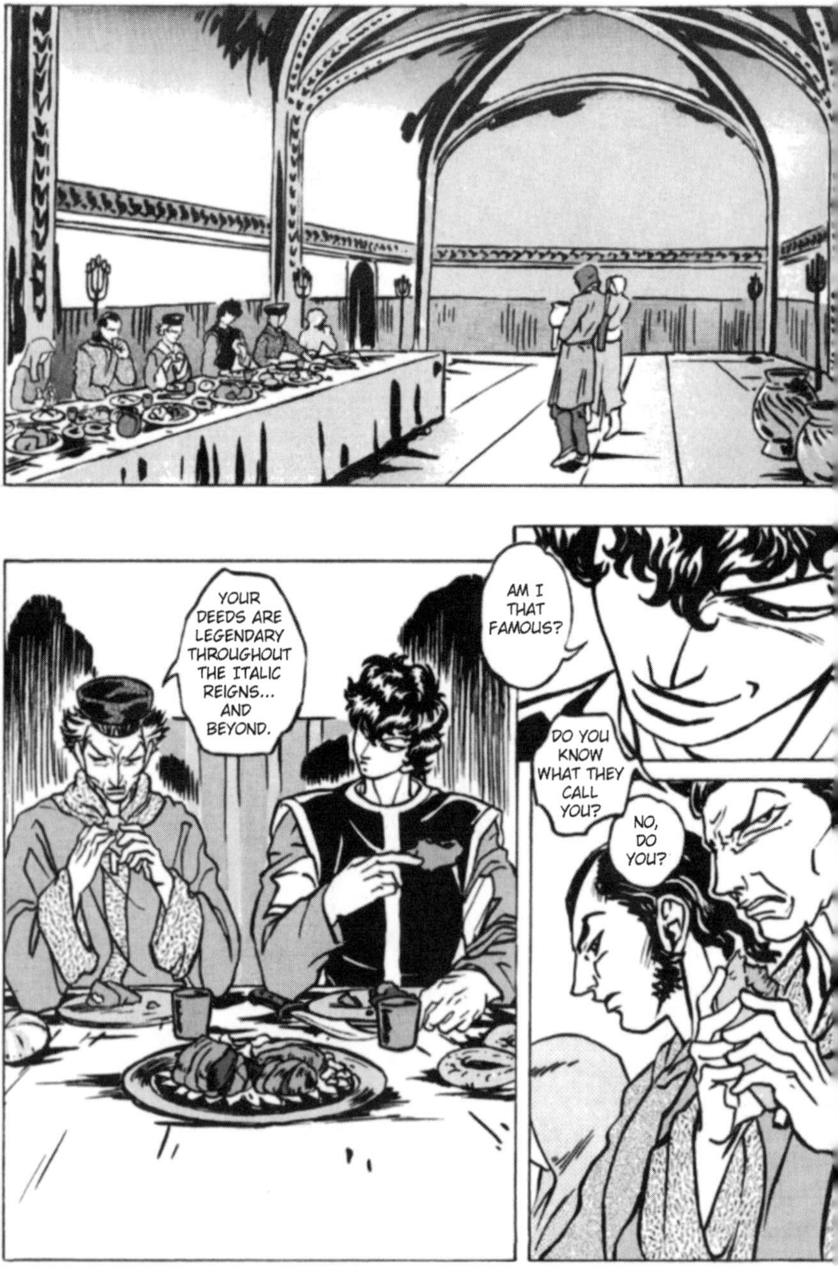
YOUR DEEDS ARE LEGENDARY THROUGHOUT THE ITALIC REIGNS... AND BEYOND.
AM I THAT FAMOUS?
DO YOU KNOW WHAT THEY CALL YOU?
NO, DO YOU?

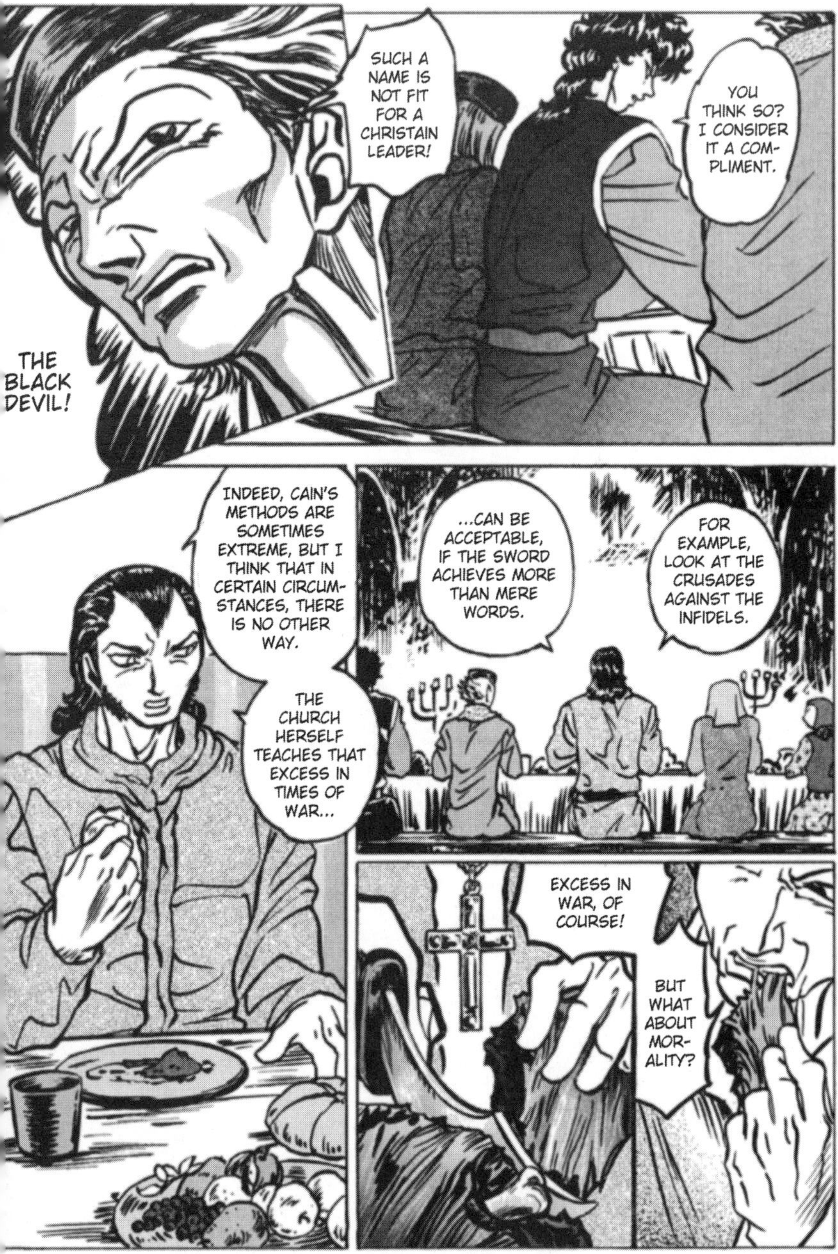

SUCH A NAME IS NOT FIT FOR A CHRISTAIN LEADER!
YOU THINK SO? I CONSIDER IT A COM-PLIMENT.
THE BLACK DEVIL!
INDEED, CAIN'S METHODS ARE SOMETIMES EXTREME, BUT I THINK THAT IN CERTAIN CIRCUM-STANCES, THERE IS NO OTHER WAY.
THE CHURCH HERSELF TEACHES THAT EXCESS IN TIMES OF WAR...
...CAN BE ACCEPTABLE, IF THE SWORD ACHIEVES MORE THAN MERE WORDS.
FOR EXAMPLE, LOOK AT THE CRUSADES AGAINST THE INFIDELS.
EXCESS IN WAR, OF COURSE!
BUT WHAT ABOUT MOR-ALITY?

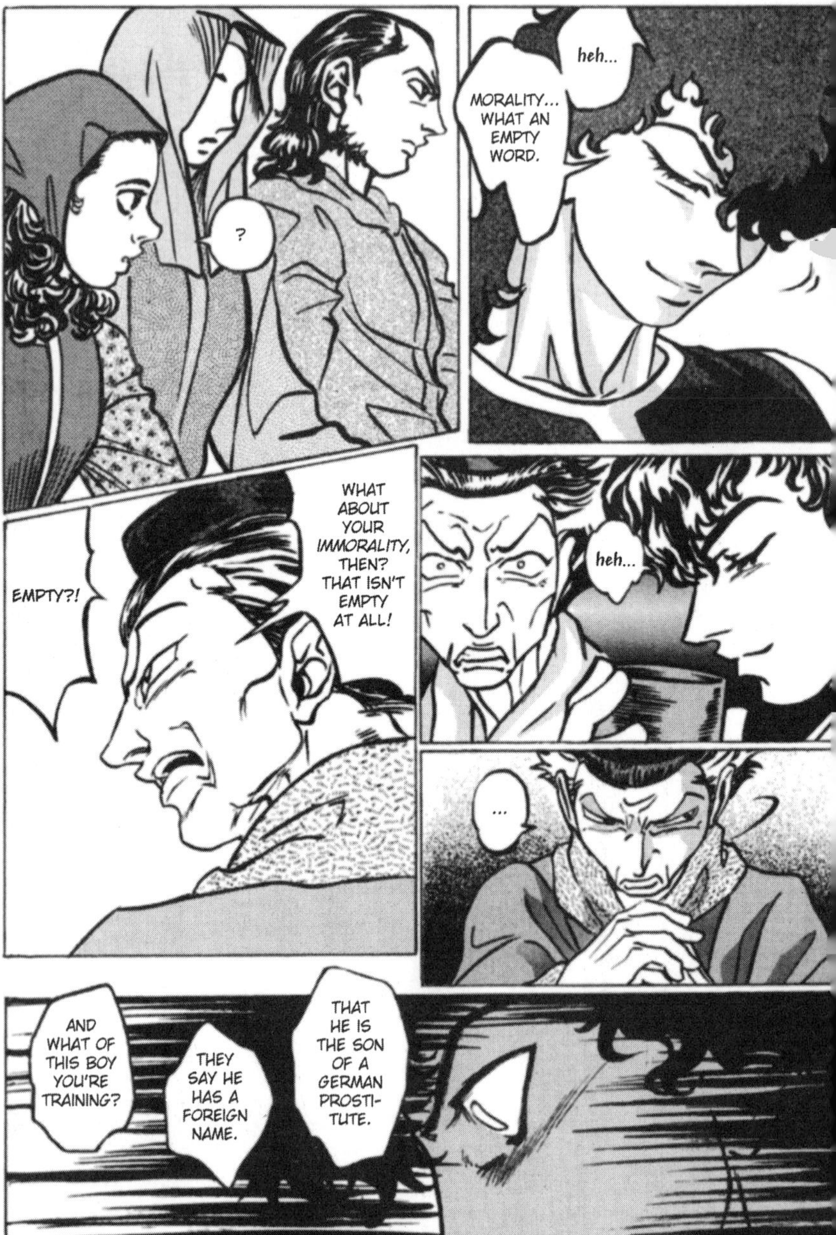
?
heh...
MORALITY... WHAT AN EMPTY WORD.
EMPTY?!
WHAT ABOUT YOUR *IMMORALITY*, THEN? THAT ISN'T EMPTY AT ALL!
heh...
...
AND WHAT OF THIS BOY YOU'RE TRAINING?
THEY SAY HE HAS A FOREIGN NAME.
THAT HE IS THE SON OF A GERMAN PROSTI-TUTE.

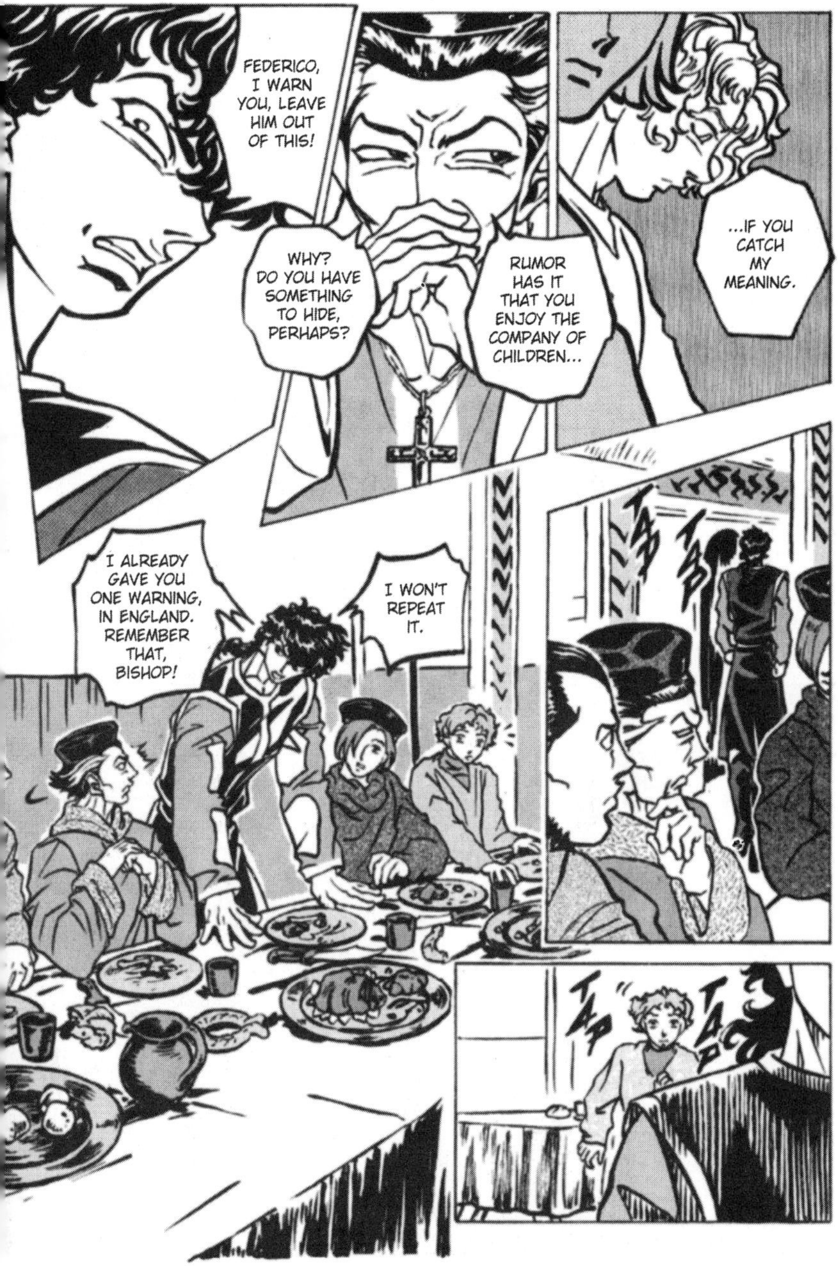
FEDERICO, I WARN YOU, LEAVE HIM OUT OF THIS!
WHY? DO YOU HAVE SOMETHING TO HIDE, PERHAPS?
RUMOR HAS IT THAT YOU ENJOY THE COMPANY OF CHILDREN...
...IF YOU CATCH MY MEANING.
I ALREADY GAVE YOU ONE WARNING, IN ENGLAND. REMEMBER THAT, BISHOP!
I WON'T REPEAT IT.

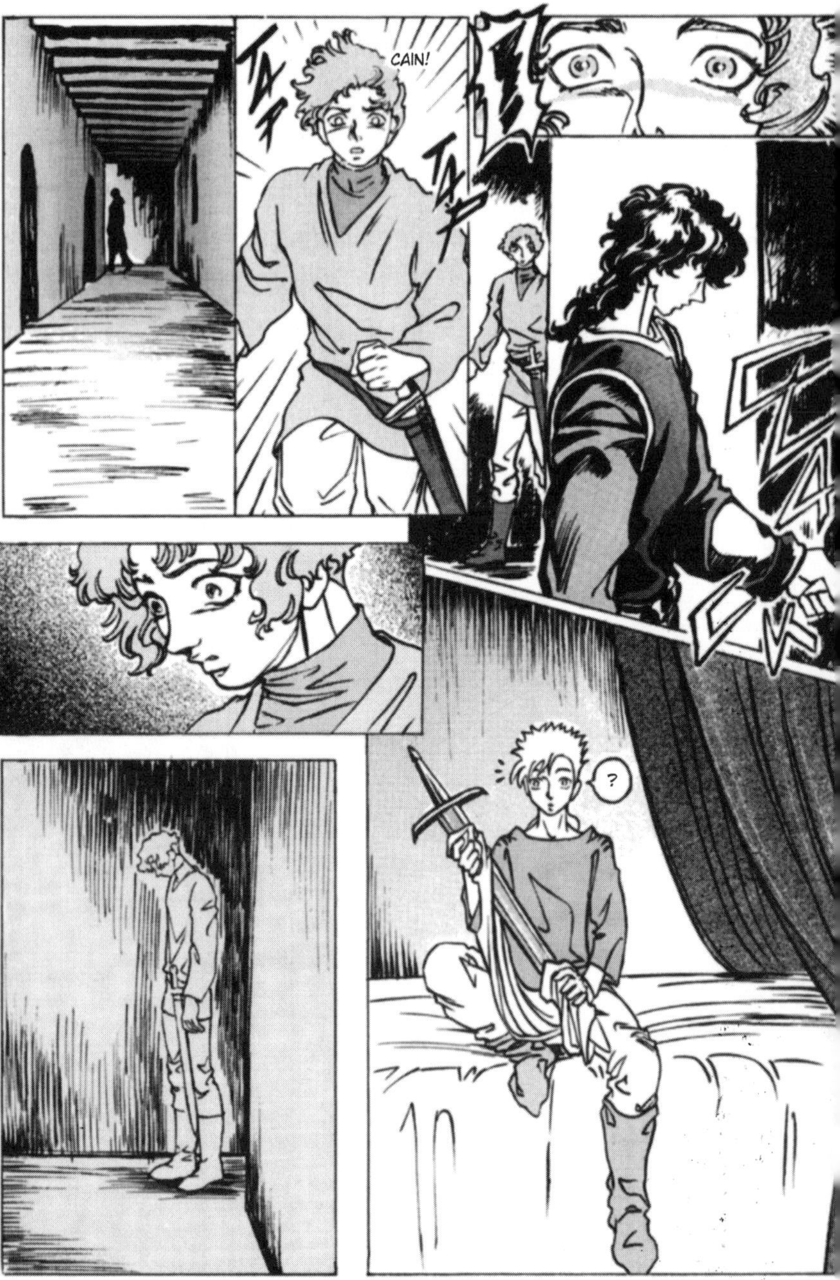
CAIN!
?

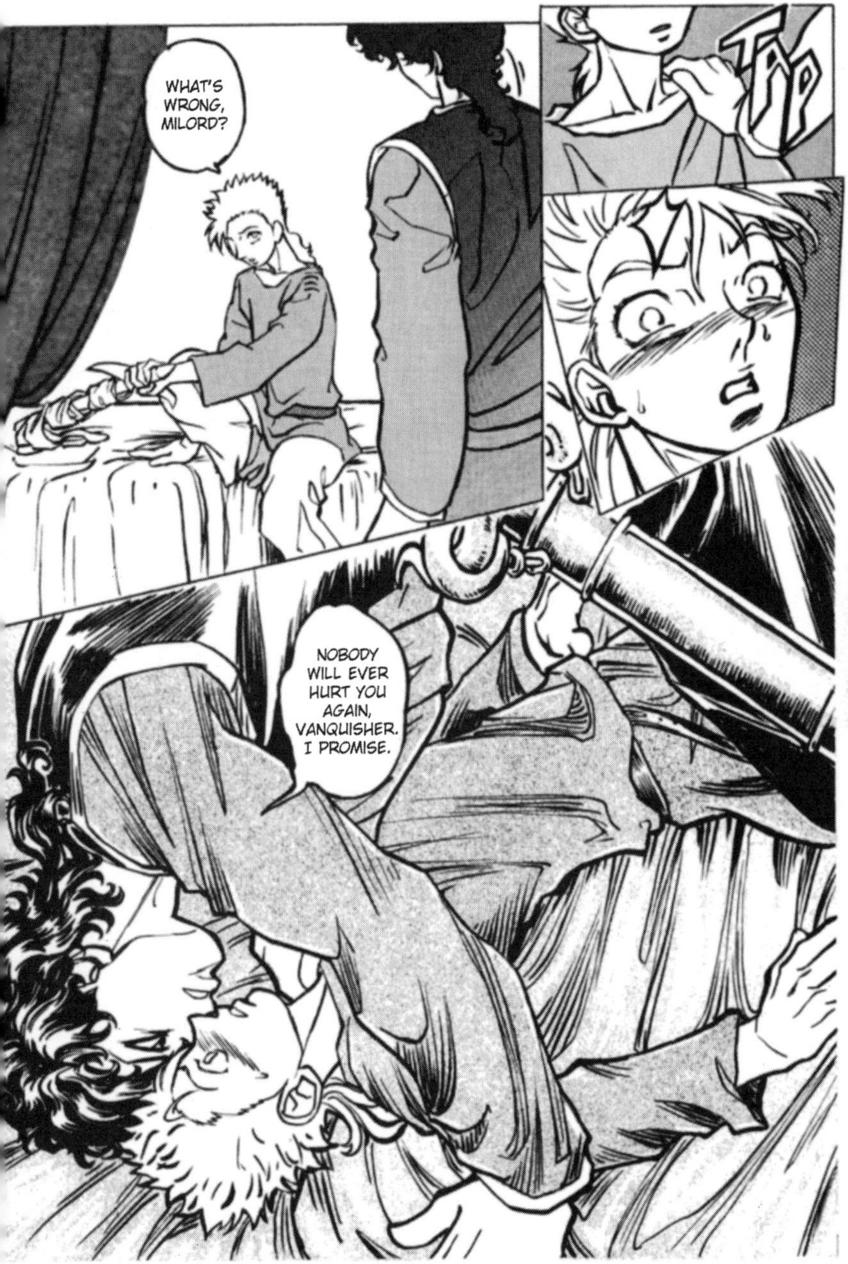
WHAT'S WRONG, MILORD?
TAP
NOBODY WILL EVER HURT YOU AGAIN, VANQUISHER. I PROMISE.

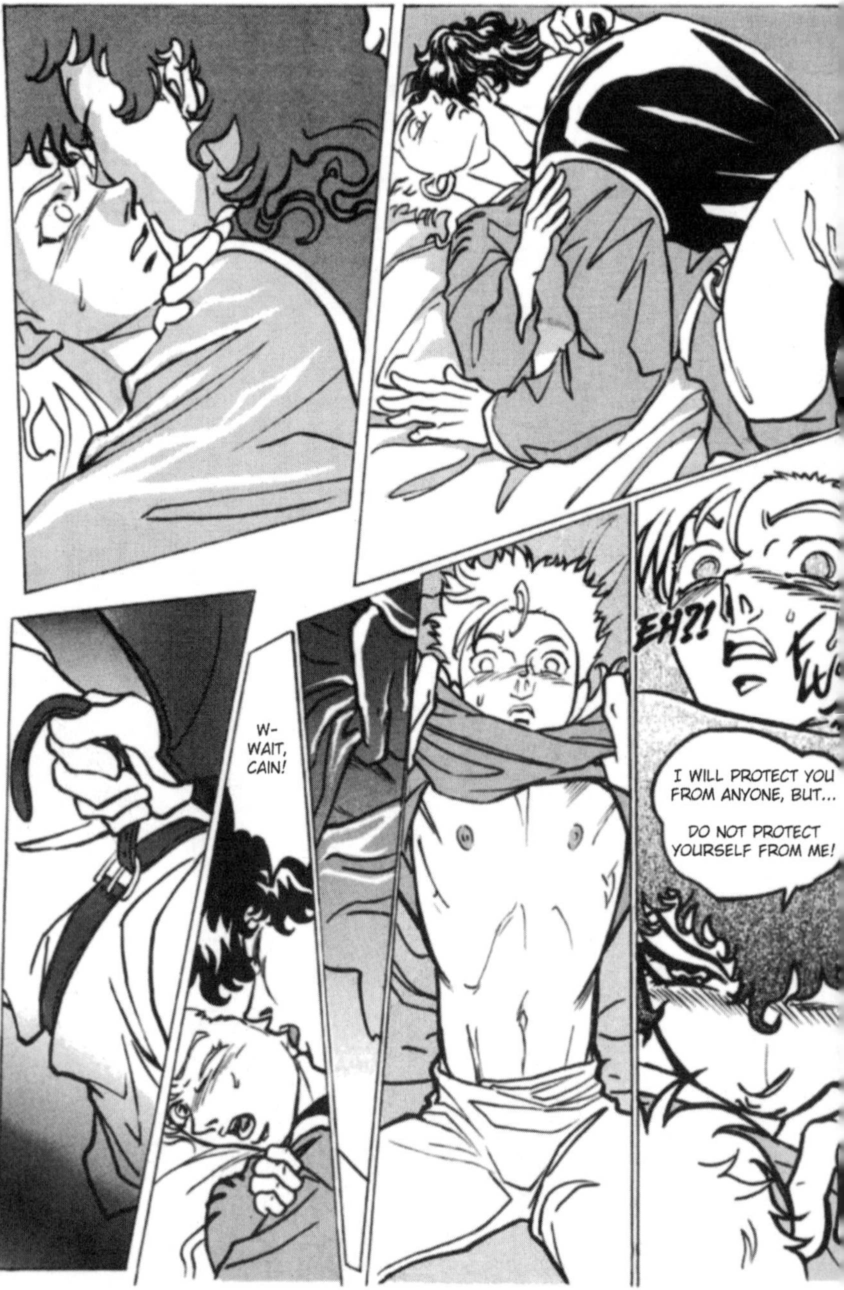
EH?!
I WILL PROTECT YOU FROM ANYONE, BUT...
DO NOT PROTECT YOURSELF FROM ME!
W-WAIT, CAIN!

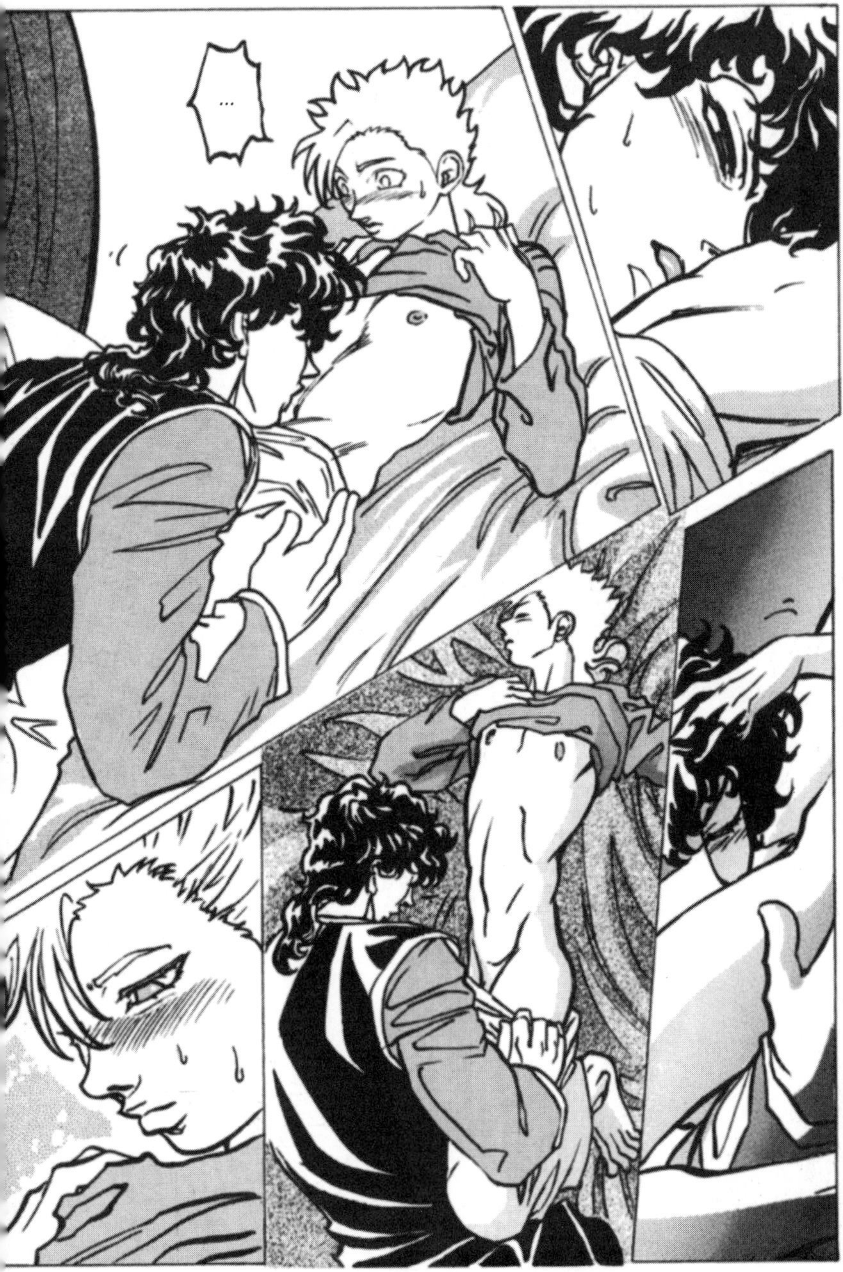
...

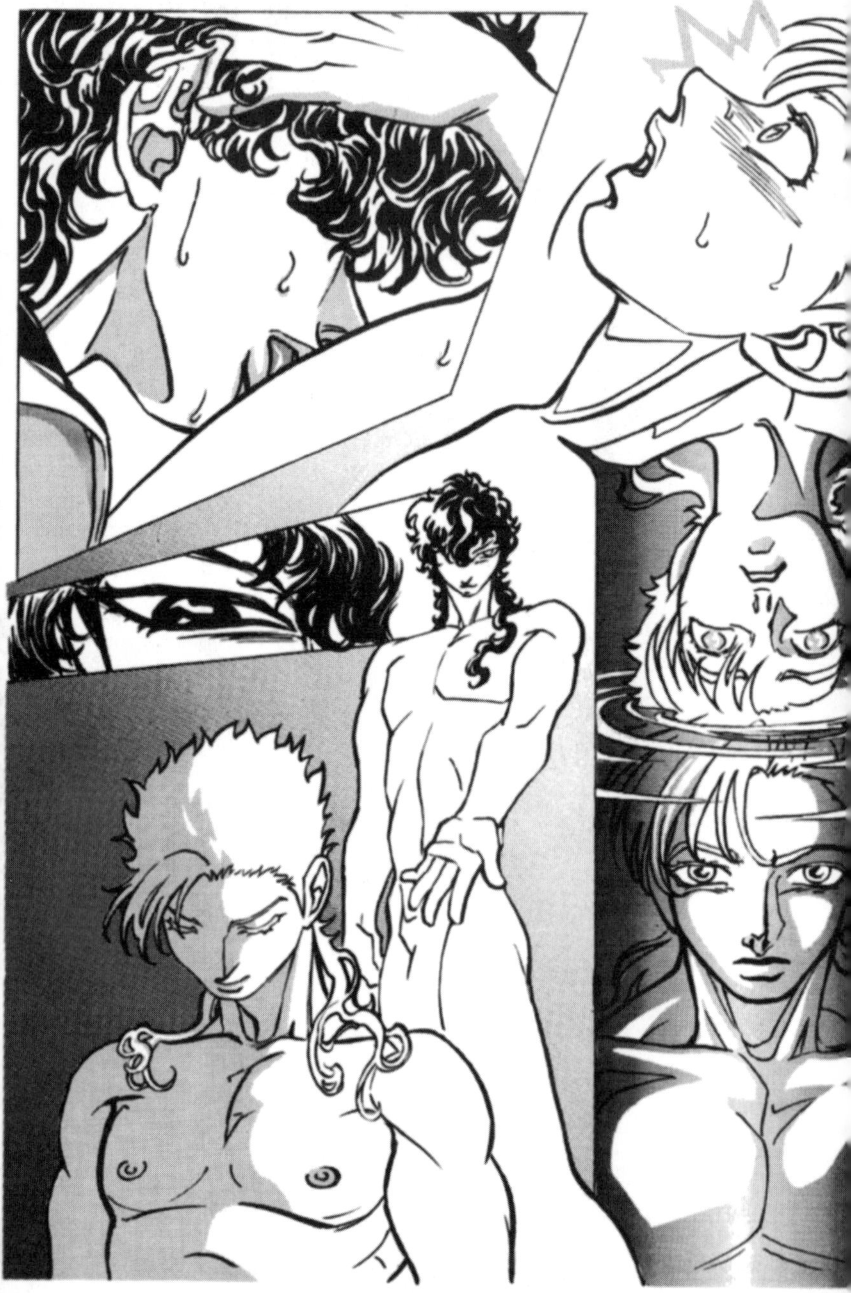

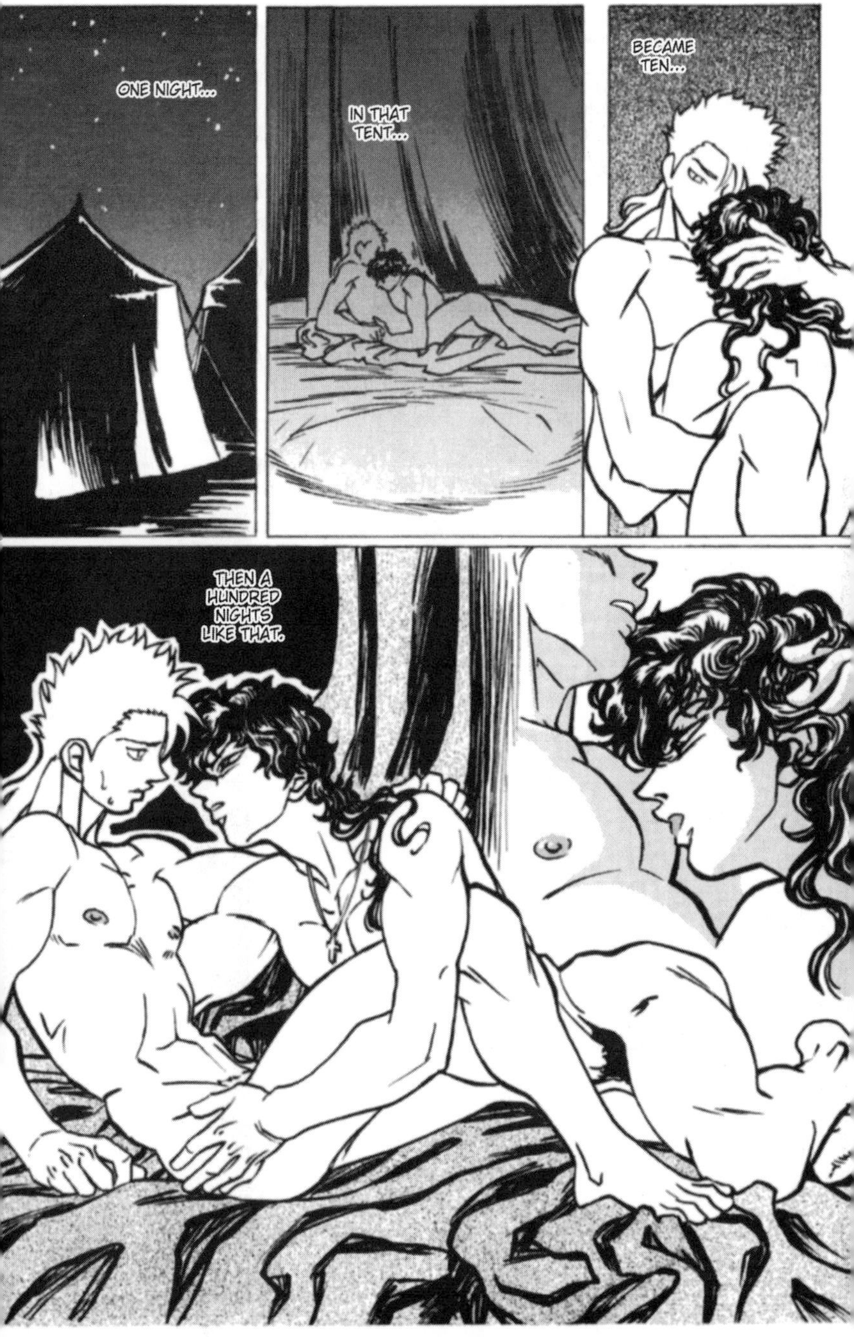
ONE NIGHT...
IN THAT TENT...
BECAME TEN...
THEN A HUNDRED NIGHTS LIKE THAT.

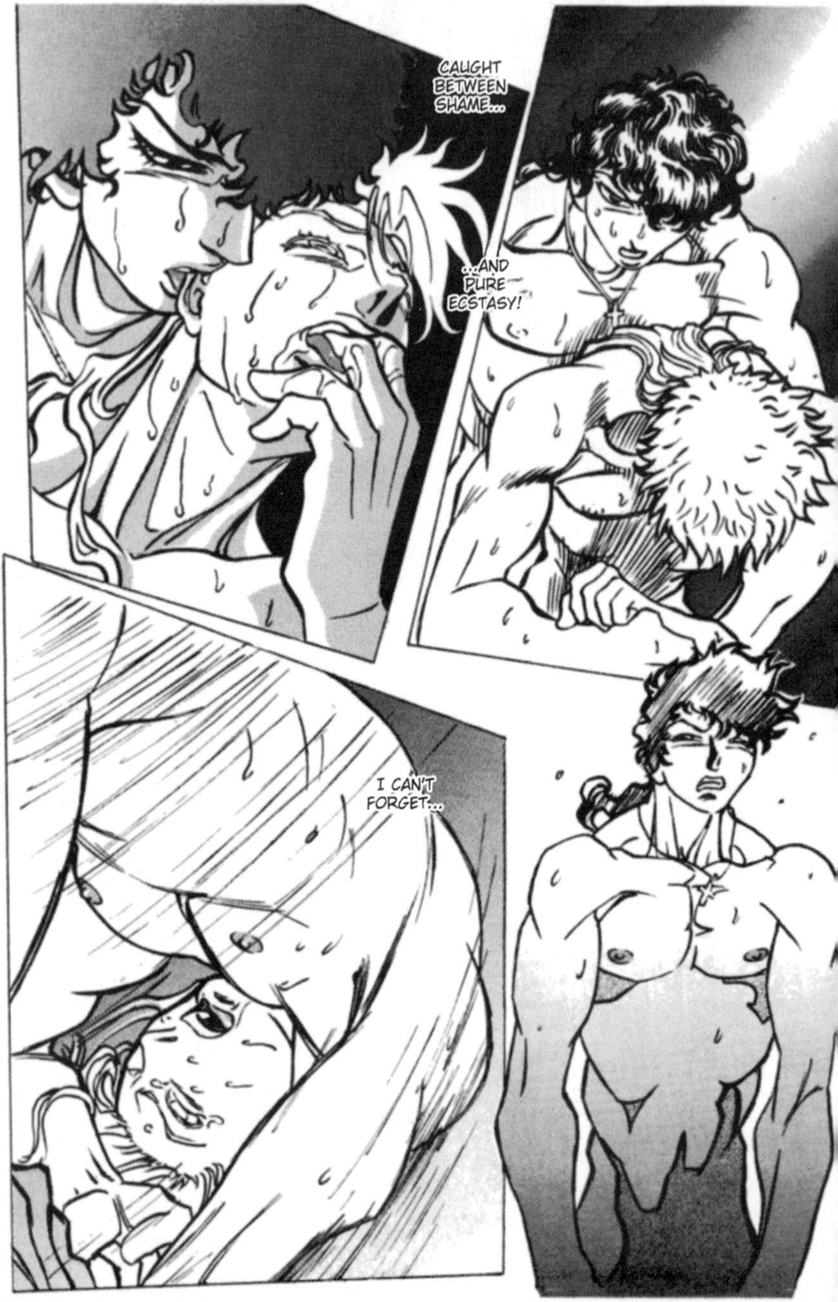
CAUGHT BETWEEN SHAME...
...AND PURE ECSTASY!
I CAN'T FORGET...

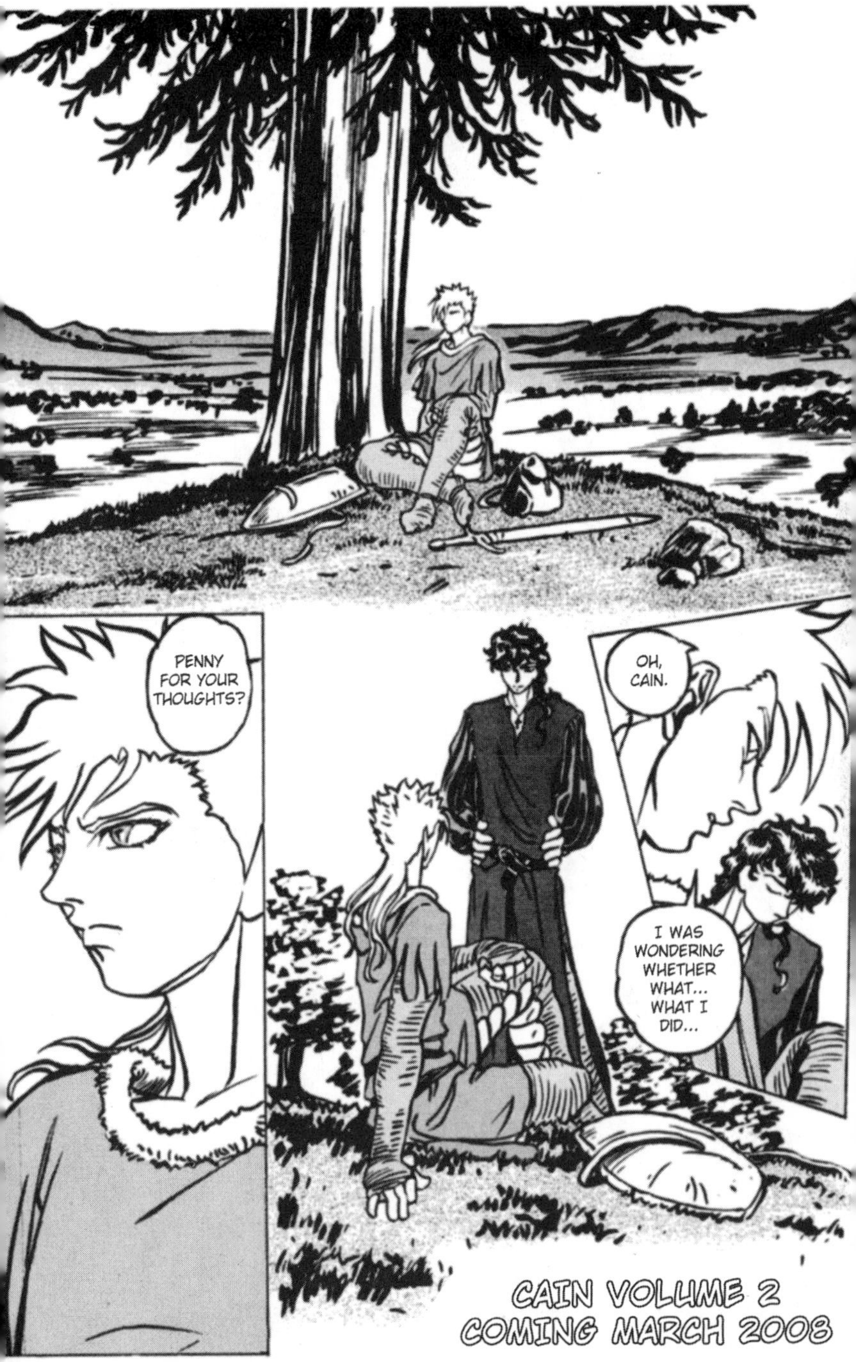

PENNY FOR YOUR THOUGHTS?
OH, CAIN.
I WAS WONDERING WHETHER WHAT... WHAT I DID...
CAIN VOLUME 2
COMING MARCH 2008

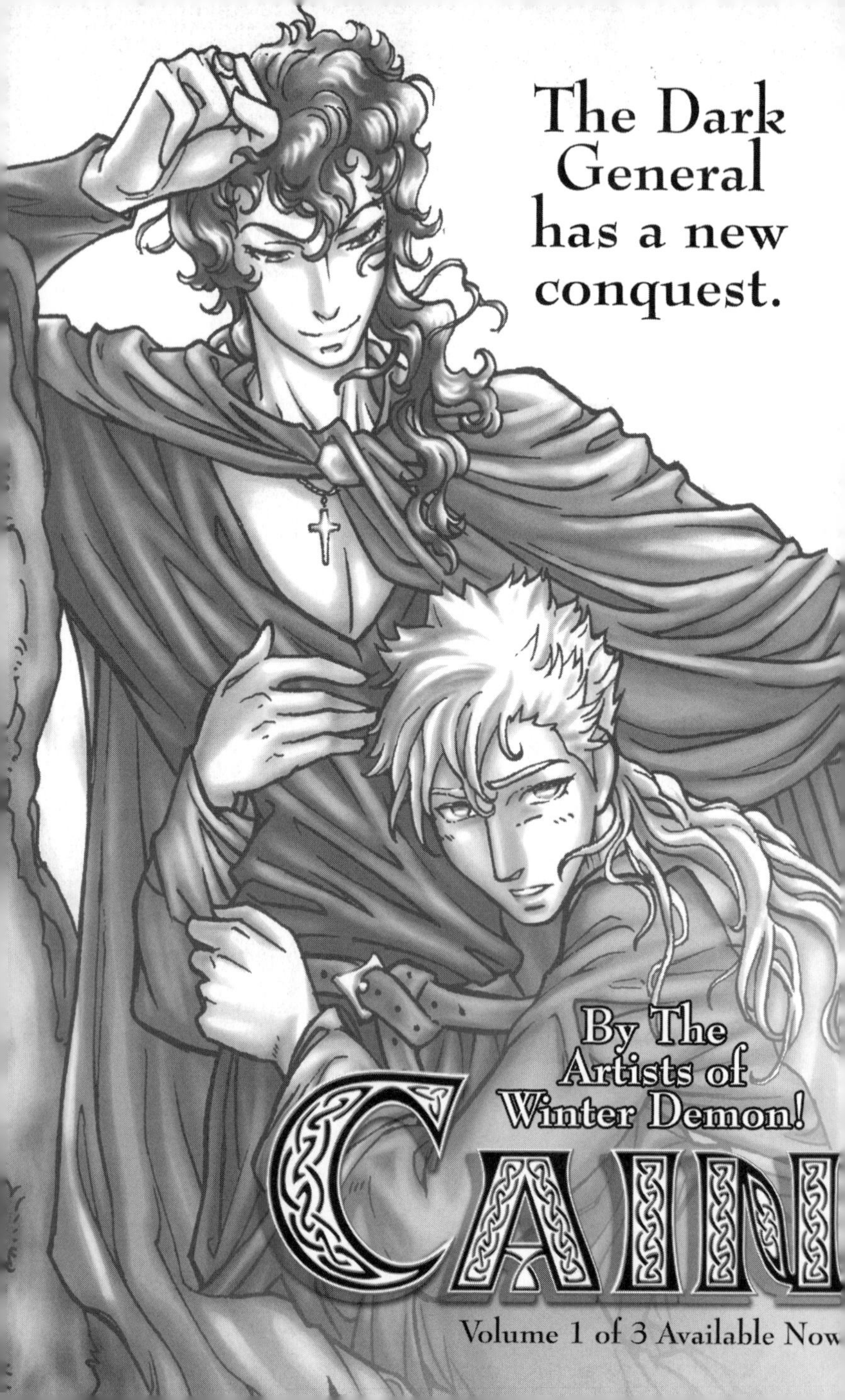

The Dark General has a new conquest.
By The Artists of Winter Demon!
CAIN
Volume 1 of 3 Available Now

By The
Artists of
Winter Demon

"What is he?"

Cain Volume 2
March 2008

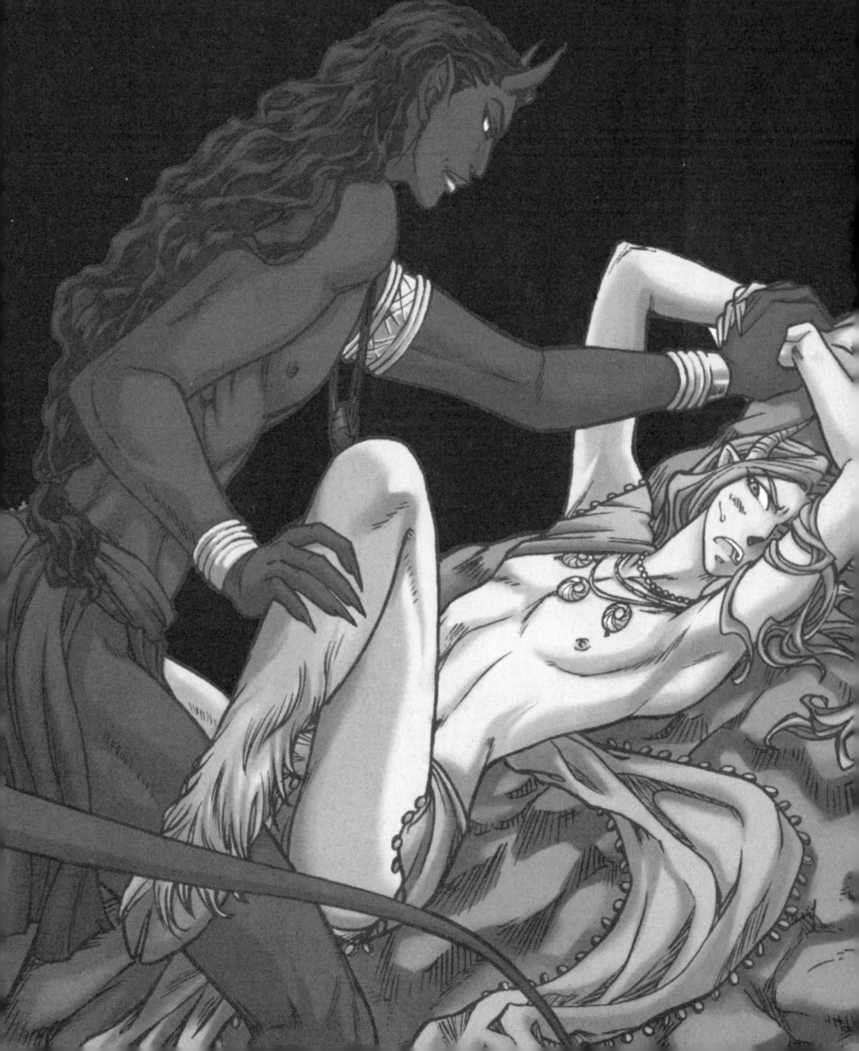

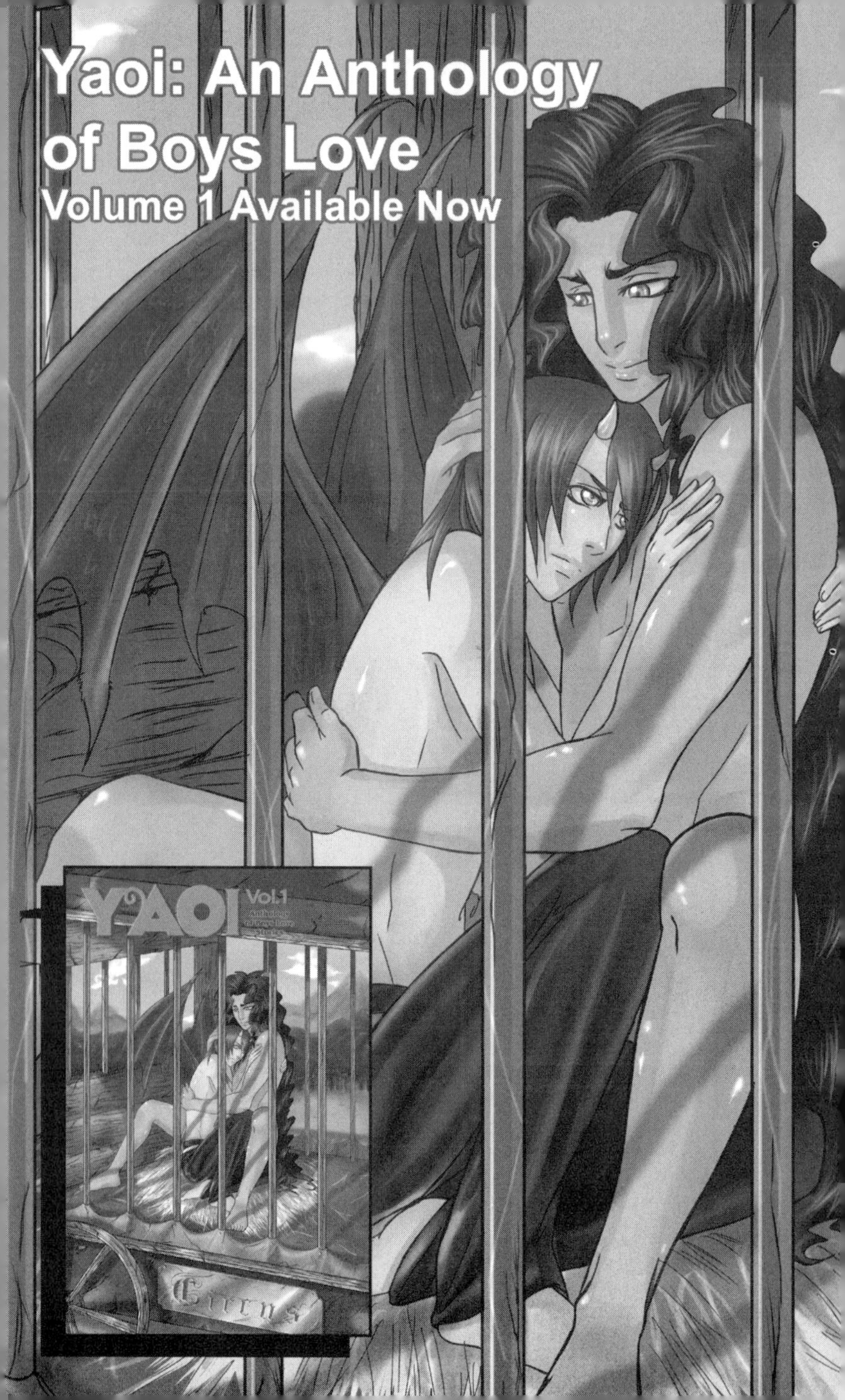
Yaoi: An Anthology of Boys Love
Volume 1 Available Now
YAOI
Vol.1

Dark Prince Vol. I
Available Now

The king's retainer Lowry has a mission to find out why Prince Davon murders boys whose names start with 'A'. He finds out Davon has a demon lover commanding him to kill, but is this demon even real? Prince Lor could help, but he claims to be Davon's lover too!

DARK PRINCE

PARENTAL
Mature Content
Not for Children
ADVISORY Yamila Abraham M.A. Sambre

Gothic
and
Macabre

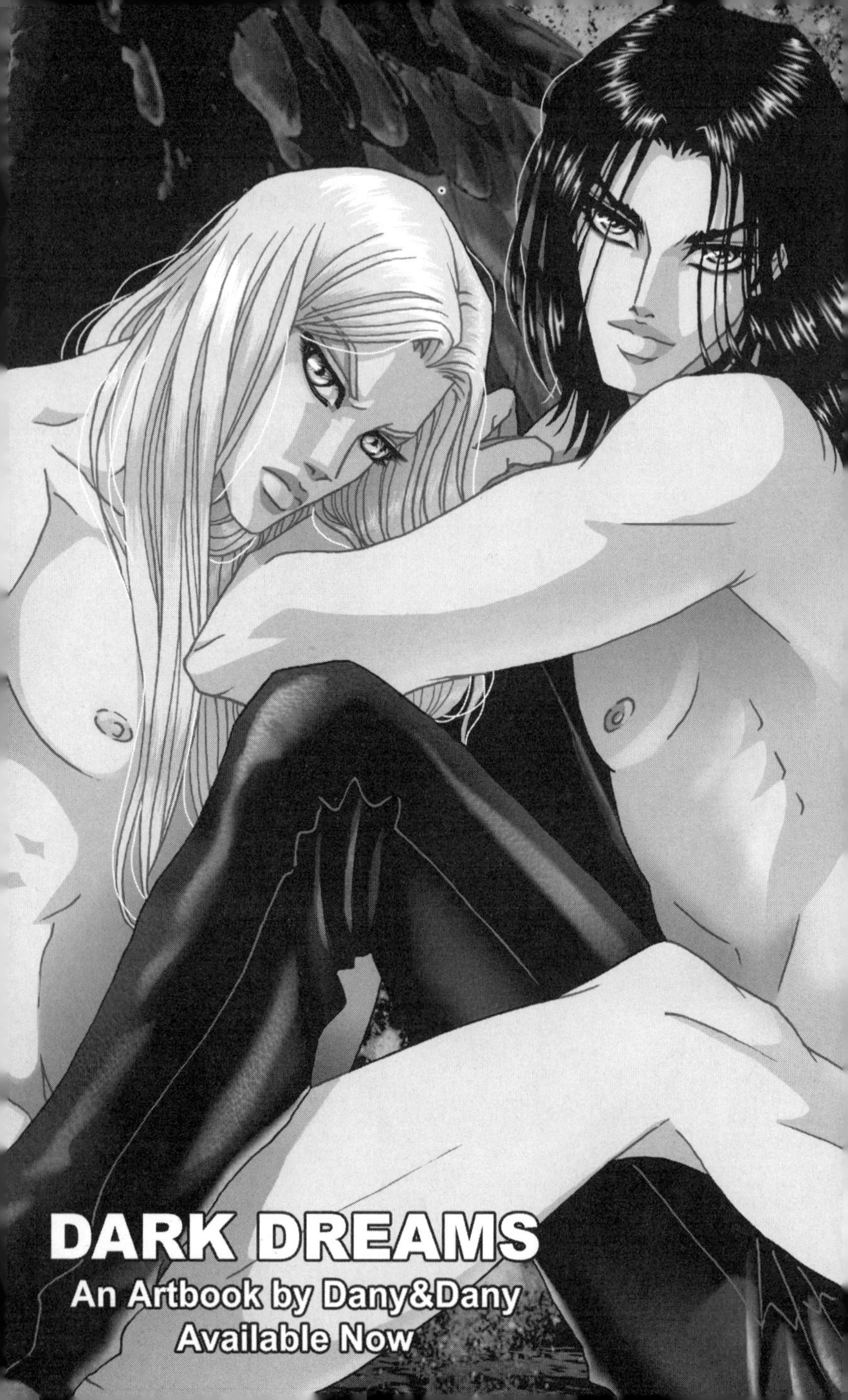
DARK DREAMS
An Artbook by Dany&Dany
Available Now